BLACK POSTCARDS

BLACK POSTCARDS

A ROCK & ROLL ROMANCE

Dean Wareham

THE PENGUIN PRESS | NEW YORK | 2008

THE PENGUIN PRESS
Published by the Penguin Group
Penguin Group (USA) Inc., 375 Hudson Street, New York, New York 10014, U.S.A. •
Penguin Group (Canada), 90 Eglinton Avenue East, Suite 700, Toronto, Ontario,
Canada M4P 2Y3 (a division of Pearson Penguin Canada Inc.) • Penguin Books Ltd,
80 Strand, London WC2R 0RL, England • Penguin Ireland, 25 St. Stephen's Green,
Dublin 2, Ireland (a division of Penguin Books Ltd) • Penguin Books Australia Ltd,
250 Camberwell Road, Camberwell, Victoria 3124, Australia (a division of Pearson
Australia Group Pty Ltd) • Penguin Books India Pvt Ltd, 11 Community Centre,
Panchsheel Park, New Delhi—110 017, India • Penguin Group (NZ), 67 Apollo Drive,
Rosedale, North Shore 0632, New Zealand (a division of Pearson New Zealand Ltd) •
Penguin Books (South Africa) (Pty) Ltd, 24 Sturdee Avenue, Rosebank,
Johannesburg 2196, South Africa

Penguin Books Ltd, Registered Offices:
80 Strand, London WC2R 0RL, England

First published in 2008 by The Penguin Press, a member of Penguin Group (USA) Inc.

Insert credits: p. 1, p. 2, p. 3, p. 4, p. 5 bottom, p. 14 top: John Wareham; p. 5 top,
p. 8 bottom, p. 10 bottom, p. 11, p. 13 bottom: Dean Wareham; p. 6 top, p. 7 bottom,
p. 8 top: Macioce; p. 6 bottom, p. 7 top: Simon Alexander; p. 9, p. 12 top, p. 16: Michael
Lavine; p. 10 top: Ebet Roberts; p. 12 bottom left: Lara Meyerratken; p. 12 bottom right:
David Mead; p. 13 top, p. 15 bottom: Yoriko Tanaka; p. 13 middle: Britta Phillips;
p. 14 bottom: Adam Fogarty; p. 15 top: Stefano Giovannini

Pages 327–28 constitute an extension to this copyright page.

Library of Congress Cataloging-in-Publication Data
Wareham, Dean, 1963–
Black postcards : a rock & roll romance / Dean Wareham.
p. cm.
ISBN 978-1-59420-155-4
1. Wareham, Dean, 1963– 2. Rock musicians—United States—Biography.
3. Galaxie 500 (Musical group) 4. Luna (Rock group) I. Title.
ML420. W184A3 2008
782.42166092—dc22
[B]   2007035280

Printed in the United States of America

1 3 5 7 9 10 8 6 4 2

Designed by Amanda Dewey

BLACK POSTCARDS

Four to Fourteen

Naomi and I had developed a strong distrust of Dean, which in the end turned out to be not nearly strong enough—we were blind-sided, despite our misgivings about the person he was becoming and the ways in which he was dealing with our modicum of "success". To give an example: during the Los Angeles show on our last tour, Dean (who almost never moved during our shows) suddenly stepped downstage front and center during a guitar solo, and a white spotlight materialized, focused directly on him. Apparently this had been arranged with the sound and lighting people beforehand. Nothing, but nothing, like that had ever been done at a Galaxie 500 show, and it completely freaked me out—I remember struggling to keep the beat while it happened, I was so surprised. In retrospect I notice that Dean chose the L.A. show to launch this new trick, when the audience was full of music industry people. We hadn't had any spotlights in Columbus or Dallas!

(Damon Krukowski, from an interview with the fanzine Ptolemaic Terrascope, *1997)*

Yes, we had been friends. We rode together in cars, vans, planes, trains, and hovercraft. We shared small humiliations and grand successes. We came in dead last in a talent show. We picnicked on Plum Island. We led a revolution and were led to the guillotine. We discovered Love and the Red Crayola. We played to six people on a snowy night and thirty thousand in a muddy field. There were hockey rinks and belly-dancing clubs, art galleries and high schools. We played Cooky's and Chet's Last Call, Bunratty's, CB's, JB's, the 40 Watt, the Casbah, the Pyramid, the Point, the Paradise, the Paradiso, Roseland, Club Lingerie, Lounge Ax, the Ecstasy, the Batcave, the Boardwalk, the Milky Way, the New Moon, the New Morning, Nightingale

Bar, Nightbirds, the Bierkeller, the Rathskellar, the Top Hat, the Falcon, and the Adelphi.

I met Damon in 1977—in ninth-grade European history class at the Dalton School. Ms. Eastman, our teacher, was cool, but the class was more exciting when her boyfriend and colleague, Vito, took over. He was an Italian Marxist and he made feudalism exciting. Instead of asking us to memorize dates and the names of kings, he drew diagrams—arrows pointing from serf to vassal to lord of the manor—that showed how the feudal system contained the seeds of its own destruction.

I was fresh off the boat from Australia, but Damon had been at Dalton all his life. His father ran a PR company and his mother was once a jazz singer. Her first album, *Wild Women Don't Get the Blues,* was produced by jazz critic Nat Hentoff (whose son Tom was also at Dalton).

Naomi Yang was also at Dalton, one year behind Damon and me. Naomi's father, a photographer and architect, was born in China but grew up in New York City. Her mother wrote gardening columns for the *New York Times.* Naomi and I took one class together—stagecraft, which taught us the art of designing and building theatrical sets. We sometimes made sketches of stage sets, and while drawing was not a talent of mine, Naomi's drawings were effortlessly perfect.

Dalton sits on Eighty-ninth Street between Lexington and Park Avenues—which may be why the *New York Observer* once wrote that my "ancestral home" was Park Avenue. You can catch a glimpse of the school, and some of my friends even, in Woody Allen's *Manhattan,* shot in 1979. In the film, an older man (Woody) dates a seventeen-year-old Mariel Hemingway, who is a senior at Dalton. Some parents were outraged at the suggestion that a Dalton girl would date an older man, but one of my teachers was forced out of the school for this very transgression (though he had waited until after the young lady graduated before starting the hanky-panky).

I was born in Wellington, New Zealand, in 1963. My great-great-grandfather Joseph Wareham had settled in New Zealand exactly one hundred years earlier. Born in Philadelphia, he served as a water boy during the Crimean War and was in Calcutta during the Indian Mutiny of 1857 before relocating to the Boston suburb of Roxbury. In 1861 he enlisted in the U.S. Navy. He served on the USS *Colorado* during the Civil War and was part of an expedition of one hundred sailors that was sent to destroy a Confederate schooner, the CCS *Judah,* at Pensacola Harbor. Joseph was injured in the battle, but recovered and made his way to Hokitika, New Zealand—gold rush territory. He later became a hotel keeper, as did his son William.

William married Evelyn Trudgeon, a beautiful woman who was hired by the Fuller Vaudeville Company to sing during the intermissions at His Majesty's Theatre in the suburb of Petone, while the movie reels were being changed.

Their son (my grandfather) Jack was the star of the family—a sprinter, cricketer, and big-time rugby player for Wellington. He wanted to be a doctor, but the Depression forced him into the catering business instead. So on my father's side it was hoteliers and caterers. My mother's father was a pharmacist, as were her three brothers.

My mother, Margaret Owles, grew up in the Wellington suburb of Lower Hutt. She loved ballet and theater, and was offered a scholarship at a drama school at age sixteen. Her father insisted that she do something more sensible, and enrolled her at Gilby's Business College in Wellington, where she studied useful subjects like typing, shorthand, and bookkeeping. Her cousin worked at a bank alongside my father, John, who worked as a teller while studying at Victoria University. It was here, in June 1958, that my parents laid eyes on each other. She was seventeen, he was eighteen. Their first date was at a coffee shop on Cuba Street. My father reports that my mother was incredibly shy on that date. Two years later they were married.

My parents, my older brother, Anthony, and I lived in a little wooden house on Tirangi Road, right by the airport, steps from the air traffic control tower itself, which is situated up on a hill overlooking the airstrip. Wellington is a beautiful little city. It reminds me a bit of San Francisco, only smaller and there's no Haight-Ashbury or City Lights Books. But its many hills are dotted with beautiful wooden Victorian homes with lovely views of the city. As Wellington lies directly on a fault line, we had earthquake drills in kindergarten, during which we had to huddle under our wooden desks.

At age four I heard "Georgy Girl" on the radio. It was a huge hit for the Seekers, an Australian vocal group who were as big as the Beatles in 1967 in New Zealand. They sounded kind of like Chad and Jeremy, or the Mamas and the Papas, but stripped down to acoustic guitar, upright bass, and vocals.

"Georgy Girl" was co-written by Tom Springfield (Dusty's brother). The Seekers had other glorious hit songs, too, like "A World of Our Own," "The Carnival Is Over," and "I'll Never Find Another You."

If we spend our whole lives trying to recapture some of the magic of childhood, then perhaps I have spent mine trying to re-create the feeling that I got from hearing "Georgy Girl"—beauty and sadness and ecstasy all together.

On August 1, 1968—my fifth birthday—I started at the public school in Seatoun. This first day away from the nest was scary. I sat under a piano all day and, knowing that Anthony was somewhere in the building, cried, "I want my brother."

In 1969 our family (there were now six of us, with the addition of my sister, Louise, and brother Jonathan) moved north to Auckland. We lived in a faded art deco duplex in Herne Bay, steps from the beach. Anthony and I attended the local primary school. It was here, in second grade, that I watched live footage of astronauts landing on the moon. At lunchtime, Anthony and I would walk home for sandwiches and a quick swim.

One afternoon we popped into a dairy (grocery store). While the shop owner's back was turned Anthony put a roll of Life Savers in his pocket.

"Anthony," I said. "Those aren't yours. They belong to the man."

Yes, I ratted on my brother. The shop owner scolded Anthony, and rewarded me with a fish—a delicious, chocolate-covered pink marshmallow fish. These candy fish are the first things I seek out when I visit New Zealand today. I still enjoy the marshmallow, even as I ponder the paths that our lives have taken—my older brother the candy thief, and me the good boy/snitch.

On April 16, 1970, we moved to Sydney, Australia, as many New Zealanders do. My dad, who was initially trained as an accountant, had built a successful management consulting business, and wanted to try his luck in Australia. We settled first in the northern suburb of Belrose, where I attended the Mimosa Public School. Across the street lived my third-grade girlfriend, my earliest sexual memory (this I gave up to my shrink)—Wendy Little. Our assignations took place in her parents' garage. It smelled delicious there, of gasoline. I remember asking her to kiss me like they did in the movies. Not little pecks—I wanted her to mash her face against mine. One afternoon we pulled down our pants for a little show-and-tell.

I told Anthony about my girlfriend, and he promptly told my mother, who gently informed me that I was a bit young for that sort of thing. So ended my relationship with Wendy. I wasn't too sad about having to break it off with her, but I was embarrassed that my mother knew all the details. Anthony had paid me back for the chocolate fish.

My dad brought new records home each week. I listened to his seven-inch singles, records such as "If You Could Read My Mind" by Gordon Lightfoot, "Both Sides Now" and "Amazing Grace" by Judy Collins, "Imagine" by John Lennon, and "It Was a Very Good Year" by Frank Sinatra.

I listened to *The Golden Hour of Donovan,* a collection of his early folk songs (before he became a pioneer of psychedelic folk rock). I would lie on the thick white carpet of the living room wearing my dad's headphones, staring at the album cover, a strange jigsaw picture of Donovan's head growing out of a country hillside.

My father also brought home Nina Simone's *Here Comes the Sun,* wherein Nina covers George Harrison and Bob Dylan and the Bee Gees, and delivers what I consider to be the greatest recorded version of "My Way." Joe Cocker's *Cocker Happy* was also a favorite, with his stellar version of "With a Little Help from My Friends," which he did far better than the Beatles. He sang "Hello, Little Friend" and "Do I Still Figure in Your Life?" (which I borrowed from lyrically for the Luna song "California"). These tracks were mixed by Tony Visconti, who later figured in my own life. Joe Cocker was big in Australia, and people were furious when the government busted him for marijuana possession in Adelaide and then ordered him to leave the country.

I was in the fourth grade on January 14, 1973, when Elvis was beamed into our homes live, via satellite, from Hawaii. The TCB (Taking Care of Business) Band featured Ronnie Tutt, Jerry Scheff, James Burton, and backing vocals by J. D. Sumner and the Stamps. Watching that concert was exciting. I couldn't stop smiling. Elvis looked handsome in his jewel-encrusted jumpsuit. I loved and admired him, especially when he handed used towels to girls in the audience, or let them give him a kiss.

Elvis's live performances from the 1970s are some of the greatest rock recordings of the era. The critics made fun of the mature, bloated King, but who had a better band in 1973? David Bowie? I don't think so. The Rolling Stones? They were good, too, but *Get Yer Ya-Ya's Out* doesn't compare with *That's the Way It Is* (which captured Elvis in Vegas and Nashville).

My fourth-grade teacher, Ms. Murphy, was a feminist. She taught the whole class, boys and girls, to sing along to Helen Reddy's "I Am Woman." Some days we listened to the radio to learn about current events. We once heard Richard Nixon answer a series of questions on the radio while Ms. Murphy paced the room, denouncing him as a liar.

I n 1974 Anthony and I were sent to the St. Andrew's Cathedral School, an all-boys Anglican day school located in downtown Sydney, headed by the Reverend Canon Newth.

Canon Newth didn't use a microphone when he addressed the student body at school assemblies. Instead, he would cup his hands around his mouth and shout at us: "There are some boys—there are some boys who are *not* standing up for old ladies on the *buses!*"

Once a week we studied "divinity," which was sometimes taught by Canon Newth himself. He had a nice set of colored markers that he used to illustrate teachings from the Bible. When the headmaster turned his back to the class, Anthony would take those Magic Markers and smash the tips in so they didn't work so well. Canon Newth stared at those pens in wonderment.

Australians are fond of suits that favor shorts over long pants. They also like a brown suit, or a green one even. But our school uniform took the cake: a light gray cotton "safari suit," worn with a blue shirt and striped tie, topped off with a ridiculous straw boater. Since we rode the ferry to school each day, our hats were prone to being blown overboard into Sydney Harbor. And if we showed up at school sans hat, why, that offense was punishable by caning. Some kids solved the hat problem by coating their hats in layers of clear polyurethane, which made them heavier, resistant to the wind, and strong enough to sit on. I was caned only once, but Anthony was often in trouble for something or other, and was frequently called before the head-master to be disciplined with six swipes to the tips of his fingers.

. . .

In 1975 I won a scholarship to attend a bigger, better, and more secular private school—Sydney Grammar School. Each class contained 180 boys. Right from the get-go they organized us into six sections ranked from A to F, based on test scores. Along with each report card we received, we were also given our rank in the class. I was a good student in every subject except for music, where I was ranked number 153 out of 180 during my seventh-grade year. My eyes glazed over when the teacher began to explain that "Every Good Boy Deserves Fudge" stuff.

Anthony loved Elton John, Gary Glitter, and the Sweet. My younger sister, Louise, loved ABBA and the Bay City Rollers. As we moved from the glam era into the disco years, I fell in love with Silver Convention—three hot German ladies named Penny, Linda, and Ramona. "Hot" wasn't really the word back then; they were "spunky." I was twelve when "Fly, Robin, Fly" and "Get Up and Boogie (That's Right)" made the charts. I didn't know that Silver Convention was really two clever dudes from Munich, while Penny, Linda, and Ramona were just hired singers. Penny's real name was Gertrude Wirschinger.

While I listened to this crap, Anthony snuck out of the house late at night and smoked pot with his friends, or sat in his room listening to Sydney's new FM station, Double J, where he discovered David Bowie and Lou Reed. He bought *Transformer* and *Diamond Dogs*. The cover image of *Dogs* frightened me—David Bowie drawn as half man and half dog. The entire album was a science-fiction nightmare.

On the back cover of Lou Reed's *Transformer* is an image of a transvestite, and another of a guy with a cucumber in his pants and a pack of cigarettes rolled into his T-shirt sleeve.

"That's Lou Reed," said Anthony. "It's all him. The guy in the jeans. And the lady, too."

He had a vivid imagination, but he was wrong about these photographs.

1977

On August 1, 1977—my fourteenth birthday—we moved to New York City. My dad rented a small office in the Pan Am Building, and bought a can of silver hair spray so that clients would think he was more distinguished. Wiser. Older.

Nineteen seventy-seven was a strange summer in the city, the Summer of Sam, the summer of *Star Wars,* the summer of the blackout and looting spree (which we missed by two weeks), the summer of Mickey Rivers, Thurman Munson, and Reggie Jackson, and the summer that Elvis died.

My mother had heard that the Upper East Side was the place to live, so my family sublet a brownstone apartment on East Sixty-fourth Street off of Lexington Avenue. My mother also insisted that we attend private school, having heard horror stories about New York City's public schools. She got me an interview at Dalton, where they asked a few questions and gave me some psychological tests, like the one where you draw a family and a house (the mommy and daddy should hold hands, and the house shouldn't be on fire or anything). I was accepted and allowed to enroll at Dalton a month later. Anthony was sent to a boarding school up in the Berkshires (from which he was expelled just a couple weeks later).

I was used to being around affluent kids, but nothing prepared me for the Dalton School, where the kids had names like Newhouse, Sulzberger, Redford, and Ross (as in not only Diana Ross, of the Supremes, but also Steve Ross, of Warner Communications). These kids were privileged.

Dalton was a brave new world. I came from that large, all-boys grammar school where we wore our suits with short pants and ties and played cricket and rugby. Here the boys wore Woolrich down jackets and preppy boating shoes. The girls wore inside-out sweatpants and Fiorucci. A few of them even wore fur coats.

My mom dressed me all wrong. I had sneakers with four stripes, not three. The extra stripe was humiliating.

In September we moved into a modern high-rise apartment building at the corner of Eighty-third Street and Second Avenue. Jonathan and I shared a bedroom until Anthony was kicked out of boarding school, and then we were three. Anthony then enrolled at Riverdale, a private school located up in the Bronx. He fell in with the stoners, joining the Columbia House record club so he could score cassettes by the Grateful Dead, Boston, and Hot Tuna, all for a penny.

Anthony got in trouble at every school he ever attended. Having been booted out of the prep school in the Berkshires, he was soon getting poor grades at Riverdale, too, and playing the sullen teen at home. My father decided that maybe Anthony would be better off finishing his schooling in New Zealand.

By summer's end he was gone. I can still picture him on his last day in New York, in his Frye boots, a red gingham shirt, and aviator glasses. I didn't mind his leaving—we had fought all summer long, so much so that I later blamed myself for his departure. It was only after he left that we really began to get along, as long-distance pen pals.

During my sophomore year at Dalton we had a cool new young drama teacher—Van Gosse, who was a recent Dalton graduate himself. Van directed the big school play that year, a production of Georg Büchner's *Danton's Death*, in which Damon Krukowski and I were cast as doomed revolutionaries. Damon portrayed Camille Desmoulins, while I played Hérault-Séchelles. This being the French Revolution, we were sent to the guillotine at the end of the play. It is well known that those who start the revolution are rarely there at its end.

Damon was a brilliant student. In 1981 he was the class valedictorian and president of our high school. Everyone liked him. He had an infectious laugh. He said he had a temper, too, and told me that he used to get into fights when he was a kid, but I saw no evidence of that. He wrote poetry and was very skilled at demonstrating how people danced.

"He dances like this," he would say, and break into a perfect imitation.

My best friends were Marc Glimcher, who lived on Park Avenue and whose dad was an art dealer, and Graham Poor, who lived in a rent-controlled apartment on Fifth Avenue at Ninety-sixth Street. Graham was not like the other children at Dalton. When he was in fourth grade, kids would pay him a dollar to say "Fuck you, God!" He was not afraid. Was it any wonder he later became a born-again Christian?

In addition to being our drama teacher, Van Gosse introduced Graham and me to Ian Dury, Television, the Clash, and Talking Heads. While the school stoners were into Pink Floyd and the Grateful Dead, and others worshipped Cheap Trick and Kiss, we listened to Devo's *Q: Are We Not Men? A: We Are Devo!* and *More Songs about Buildings and Food* by Talking Heads.

Talking Heads, in their button-down shirts and straitlaced haircuts, became my favorite band. They weren't trying to be rock stars, punks, or the second coming of the Rolling Stones. David Byrne affected a shy, bug-eyed persona. His style of guitar playing was scratchy and angular—a far cry from the popular guitar heroes with their rock poses.

We bought our vinyl at King Karol Records on Eighty-fifth Street and Third Avenue, where Lux Interior from the Cramps worked, or at Disc-O-Mat in Grand Central Station. We would venture downtown to Freebeing Records on Second Avenue (next to Gem Spa) and Bleecker Bob's on MacDougal Street, where I tried to get a job.

"Who recorded 'In the Still of the Night'?" asked Bob himself.

I didn't get the job.

Graham and I bought old clothes at the three-dollar store (Revenge) on the Bowery—skinny ties and jackets with holes in them. I didn't notice that my jacket was actually cut for a woman until I got it home. We were what the TV personalities referred to as *part-time punks*—private-school kids dressing up as something we were not.

Together we went to CBGB to see Richard Hell and the Voidoids. This was my first time at CBGB and the walk down that long corridor made me nervous. I discovered the basement bathrooms, which were just plain scary. No lid on the toilet, no door on the stall. In those days they didn't book seven bands a night at CB's, but instead had two bands play two sets each. The Voidoids were fantastic, especially their guitarist Robert Quine, he of the bald pate and dark glasses. I came to know Quine many years later, after he had played with Marianne Faithfull and Lou Reed and Matthew Sweet. I would run into him at Mojo Guitar Shop on St. Marks, Carmine Street Guitars, and Subterranean Records. He advised me which Fender Telecasters

were the best (the Japanese ones), or how to track down records by James
Burton. He had a sharp tongue.

"*Matthew* Sweet . . . I hope he gets hit by a *bus.*"

W e saw the Ramones perform an afternoon rock show at a record fair.
We saw the Stimulators and the Speedies and the Student Teachers.
We saw the Clash perform at the Palladium on Fourteenth Street, with the
Undertones and Bo Diddley opening.

We saw Public Image Limited (PiL) at the Palladium, around the time
they released *Metal Box.* They played for about twenty minutes before John
Lydon invited a dozen audience members onstage to dance and then exited
stage left. He did not return. The band finished the set without him, their
great bassist Jah Wobble lying down on his back, playing the bass on the
floor.

In the tenth grade I dated Donna, a senior. I don't know what she saw
in me. I was cute and nonthreatening, I suppose. I knew what I saw in her:
She was a woman. She invited me over to her mother's high-rise apartment,
where we would make out and play records. She played me "I Will Survive"
by Gloria Gaynor and "Just the Way You Are" by Billy Joel. I played her "Beat
on the Brat" by the Ramones and "Sex and Drugs and Rock and Roll" by Ian
Dury. Donna introduced me to sex and Quaaludes.

In June of 1979, on prom night (and since I was lucky enough to be dating
a senior, I attended the prom), Donna and I saw the B-52's at the Mudd Club,
right before their first album was released. The bouncer hesitated before
letting me in—I was sixteen years old and wearing a pastel blue tuxedo
jacket, but Van Gosse's friend Danny Heaps was the DJ (Heaps later helped
found Rockpool and the New Music Seminar and became an A&R man at
Geffen Records).

I spent the summer of 1979 back in Wellington, New Zealand, at my grandfather's house in Lyall Bay. It was not summertime in Wellington, but
rather a bleak and windy winter. I worked as a bartender for my granddad's catering business, which was a family tradition, and hung out with
Anthony.

Although he still liked his Hot Tuna and Grateful Dead records, Anthony was also getting into punk and New Wave. He played me *Secondhand Daylight* by Magazine and *The Modern Lovers*, the incredible first album by Jonathan Richman's eponymous band, one of those rare albums on which every single track is perfect. Recorded in 1972, but not released until 1976, this record was a crucial link from the Velvet Underground to the punk generation (the Sex Pistols did a version of "Roadrunner"). The record was available in New Zealand, but was impossible to find in the United States.

At summer's end I returned to New York, but Anthony and I continued to exchange music. He sent me cassettes of Joy Division and John Cooper Clarke. I sent him *Crazy Rhythms* by the Feelies. Released in 1980, when I was in eleventh grade, this was another perfect record, and one that later changed my life (though I had no inkling at the time). I had read about the Feelies in the *Village Voice,* one of the few sources of information on good music. *Rolling Stone* generally paid little attention to the punk and New Wave bands. They may have hailed the record as a masterpiece years later, but in the late '70s and early '80s, when it counted, they ignored all the best music.

In high school, the same year *Crazy Rhythms* came out, I took a class called Men and Ideas, an introduction to philosophy taught by my favorite teacher, Paul Poet. We read Plato and David Hume, Bertrand Russell and René Descartes. We read *The Communist Manifesto* and *Civilization and Its Discontents.*

My high-school German teacher, Frau Prokuda, introduced me to Bertolt Brecht. We read *Der Gute Mensch von Sezuan* and *Der Kaukasische Kreidekreis,* and I read everything I could about Brecht and Erwin Piscator and German expressionist drama. Here I was at a fancy private school for rich kids being exposed to Marx and Brecht, writers who wanted to change the world, not just explain it.

I developed some kind of primitive theory that art should serve politics, that art for art's sake was frivolous. Senior year I staged my own expressionist presentation of a German play, Wolfgang Borchert's *The Man Outside.*

It was a great time to be young and in New York City. The legal drinking age was eighteen, but no one cared to enforce it, and I was never turned away from a rock club. And the New York music scene at that time featured the best bands in the world—the Ramones, Talking Heads, Suicide, Richard Hell and the Voidoids, Blondie, and Television.

I saw Blondie and Devo in Central Park, the Au Pairs at the Mudd Club, 999 and Pere Ubu at Irving Plaza, Talking Heads at the Capitol Theatre in Passaic, New Jersey (for the *Fear of Music* tour), and at Radio City Music Hall (for *Remain in Light*). Graham and Marc and I waited by the stage door after the Radio City show, hoping to meet the band. After we stood in the cold for an hour, David Byrne, Tina Weymouth, and Chris Frantz appeared. Graham was so excited that he fell to the pavement and rolled on his back like a puppy.

"I love you, Tina!" he squealed.

"I love you, too," she laughed.

O n May 28 of 1981, two weeks before my high-school graduation ceremony, I saw the Clash perform at Bond's International Casino (now the Virgin Megastore) on the opening night of a legendary series of shows they played in New York in support of their *Sandinista!* triple album. These shows were legendary in part because the fire marshall declared them dangerously oversold after that first night, forcing the Clash to double the number of performances from eight to seventeen in order to honor every ticket.

Out in the lobby of Bond's was a table piled with literature about the Sandinista revolution. The opening act that first night was New York's own Grandmaster Flash and the Furious Five. Joe Strummer was an early fan of hip-hop, and you can hear that influence on tracks like "The Magnificent Seven" or "This Is Radio Clash." The audience that night was not so enlightened, caring neither about Nicaragua nor about hip-hop. They threw beer cups at the Furious Five, booing them off the stage to chants of "Disco sucks!" and "Nigger!" I was ashamed to be a Clash fan that night. Was this the religious, communal feeling people talk about at big rock shows?

Joe Strummer himself looked disgusted when the Clash took the stage. This was the true meaning of the DISCO SUCKS! buttons and T-shirts that had proliferated in the late '70s—ostensibly the slogan championed rock and roll, but it just as significantly contained antigay and antiblack biases.

It is a sad truth that the bigger a band gets, the higher its quotient of meathead/lout fans. Apparently, Kurt Cobain struggled with this; it killed him that a large portion of his audience was comprised of converted metal fans.

The *New York Times*'s Stephen Holden gave the Clash show a mixed review, writing that Strummer could "technically hardly carry a tune" and that his melodic range was "not much greater than 'Three Blind Mice.'" Yet somehow they had just released a magnificent triple album—too long, perhaps, but a triumph nonetheless.

Speedy and the Castanets

In 1981 I enrolled at Harvard University. My parents, my two younger siblings, and I all drove up to Cambridge. There was a tearful goodbye—well, my mother cried. I wasn't going to be too sad or lonely, because I had a couple of high-school friends here—Damon and Marc. Marc and I celebrated our first night at Harvard by dropping acid and exploring the campus till the sun came up.

My freshman-year classes did not thrill me, whether it was computer science or Roderick Firth's Types of Ethical Theory (a class recommended by my advisor, a law student who lived one floor below me and screamed about the loud music coming from my room). I did like Harvey Goldman's freshman seminar, where we read *The Rebel* by Albert Camus and Nietzsche's *Thus Spoke Zarathustra.* "What does Nietzsche mean by the *eternal return*?" asked Professor Goldman. I was hoping he could tell me.

My last high-school girlfriend, Toni, was enrolled at Brown. Some weekends I took the Amtrak train down to Providence to visit her. I couldn't afford the train fare, but I learned that you could hide in the bathrooms when the conductor came around.

Toni and I had been an item since the eleventh grade, but lately we were growing apart. Toni called herself a feminist. This didn't bother me. What bothered me was that she was a *Republican* feminist—like Jeane Kirkpatrick. Toni believed that women deserved equal pay. But she also admired Ronald Reagan and believed that income tax should be abolished. I, on the other hand, was getting more serious about left-wing politics. I broke up with Toni over the Christmas break that year. I wasn't in love with her anymore.

Marc and I took mushrooms and saw Pere Ubu at the Paradise that fall—this was the period where Mayo Thompson of the Red Crayola was on guitar. The Red Crayola was a pioneer of psychedelic rock in the 1960s, but the great Texas psychedelic bands were overshadowed by the inferior ones from San Francisco, just as Pere Ubu (from Cleveland) toiled in the shadow of punk bands from New York and London.

Pere Ubu was fantastic that night. David Thomas (a Jehovah's Witness, the greatest Jehovah's Witness in the history of punk rock) sang about being underwater, swimming with the fish and talking to them, and we were right there with him.

We saw Gang of Four at the Metro, with a new band from Georgia called R.E.M. opening up. I thought that R.E.M.'s singer danced in a pretentious way, with that long curly hair dangling in front of his face, but I did like their single *Radio Free Europe,* which I was able to sell for $40 a few years later.

It was Marc who suggested that he and I and Damon start a band, reasoning that it might be a good way for him to get a girlfriend. We called ourselves Speedy and the Castanets. I was Speedy. Marc was Conchico. Damon was Maurice.

In a tiny studio in Harvard Square, right above the Tasty Diner, I took four guitar lessons during the fall semester, just enough to learn a few basic pentatonic scales for soloing. I sat in my room and practiced those scales, as well as a few country and blues riffs that my teacher taught me. My Chinese American roommate, Patrick, a physics major who also played the bass guitar, laughed at me. He said my playing sounded "so white."

There were two music rooms set aside in the basement of the freshman dining hall, and that's where we practiced cover versions and wrote our own songs. We didn't own a drum kit, but we used one that belonged to a fellow student named Conan O'Brien. We didn't know how to play, but we thought we were cool. Our friends dropped by to laugh at us while we struggled with "I'm So Bored with the U.S.A." by the Clash, "Shadowplay" by Joy Division, "Submission" by the Sex Pistols, "Armalite Rifle" by Gang of Four, and "Human Fly" by the Cramps. We were terrible, of course, since none of us could play our instruments. It would have been better if at least one of us was proficient, because one good musician makes the others sound better.

Not only could we not play our instruments, but we didn't actually own any. Marc eventually bought us some real equipment so we could play gigs around campus. Damon got a nice old Gretsch drum kit finished in green sparkle. I received a Music Man 112RD amplifier and a beautiful alpine white Les Paul Custom with a cracked headstock.

In addition to the punk-rock covers, Speedy and the Castanets worked up some original songs, like "Back to Beirut." Marc wrote the lyrics for this one:

Take me back! Take me back!
Take me back! Take me back!
Take me back
Back to Beirut
Where the girls are cute
And the boys all wear
Machine guns!

I developed a crush on a beautiful girl I would see in the dining hall each night. I didn't know her name, but Marc dubbed her Chiquita Banana, and the Castanets wrote a song for her.

Oh oh
Banana Chiquita
Oh oh
You know I'm gonna eat you
Oh oh
Chiquita Banana
You and me on a trip to Havana

She was beautiful, but she didn't know I existed. Then someone told her about the song, and she started to look at me with a smirk, as if she knew.

In the spring of 1982, we entered ourselves in Harvard's Battle of the Bands at Memorial Hall. Marc wore a plaid tuxedo jacket, complete with plaid cummerbund. I wore pleated black wool trousers and a striped shirt buttoned all the way to the top, trying to emulate the Feelies as they appeared on the sleeve of *Crazy Rhythms.* I had my hair slicked back with grease and wore eyeliner. We hung castanets from the microphone stands.

I broke a string during our second song. This was not something I had anticipated. I had no backup guitar, so I had to restring it right there on the stage. I had a bitch of a time putting the guitar back in tune. That broken string killed our whole set. Marc resorted to telling jokes while I tuned that string up and down.

"What am I?

"Scotch tape. Get it? Scotch tape!"

He pointed to the plaid cummerbund.

We did not win the Battle of the Bands. A committee graded each band on four criteria: presentation, songs, musicianship, and appearance. We came in last in every category. Surely that was worth something. The winning band was the Love Monsters. They had spent a good deal of time on their costumes—they wore matching button-down shirts, each member's shirt with a different section cut out of it. The Love Monsters featured two brothers, Matt and Dan Wilson, who years later would form a band called Trip Shakespeare, based out of Minneapolis. Dan Wilson went on to far greater heights with Semisonic, who had a bona fide radio hit that is probably still paying his mortgage—"Closing Time."

We were the last ones to clear out of Memorial Hall that night. We had come in last, but being last in every single category somehow made us feel better. We sat there till 2:00 A.M. smoking cigarettes, waiting for a taxi to come and help us with our equipment. It was fun to be in historic Memorial Hall so late, with the lights out and no one else there.

Speedy and the Castanets sucked. We were clueless and talentless. And yet we felt we were the only interesting band on campus. So what if we couldn't play? If nothing else, we had our arrogance.

My Toes Can Talk

G raham Poor had been on a spiritual journey since leaving high school for the confines of Tulane University. Freethinker that he was, he had started experimenting first with LSD, then with meditation and Buddhism—a natural progression for kids who read Alan Watts at age seventeen.

One night a funny thing happened to Graham. There he was, walking down the street, tripping on acid, when he ran into a group of born-again Christians who were out distributing their literature and spreading the message of salvation.

"No thanks," Graham said. "I'm a Buddhist."

"If you died right now, what would happen to your soul?"

Graham froze in his tracks. He had no answer to that question. It blew his mind.

"What did you say?"

Graham, the lifelong atheist, who had earned extra cash by shouting "Fuck you God!" at a dollar a pop, was born anew.

The best thing about Graham's becoming a born-again Christian was that he decided he couldn't listen to his punk-rock albums anymore, and gave them all to me.

I got the Slits' *Cut* LP. They sing about shoplifting and shooting up, and the three girls who made up the band are topless on the front cover, each wearing only a loincloth and a slathering of mud. Graham couldn't keep that one. He gave me the Buzzcocks' *Singles Going Steady,* which has that song "Orgasm Addict." God frowns on masturbation. And the X-Ray Spex classic *Germfree Adolescents.* Their singer, Poly Styrene, was later to be born again herself, joining a Krishna sect and denouncing the Sex Pistols for their lyric "I am the Antichrist."

Graham also gave me the eponymous first album by Suicide. I can see that the Suicide album wouldn't be so popular in church, what with "Frankie Teardrop," a long and terrifying dirge about a factory worker who can't make ends meet, and who eventually shoots his wife and blows his own brains out.

Frankie with a gun to his head . . .
Frankie's dead.

Then Frankie goes to hell. Alan Vega makes his point:

We're all Frankies
We're all lyin' in hell

In the summer of 1982, Graham invited Marc and me to his aunt's house in New City, which is in Rockland County, to drop acid and walk in the woods. We drove out there in Marc's Toyota Camry. On the way, we loaded up on junk food at the supermarket, and were so bold as to simply walk out of there, holding bundles of food, without paying. Nobody stopped us.

We ate the tiny windowpanes (so named because the acid was on these tiny pieces of see-through plastic) that Graham had procured from behind the band shell in Central Park. An hour later we were wandering about in a creek, slowly making our way upstream. We took off our shoes and sat in the mud. I stared at my toes, and they seemed so happy. They were smiling at me. Smiling and talking. I looked closely at the mud, picking it up and crushing it in my fingers. I thought about mud. This was fresh mud. What *is* mud? I examined it again. This mud was made of leaves! Decomposing leaves, which come from trees. The leaves turn into mud. And the mud in turn nourishes the trees that are growing by the side of the creek. The mud turns back into leaves. And my mind had turned to mush.

We walked farther upstream. I found an old pickax by the side of the creek. I picked it up and started swinging it around, just for fun. I didn't realize that the pickax's handle was also decomposing, and the head of the ax came flying off, narrowly missing Graham. Holy shit. That's the thing you hear about LSD—kids take acid, and one of them gets a crazy notion that maybe he can fly, or put his hand in the fire. I needed to chill out a bit.

Just then, something slightly magical happened. The sun came out from behind a cloud. The acid was really kicking in—we were peaking. My head felt warm. Waves of warm, good feelings washed over me. I looked at Marc and at Graham and they were feeling exactly the same thing. It was one of those rare moments in life when you feel totally at one with the world and with your friends and everything is just perfect.

"What is it?" I asked.

"I know what it is," said Graham. "It's God. God is revealing himself to us."

Although I didn't believe in God, I knew, in a way, that Graham was correct. The LSD had revealed the oneness of the universe and all that jazz. The mud, the leaves, the trees, the bees, my toes, my best friends—we all belonged to the same thing. Which some people call God. Graham told us what an important moment this was, how special it was that God had chosen to reveal himself to us. And Graham believed that God was doing it for a reason.

He had me convinced for about sixty seconds that the Lord himself had come out from behind the cloud. But then the sky clouded over again, and I said, "Hold on a minute," and just like that I stopped believing.

Two hours later we were driving down the Palisades Parkway listening to "I Will Follow" by U2 and "What a Day That Was" and "Big Blue Plymouth (Eyes Wide Open)" by David Byrne (from his *Catherine Wheel* album), and Marc and Graham were pretty excited about the big epiphany that we had just had.

I was not excited. I didn't want to get religion. I didn't want to like U2. I didn't want to give myself to Jesus. I was selfish. Graham said that Satan is happy when you put yourself first, that Satanism is essentially selfishness. If that's true, then I am an occasional Satanist, because there certainly are times in my life when I have put me first.

Speedy and the Castanets played a few shows during my sophomore year at Harvard, but Marc and I drifted apart. I became more active in politics, while he became more interested in religion—and in his annoying girlfriend—and lost interest in rock and roll. Finally, he said he didn't feel good about playing this music, and quit the band.

Damon and I formed a new band—Johnny Guitar—named for the Nicholas

Ray Western starring Sterling Hayden as Johnny Guitar and Joan Crawford as Vienna. Johnny Guitar shows up in Vienna's saloon. He carries a guitar, but no gun. But Johnny has a secret past: In truth, he is Johnny Logan, the fastest gunslinger around, but he is trying to put all that behind him now.

"I loved a woman once," he says. "She wasn't good. She wasn't bad. But I loved her anyway."

Johnny Guitar's lineup was myself on vocals and guitar, my friend Claudia Silver on guitar, Damon on drums, and a guy named Shaun on bass. We had our moments, but it wasn't as fun as Speedy and the Castanets. The magic was gone.

Sophomore year I lived in Quincy House with my roommate, Bill Gump, who chewed tobacco and left cups filled with brown spit on my desk. I painted the pipes and radiator bright red, but kept the walls of my room bare.

Every afternoon I sat in my room and listened to my Joy Division and New Order records. Ian Curtis, the tragic figure who hanged himself in 1980 on the eve of their first U.S. tour, was our young Werther, our Rainer Maria Rilke. Following the death of Curtis, Joy Division renamed themselves New Order. I loved their first album, *Movement,* and eagerly awaited their every move. In 1982 they released a string of beautiful singles—*Everything's Gone Green, Procession,* and *Temptation.*

Most of the punk bands that I loved in high school were breaking up or just plain losing their way by 1982. The Clash was self-destructing. This happens to most bands, but the Clash probably faced more pressure than most—the pressure of being important. PiL started to suck, as did Devo and all the other bands that had seemed so important only a few years earlier.

I signed on to be a DJ at WHRB, Harvard's radio station. They gave me the graveyard shift—2:00 to 6:00 A.M. on Wednesdays. This was not good for my studies, but it opened my ears to some new music.

A new crop of L.A.-based bands appeared in the early '80s—bands loosely referred to as the Paisley Underground. There were great albums like *Sixteen Tambourines* by the Salvation Army (who were sued by the real Salvation Army and renamed the Three O'Clock), the Dream Syndicate's *The Days of Wine and Roses,* and *Emergency Third Rail Power Trip* by Rain

Parade (whose leader, David Roback, later formed Opal, who then became Mazzy Star).

New Wave had run out of steam, and there was an inevitable turn toward the past, toward garage music and psychedelic rock indebted to the Velvet Underground, the Seeds, and the 13th Floor Elevators. You can dismiss the Paisley Underground bands as retro, but they sure sounded fresh in 1983, after Frankie Goes to Hollywood, Duran Duran, and U2.

Marxist-Leninist-Bonkerist: Socialism or Barbarism

My first week at Harvard, I encountered a guy named Alden, who was selling a paper called the *Workers Vanguard* outside the Freshman Union.

"We're Trotskyists," he said.

Over the next year I became something of a Trotskyist myself, though not a very good one. I am glad I didn't run into any Maoists.

I knew nothing about Trotsky, who was, after Lenin, the most important leader of the Russian Revolution, and who subsequently became the leader of the Left Opposition to Stalin (a group inside the Communist Party). Stalin had him expelled from the party in 1927, exiled to Alma-Ata, and then deported from the country in the dead of night in February 1929. In 1940 he was murdered at his desk with an ice pick in Mexico City by an agent of Stalin's secret police.

But I was interested in socialist politics. I read the *New York Times* every day and became incensed about the dirty war that Ronald Reagan was conducting in Nicaragua, and the billions of dollars that the U.S. government sent to a regime in El Salvador that killed peasants, nuns, and archbishops.

Alden was in his mid-twenties, tall, blond, and sarcastic. He wasn't a Harvard student, though rumor had it he was from a very wealthy family. He belonged to a group called the Spartacist League (SL), who had been expelled from the Socialist Workers Party in the early 1960s. They called themselves the Spartacist League in tribute to the original German Spartacist League led by Rosa Luxemburg and Karl Liebknecht, socialists who spent World War I behind bars for their principled opposition while the bulk of the Social Democrats gave full support to the war effort.

In 1919 Luxemburg was arrested in Berlin by right-wing Freikorps militias who beat her with rifle butts, shot her in the head, and dumped her body into the River Spree. Liebknecht, too, was arrested, and famously "shot while trying to escape." Isaac Deutscher called these murders the first triumph of Nazi Germany.

I started attending educational forums that the SL held on campus, reading Trotsky's *History of the Russian Revolution* and *The Revolution Betrayed, State and Revolution* by Lenin, and James P. Cannon's *History of American Trotskyism.* Trotsky, a literary critic during his early years in Siberian exile—where he signed his articles Antid Oto—wrote beautifully. In *Literature and Revolution* (1923) he defended poets, scientists, and artists against those who wanted to establish rules for proletarian culture. "No one is going to prescribe themes to a poet or intends to prescribe them. Please write about anything you can think of." His position did not carry the day in Stalin's Soviet Union.

The Spartacist League (and their youth group, the SYL) was reviled by the rest of the American Left, because it spent much of its time polemicizing against other leftist groups, especially anyone who gave support to the Democratic Party come election time (this describes most of the American Left).

The biggest political issue on campus in the early '80s was divestment from South Africa—a movement urging the university to pull its money out of any companies that did business in the apartheid state. The SL refused to join this movement, arguing that it was sheer hypocrisy to urge American bankers to take money out of South Africa. Did not this wealth properly belong to the South African workers? The SL had a knack for coming up with controversial slogans that would draw a hard line between their own stance and everyone else's, and they had a few positions that were unique on the Left. For example, while most of the Left supported the Ayatollah Khomeini's 1979 Iranian revolution, the SL denounced him as a reactionary.

When the Soviet tanks rolled into Afghanistan at the request of its government, which had been embroiled in a civil war for some time, *Workers Vanguard* proclaimed HAIL RED ARMY IN AFGHANISTAN!

This was not a popular position in 1981. The United States pulled out of the Moscow Olympics and Jimmy Carter reintroduced draft registration. As a green-card holder, I, too, was required to register.

The SL argued that the Soviets had intervened on the correct side, the side of a pro-Soviet government that was attempting to bring land reform and women's rights to Afghanistan. On the other side, funded by the CIA and Pakistan's Inter-Services Intelligence (ISI), were the freedom fighters (like Osama bin Laden), the warlords and future Taliban. Dan Rather appeared on TV in tribal headgear, championing the cause of these rugged fighters— the salt of the earth—in their battle against the evil empire.

Gulbuddin Hekmatyar, America's favorite freedom fighter/warlord, and founder of the Hezbi Islami, was reported in his university days to hurl acid at young girls who dared to wear short skirts instead of the veil. (Hekmatyar later called for a jihad against the United States, and claimed to have assisted Osama bin Laden in his escape from Tora Bora.) Dan Rather, Bernard-Henri Lévy, and Rambo lined up in 1980 in support of the courageous mujahideen. The SL position seemed outrageous in 1980, but in light of the subsequent horrors visited on Afghanistan, perhaps they were right.

They were right about a lot of things, but no one was listening much. It seemed no one in America (and certainly not Harvard students) paid attention to words or phrases like "imperialist," "worker," "vanguard party," "bloodthirsty rulers," and "armed fist of the capitalist state." The 1980s were a bleak time for campus radicals, and for the Left in general. The whole country shifted to the Right under Reagan, and it was the conservative student groups that were on the upswing.

I was enlisted to sell *Workers Vanguard* in front of the Harvard dining halls at 6:00 P.M. and to transit workers outside subway stations at 6:00 A.M. I stood in front of the Freshman Union with the headline REAGAN IS WAR CRAZY.

"So's your mother!" one football player answered.

There was no such thing as radical chic. I read about the campus during the 1968–69 school year, how the students took over the dean's office and kicked ROTC off campus, and wished that I could have been a student back then, in an era of free love and student activism, the Weathermen, SDS, LSD, and the Panthers.

There was some positive, too, like raising money for striking English coal miners in 1985, or for the defense of the Nicaraguan revolution (to which the SL gave critical support) against the contras.

One afternoon I was sent to Harvard Law School to collect signatures from law professors for a petition simply stating that the SYL had a right to be on campus.

I wandered into the office of Professor Alan Dershowitz.

"Yes, I will sign your petition. Yours is a despicable anti-Semitic group, but you have the right to demonstrate."

"Anti-Semitic? But it's a Trotskyist group."

Trotsky, born Lev Bronstein, was a Russian Jew, but probably just one more self-hating Jew to Professor Dershowitz.

Village Voice columnist Alexander Cockburn called the SL "Marxist-Leninist-Bonkerist." The SL, meanwhile, came to his defense when he was fired from the *Voice,* with an amusing article titled "Defend the Scoundrel!"

I came to realize that these people were not going to lead an American revolution anytime soon. Not only that, they were ruining my social life. My lovely girlfriend at the time, Eve, complained that she never saw me—there were too many meetings of one sort or another. I pulled away from the SL and was happier when I did so. I got my life back—my life as a petty bourgeois student.

Had I wasted my time? My grades had suffered, but reading Lenin and Luxemburg was more interesting than reading Weber and Durkheim. No one at Harvard taught me a thing about Lieutenant William Calley, the Spanish Civil War, or the 1956 Hungarian uprising against the Soviets (an uprising that the Trotskyists supported). I did learn a few things from these people. Some of them were brilliant, and could talk for hours about the Paris Commune or the history of Students for a Democratic Society. They came from different walks of life—an emergency room surgeon, a young female electrician, and a former minimalist painter who had become an activist. A couple of them were just plain weird—any group on the fringes is going to attract a few nuts. One poor guy wanted to be a Trotskyist and an animal liberationist both, but the SL didn't want him spouting that crap at demonstrations, and rejected his application for membership.

As stated earlier, I was not a good Trotskyist. I lacked revolutionary optimism. I admired people like Victor Serge for their unflagging optimism and dedication, but pessimism and cynicism seemed more appropriate in 1983. Rosa Luxemburg posed a choice for humanity—between socialism and barbarism. Barbarism seemed to be winning.

I was also not a good guitarist. And I was not a good student. I would sit in Lamont Library, staring at the pages for hours, only to discover that I had read a total of three pages of Tocqueville. At the end of each year I found myself hopelessly behind, and would have to sick out of at least one final exam. I became expert at showing up at the university's health services office, complaining of a terrible stomach ailment.

It may be hard to get in to Harvard. But once you're there, it is sure hard to fail. I did my best to get an F in computer science. I was the first student to complete the final exam, standing up after ninety minutes (you're not allowed to leave before that) because I couldn't answer any of the questions. I was certain I had failed, but the teaching assistant let me off with a D, explaining apologetically, "You really bombed on the final."

Somehow I graduated with a degree cum laude in social studies. Technically, then, I was an honors student, but only because all social-studies majors graduated cum laude. It was a rigorous major—once accepted by the department, we took courses in economics, history, sociology, and anthropology. We read months and months of Tocqueville, Marx, Durkheim, Weber, and Freud, and were required to write a senior thesis. Mine was on the sad history of the German Communist Party in the 1920s.

I graduated in 1985. Paul Volcker of the Federal Reserve spoke at the ceremony, single-handedly putting two thousand people to sleep.

I spent the summer in New York City, and then, with no idea of what to do with myself, followed my brilliant and focused girlfriend, Eve—Phi Beta Kappa, Fulbright scholar—to Germany. We spent six lonely months in the city of Kiel. This former member town of the Hanseatic League was once the main base of the German navy, and it was a sailors' mutiny here that began the German Revolution of 1918. If it was once a pretty town, this beauty did not survive—80 percent of the city was destroyed by bombing at the end of World War II.

We settled into a dark and moldy little studio apartment that had formerly been a butcher shop. I found a job teaching English to workers in the submarine and shipbuilding factories. While Eve attended classes at the university, I sat in our backyard apartment and read books that I was supposed to have read in college, like *Dead Souls* by Gogol and *The Magic Mountain* by Thomas Mann, *Man's Fate* by Malraux and Victor Serge's *Memoirs of a Revolutionary*. When I wasn't reading I played my guitar, practicing pentatonic scales for hours on end.

Stuyvesant Town and the Age of Reason

A year later I was back in New York, living at 248 Front Street in Manhattan, between Frankfort Street and Peck Slip, by the fish market at the South Street Seaport. The neighborhood did not yet boast fancy condominiums, but it was in transition. Once I got used to the long walk to the Chinatown Pathmark (the biggest supermarket in Manhattan), the mosquito problem, and the smell of fish, I liked living there.

My roommates were Jamie and Sarah. Jamie was an unemployed actor, Sarah a documentary filmmaker. They fought a lot. The walls were thin and I could hear them yell at each other, with an occasional slap thrown in for good measure. Sarah kept two cats: Shrimpie (the mother) and Weenie (her son). It so happens that Weenie was my nickname, too, but I trained myself not to answer when Sarah called for the kitten.

April was a miserable month. Eve and I were no longer together. Not after she discovered that I had been dating my friend Claudia off and on. Claudia wasn't my girlfriend exactly, but we were old friends who slept together now and then. I wanted something more, but she was happy enough with the arrangement we had.

We would go out on Saturday nights, either go to a party together or drink at Joe's Bar on East Sixth Street or Milano's Bar on Houston, and then go back to Claudia's NoHo loft, where we would stay up all night listening to Al Green's *Greatest Hits, Volume 1,* or *The Good Earth* by the Feelies. Those were fun nights. But upon waking in the morning, Claudia would make it clear that I should leave as soon as possible, preferably without eating breakfast. That wasn't so hard, because her refrigerator rarely contained so much as a stick of butter. I thought it was sexy of Claudia to have an empty fridge.

One day Claudia told me that we shouldn't see each other anymore. It wasn't me, it was her. She wasn't ready for love. I was heartbroken. No one had ever done this to me, and it hurt plenty.

I had a succession of temp jobs that year. I started at Chase Manhattan Bank's offices downtown, the big black building with the giant Dubuffet sculpture out front. I did data entry and typed letters. When my boss discovered that I had attended Harvard and lived in Quincy House (just like her), she offered me a full-time job.

"What are you doing here?"

There are days I think I should have taken that job. But I didn't. I told her I wasn't interested.

I found a new temp job, as the assistant to the assistant to the vice chancellor at New York University. I worked alongside the assistant in her office on the eleventh floor of Bobst Library. She was abrasive and demanding. I typed letters and ran errands and ordered car service. And I combed the back pages of the *Village Voice* looking for bands that needed a guitar player.

One ad looked interesting—a self-described minimalist was searching for a bass player. I couldn't play the bass guitar, but I thought it sounded like something, so I went along to the minimalist's East Village storefront on a Saturday afternoon. He was a long-haired, forty-ish hippie whose favorite band was Vanilla Fudge. But he had a new concept.

"I play one chord, and one scale: A minor."

The band would only perform instrumental pieces comprised of scales in A minor. He saw himself as some kind of minimalist visionary, but I thought of him more as an East Village nutcase.

I went to another audition in the music building on Thirty-eighth Street. The music building was a horrible place. Bad metal blared from dank, dark practice rooms. But the guys I went there to meet weren't like that. They called themselves the Age of Reason. I didn't know about the name until after I had joined. Had their advertisement read "Age of Reason seeks guitar," I would not have called. But they were three cool guys from Albany who had moved down to New York City together. They lived together in a two-bedroom apartment in the West Village, right above a hardware store on Bleecker Street. I liked their songs. We shared a love for midperiod Jonathan Richman, records like *Rockin' and Romance* and *Back in Your Life.* The singer, Robert, wrote all the lyrics and played the cornet. He was way into Jack Kerouac. They all were. They thought they were born too late.

"Wouldn't it be cool to live in Berlin in the twenties?"

"What's wrong with New York City, 1987?"

Robert's kid brother, Frank, played the drums. The bassist, Paul, drove into town in a beautiful old car—a Galaxie 500. That was the first I had heard of that particular automobile.

We couldn't afford a practice space, so we practiced in their apartment until the angry neighbors forced us to look elsewhere. We next rehearsed in the basement of Stuyvesant Town, the big housing complex in the East Twenties, only because Frank had a friend who lived there and they had figured out how to sneak into the basement, where there were long empty corridors, perfect for rehearsing. We couldn't set up a drum kit in the basement of Stuyvesant Town, so Frank played the rhythm on a phone book instead.

We practiced four times a week. The songs were good, and we were making progress, but their favorite thing was to stop the rehearsal and tell AIDS jokes, in lisping tones. That was about the funniest thing they could think of. They also liked to talk frankly about their sexual experiences. Frank told me he would never ever go down on a woman, because it was dirty down there. It began to dawn on me that these guys weren't really hipsters at all. Is it hip to be obsessed with Kerouac and wear a porkpie hat?

Robert loved to chase after women he saw on the street or in the subway. He was not afraid to strike up a conversation anytime an attractive woman appeared. He would happily follow her down the street for a few blocks, trying out various pickup lines. Most of the time it would come to nothing. But Robert insisted that if you made this daily effort, you would get actual results.

On Friday nights the boys liked to go dancing at Nirvana, a bridge-and-tunnel club high above Times Square. They took me along one time, but I didn't understand the attraction of this club. Why would you move all the way to New York City to hang out at a place like this?

After months of rehearsing, we booked a Monday night gig at CBGB. This was exciting. I invited all my friends (which is how they made their money at CBGB on a Monday night—booking half a dozen bands and, by extension, all their friends and families).

The rehearsals did not prepare me for the transformation that took place with our singer. I now know that singers are often completely different onstage than they are off. The moment Robert hit the stage, he began channeling David Lee Roth and Freddie Mercury. He was a clown. He sang. He danced. He wiggled. He made funny faces. And he would not shut up between songs.

I was embarrassed. There I was, under the lights at CBGB for the first time in my life, just now realizing that I was onstage with a fool, and that I needed to quit the band immediately.

Back in Your Life

I now had no band, no girlfriend, and a thankless job. I didn't enjoy waking up in the mornings. Waking up meant realizing that my heart was sort of broken and that I didn't know what I was doing. One hazy summer morning, as I walked the long walk up the hill to the subway station, I came across a couple of dead fish swarming with maggots. I started to cry.

My favorite album that summer was *Back in Your Life* by Jonathan Richman and the Modern Lovers. The album is spotty, but I listened to the title track every day, and felt sorry for myself. I went so far as to include it on a mix tape that I gave to Claudia. Claudia was not impressed. She thought I was pathetic.

The good news was that Damon and Naomi, now grad students at Harvard, were spending the summer in New York, and we were going to try making music together.

Galaxie 500 was born the day that Naomi volunteered to play the bass guitar. Damon and Naomi had been an item since high school.

She had seen all the Speedy and the Castanets gigs, had designed our stage backdrop and our handbills. Now she was studying architecture at Harvard, where Damon was a grad student in comparative literature.

You can spend your time placing ads in the *Village Voice* and sifting through messages left on your answering machine by idiot musicians, or auditioning for other people's bands, but the best thing is to start a band with your friends. Your friends are tasteful and smart and like the same things you do. Who cares if one of you doesn't play an instrument? She can learn.

Mary Harron wrote that rock and roll "is the only form of music which can actually be done *better* by people who can't play their instruments than by people who can." I'm not sure how the Jimi Hendrix Experience fits into that equation, but she has a point—to a point. At any rate, you don't all have to be ace musicians. Great guitar players are a dime a dozen. It is sometimes your very limitations as players that set you apart from the crowd.

In addition to learning the bass, Naomi was becoming a uniquely talented graphic designer, and graphic design is at least as important to a band as the bass guitar. Naomi was always thinking about visuals. Where I saw a gas station, she saw something else altogether. She took photographs of ugly things, but her photographs made them beautiful.

Damon and Naomi were explorers. They liked nothing better than to get in their little yellow Fiat and drive out to Concord or Plum Island or Walden Pond.

We had our first rehearsal on May 27, 1987. Our plan was to work up some cover songs and perform in Washington Square Park. Naomi suggested "Where Have All the Flowers Gone?" Peter, Paul, and Mary had the big hit, but *my* favorite version is by Marlene Dietrich, backed by Burt Bacharach and his band. We also worked out "I Can See Clearly Now" by Johnny Nash, the Temptations' "Just My Imagination (Running Away With Me)," and Dylan's "Knockin' on Heaven's Door." Every band takes a crack at this Dylan tune. It's easy to play and lends itself to stretching out—and Axl Rose had not yet ruined the song for the rest of us.

We rehearsed all summer long. Sometimes Damon and I met during my lunch break. He was studying surrealist poetry that summer, and his investigations sometimes led him to the Bobst Library downstairs. At summer's end we played a gig at my apartment on Front Street. Naomi made up little flyers for the event. It was the best gig of my life. I didn't break a string. I didn't forget the words. We played for twenty minutes, and it was just perfect.

In August we took ourselves into 6/8 Studios, in the Cable Building, at the corner of Broadway and Houston. These were the first Galaxie 500 recordings, two sessions on a Thursday and Saturday night, with an engineer named Perkin Barnes. We recorded seven songs.

My favorite song from the session was "The Other Side," which Naomi wrote. Her singing was shaky (and mine was, too), but it worked. The best moment in the song came when I hit the wrong chord and had to slide into the correct one. I incorporated that wrong chord into the song when we played it live. If you make a mistake, you should repeat it, because then everyone will think you did it on purpose.

I took that cassette home and listened to it again and again. Sometimes, if you listen to something again and again, it gets better. But not this tape. It was decidedly mediocre. I had two guitar sounds—thin and scratchy. I could have used some singing lessons. Since we always rehearsed without a microphone, I never got to hear myself sing. When I stepped up to the microphone in the studio, I could hear myself all too well. Since I was self-conscious about my lyrics, I mumbled my way through the songs and we buried the vocals in the mix.

What I didn't realize is that we were halfway there. We were a half-baked, primitive version of the band we later became. We droned along, playing simple chord progressions, building them up and breaking them down. We weren't good, but we were different.

I was still thinking about Claudia, but tried dating other girls. One Thursday night in June there was a little office party at NYU. Some of us got a little tipsy and I wound up kissing a girl from the office. A week later we went on a date, and she took me home to her apartment in Greenpoint. Her bedroom had nothing on the walls except a wooden crucifix. We made love right there and in the middle of our lovemaking she told me she loved me.

What? Hadn't she ever been told not to say that on the first date?

September rolled around and I realized that I had no particular reason to stay in New York City. Damon and Naomi were heading back to grad school in Boston and I decided to follow them, to see where this band thing would lead.

Chet's Last Call

Naomi knew some architecture students with a room to rent in Somerville. The address was 32 Adrian Street, near Inman Square. Adrian was very briefly my middle name—I was born Michael Adrian Dean Wareham, before my grandfather argued that it was a sissy name, and Adrian was dropped.

A Cambridge temp agency placed me in a secretarial job at MIT, working for the dean of student affairs. The office was a collection of assistant deans that offered psychological counseling to students who were having a hard time adjusting to the rigors of life at MIT. And plenty of students had a hard time there. There were several suicides that semester, and on those days no one smiled.

My roommates were never at home—they were always at the charrette. I had my own little room, which I painted a shade of blue called November Sky. I didn't have a lot of possessions, just my Epiphone Riviera and my guitar amplifier and a stereo system and my record collection. My rent was $325 a month.

We found a rehearsal space in a converted warehouse on the corner of Wareham and Albany Streets in South Boston, right by the expressway. We shared the rehearsal room with Damon's former band, I Heart My Doghead, or the Dogheads for short. Having a domestic animal in your band name was popular in Boston. There was Dogzilla, the Raindogs, the Cavedogs, and Scruffy the Cat.

I was living on Adrian Street, rehearsing on Wareham Street, and working in the dean's office. Surely this was where I was supposed to be.

I needed wheels—you need transportation if you want to be in a band. It usually says that right in the classified ads—"transportation a must."

Damon and Naomi drove me out to the leafy suburb of Newton, where I purchased an orange 1972 VW Beetle from a gentleman who had recently upgraded to a brand-new Mazda. We returned with two cars, their yellow Fiat and my orange Beetle. That's how we rolled into our gigs, looking like a couple of Jujyfruits.

If a band doesn't have a manager or a booking agent, then someone in the band assumes that role. In our band, Damon was that someone. He started booking our shows, making the annoying phone calls to clubs around town, and sending out our demo cassettes. He immediately got a call from Chet, the owner of Chet's Last Call. Chet offered us our first club show, on Thursday, October 1, at midnight. Thursday is a good night—it's almost Friday.

Chet's, formerly known as the Penalty Box, was located on Causeway Street, directly across from the old Boston Garden. The downstairs bar catered to hockey fans and police officers. The club upstairs was for up-and-coming bands who were going absolutely nowhere, bands who weren't established enough to play at the Rat in Kenmore Square. Apparently Chet's was also *the* place to buy a bag of heroin (from one of the guys who worked the door). They had an ingenious system at Chet's whereby you hand out cheap tickets to your friends, and when they show up at the door, Chet knows which band they came to see, and he knows who is bringing in the crowd.

We weren't quite ready for the gig, but we weren't going to turn down a Thursday night at Chet's. I was terrified onstage. But we got through the show, and enough of Damon and Naomi's friends came out to see us and bought drinks to make Chet think that we must have a following. We recorded the show on a portable boom box and listened to the cassette the next day. It sounded like shit. *We* sounded like shit. Still, Chet asked us back just six days later. Chet loved us!

The college radio stations in Boston encouraged local bands to submit cassette tapes, and if they liked your song, you'd get radio play. No matter that you didn't even have a record out, you could have a hit single on WMBR (the excellent radio station affiliated with MIT) without there being an actual physical single. We sent them "The Walking Song," which sounded not unlike the Feelies, if the Feelies had been a three-piece band who couldn't play their instruments instead of the amazingly precise musical machine that they were.

I mailed tapes from work to a handful of independent record companies: Coyote, Big Time, Homestead, Celluloid, Relativity, Taang!, Ace of Hearts, and Slash. Today there are thousands of independent record companies, and anyone can release a record. Back then, there weren't so many.

One day in October Claudia called. She said she had been walking down the street and she stopped dead in her tracks and realized that she missed me. I certainly hadn't stopped missing her. I still thought about her all the time. Every day. So she came up to visit me for the weekend, and it was nice. Still, she reminded me that it wasn't a good idea to go falling in love with people, because it would only end badly. In response, I wrote pained lyrics about her, for a song called "Oblivious":

Came to the door but she wouldn't see me
So I turned away to leave
She leaned out the window and said, Where you goin'?
Now I have no time to grieve

These were not my best lyrics, but they were heartfelt. My confusion was real.

One snowy night in November we played at Green Street Station, a club in Jamaica Plain. A major snowstorm hit the city. We took the stage at midnight, playing our songs to half a dozen regulars who were hanging out at the bar, watching the weather report on TV. We earned $12. I sang badly, and so did Naomi. But no one was there, so it didn't matter. It's good to play shows where no one is listening. It's good practice for the shows where people will be listening.

Soundman Chuck White was listening and he said he liked our sound. We gave him a cassette. Joyce Linehan, who booked the club (and later went on to work for Sub Pop), liked us, too, and promised she would have us back on a night when there wasn't a snowstorm. We drove back to our rehearsal space at fifteen miles an hour, the Fiat leading the way through the blizzard. I had lost the driver's-side windshield wiper, so I drove with one arm out the window trying to clear the snow off the windshield with my hand.

.   .   .

We returned to Chet's for another Thursday night show. We shared the bill with the Well Babies. Their band name did not mean "babies who fell into a well." Rather it signified the room in the hospital where they put the babies who are doing well. The Well Babies had a good-size crowd, which at Chet's meant about forty people. The singer was a chubby guy who dressed in a diaper, tube socks, and sneakers, and wore his hair in a bun. He rather resembled a sumo wrestler. During their final song, he punched a hole in the dropped ceiling over the stage. They were friendly people, though. They liked our show, and said let's play together again sometime. Others in the crowd were less hospitable. We had a couple of hecklers. "College boys!" they yelled at us.

By the time we finished our set, the club was empty. Chet added up the tickets and paid us $6. A new low. The soundman said we needed to promote our shows better.

"Promotion, promotion, promotion!"

It's hard to get your friends to go out of their way to see you at midnight on a Thursday. They'll do it once, but you can't really ask them to come back again two weeks later. People have stuff to do.

The Rat

Paying the rent was a struggle. One Friday in November I found myself with $7 to last me till payday on Tuesday. Fortunately, Damon loaned me some money. I now owed money to Damon and Naomi *and* rent to my roommates. I was saved by Anna Poor (Graham's sister) and her husband, Francis, who rented me a room in their house on the edge of Jamaica Plain and Roxbury (where my great-great-grandfather lived in 1860).

My job at MIT was a bummer. I didn't like the lunch options around MIT. And I felt like I was working at the State Department. Sure, they had Noam Chomsky, but other than that the school felt like an extension of the military. There were ROTC cadets everywhere. And the suicides.

I found a new temp job at the Brigham and Women's Hospital, filing and copying and typing for the head of the pulmonary division. My boss was a gentle professor, with a dirty secret. He smoked a pipe. The head of the pulmonary division hid in his office and smoked, while the other doctors wrote technical articles on the harmful effects of this or that chemical on the lungs—asthma, humid air versus cold air, tobacco.

I investigated the refrigerator and storage closet in the pulmonary division, and found a small bottle of liquid ketamine. My brother Anthony had told me several times how wonderful ketamine was. It's an animal tranquilizer, but it is also a fantastic psychedelic drug. Which is why they won't give it to humans—it's too much fun.

I studied the ketamine bottle, but I wasn't sure how to administer it. Was I going to have to shoot this stuff into my veins? I was a little put off by the label: POISON.

I could have called Anthony for advice. Anthony had been back in the United States for some years, but he had just recently checked out of rehab—he had developed an addiction to cocaine, and whatever else he could get his hands on. I didn't feel right asking him for advice on how to administer the ketamine. After staring at the vial each day for a couple of weeks, I flushed it down the toilet.

S oon Galaxie 500 was deemed good enough to score a Wednesday night show at T. T. the Bear's Place on Brookline Street. T.T.'s was a step up from Chet's. Real national touring acts booked shows here. We pulled in thirty-five paying customers, which was a grand success. After the show, there was a party at an apartment house in Central Square. Meltdown was playing in the basement. Scenester/impresario Billy Ruane was there, completely soaked as usual. Rock critic Francis DiMenno sat out in the backyard eating a McDonald's salad with his bare hands.

Francis wrote for a free biweekly fanzine called the *Noise,* the kind that you find in the entranceways to rock clubs and record stores. He had seen our show, and said he liked it well enough, though we still needed some work.

When you're starting out as a band, people like Francis DiMenno are gods. Unemployed geeks who are addicted to science fiction and write for free magazines that no one reads. Overworked club promoters who answer the phones only on Tuesday afternoons between three and six o'clock. They seem like immensely important and powerful people.

The party's hosts had built a special slide, like a supermarket conveyor belt, that ran from the kitchen to the backyard. You could get on a wooden cart, hurtle down the slide, and land on a big cushion in the yard. They had an old black-and-white TV set up out there, so you could watch TV in the freezing cold. I rode the slide and got a splinter in my hand. Some guy punched out the glass in the front door of the apartment. A weird girl kept saying my name.

"Dean."

"Dean."

"Dean."

"Dean."

I went home and wrote the lyrics to "Tugboat."

I don't wanna stay at your party
I don't wanna talk to your friends

I don't wanna vote for your president
I just wanna be your tugboat captain

I kept it simple—I sang the same verse three times. Maybe I was lazy. But plenty of great songs only have two lyrics—"Fly, Robin, Fly" by Silver Convention, for example, or "I Don't Wanna Walk Around with You" by the Ramones.

Lois from the Rathskellar (aka the Rat) was another person who seemed powerful. The Rat was located in Kenmore Square, around the corner from the hotel where they fixed the 1919 World Series. Lois had a cancellation, and needed us to fill in one Saturday night at the upstairs bar (not the rock club itself, which was in the basement). She paid us $30 for three sets, and it cost us $20 to put our cars in the parking lot, so we made $10, but we were pleased to be playing at the Rat on a Saturday night.

After the second set, a guy named Lloyd sent three Budweisers to the stage with a note saying he wanted to talk to us.

"How would you feel about adding a vocalist?" he asked me.

Lloyd said he was a scout for the Roxy in Los Angeles. He brought people to L.A. Not only that, but he lived next door to Jon Bon Jovi.

"Bon Jovi are great. Cinderella are terrible. I guarantee you, Dean, you will not hear another album from Cinderella. I hear early Beatles in your music, and Crosby, Stills, and Nash—am I right?"

Noise New York

After five months of rehearsing and gigging around Boston, we had half a dozen new songs ready to record. All the Boston bands recorded at the same couple of studios with the same engineers and producers. We decided to record in New York City with a real record producer. I put in a call to Kramer at Noise New York.

Kramer had been a member of Shockabilly and Gong and (briefly) the Butthole Surfers. Now he played in two great new bands, Bongwater and B.A.L.L.

I had seen Shockabilly perform at 8BC a couple of years ago, with Anthony. Anthony loved Alphabet City, maybe because it was easy to buy coke and smack in that neighborhood. 8BC was located in a basement on Eighth Street between Avenues B and C, amid abandoned and burnt-out buildings. They sold Budweisers out of a large bucket for a dollar each. 8BC didn't last long, as it was quite obviously lacking in the proper permits. But it was great while it lasted. It was there that I was introduced to Shockabilly and to comedy acts like the Alien Comic and They Might Be Giants.

Kramer had recently produced the terrific new Half Japanese album, *Music to Strip By.* We could record with Kramer for $35 an hour—a bargain. I couldn't afford my share, but Damon loaned it to me. He was generous like that. I don't know why they always had money and I was always broke even though they were students, while I had an actual job, but there it was.

In February 1988, we drove the Fiat and VW down to the city for our session at Noise New York, a fourth-floor walk-up at 247 West Broadway, close to the exit from the Holland Tunnel. One side contained Kramer's apartment; the other was the recording studio, a single room without any soundproofing treatment or gobos or isolation booths or rugs—just a wooden floor and brick walls. He had a sixteen-track, one-inch tape machine, but one of the tracks was permanently broken. So officially we made fifteen-track recordings. But equipment is overrated—it's the people behind the gear who make the difference.

Kramer was the skinniest man I had ever met. He had long, dark hair, halfway down his back, tied in a ponytail, and he smoked weed vigorously.

We didn't have the foggiest idea how to record a song. Our basic formula was to play the verse and the chorus for a couple of minutes and then let the song wander where it pleased, not bothering to go to a bridge or come back for another chorus. Kramer later said he thought we were retarded when he first heard us bashing out those chords.

"Tugboat" was comprised of a single repeating chord change (one that Damon came up with) to which I added a very simple guitar line. Kramer drenched my voice in reverb and echo, and sent me out to play some kind of guitar solo. I was given one take. The song explodes in ecstasy a little over halfway through, riding out with cymbal splashes and a guitar phrase that repeats over and over before the song breaks down and it feels like the clouds have lifted.

We walked out of Noise New York with recordings of our half dozen songs. Some of them were unfinished. But, incredibly, "Tugboat" was good. It was like a trip to another planet—we didn't sound like the scratchy three-piece band that had been gigging at Chet's Last Call. Somehow I had stumbled on my own guitar sound. And together we sounded like Galaxie 500. We didn't sound like the Modern Lovers, Big Star, the 13th Floor Elevators, Love, Joy Division, or the Feelies, or like anything else we had been listening to. And we didn't sound like every other protogrunge band that was popular in Boston. This in itself was an achievement.

We made up a box of cassettes and started sending them around. Billy Ruane was booking shows at a new place, the Middle East—a Lebanese restaurant and belly-dancing club in Central Square.

I first met Billy in 1981 at a gig by Human Sexual Response, at Harvard's Freshman Union. I was watching the band do their signature New Wave tunes "Jackie Onassis" and "What Does Sex Mean to Me?" when suddenly someone was climbing on my back and doing the pogo, bumping into people. That was Billy. Sloshed. Wearing a rumpled suit and tie, which was his uniform for many years to come. If not a suit, then he would wear a black full-length winter coat. Billy's day job was working at Widener Library, in the room where they kept the obscene books.

Billy could be seen at any important gig in town, getting loaded, jumping up and down while holding a drink, which he sometimes spilled all over himself. Some nights he would jump onstage and urge the crowd to make some noise for an encore. He was routinely banned from certain clubs for a couple of months for such behavior, but they invariably took pity on him and let him back in. He was Billy Ruane.

Billy gave us one of our big breaks, a Saturday afternoon show at the Middle East, on a bill with Beat Happening, a trio that actually swapped instruments as if to make sure that no one ever became too proficient on either guitars or drums. We went over well that Saturday afternoon.

Calvin Johnson, their leader, was later called the Andy Warhol of Olympia, Washington, an unrepentant punk rocker and leader of the International Pop Underground. Calvin's version of punk did not mean wearing a leather jacket and playing loud and fast. "As it turned out," writes Michael Azerrad, "Beat Happening and K [Records] were a major force in widening the idea of a punk rocker from a mohawked guy in a motorcycle jacket to a nerdy girl in a cardigan." Of course, this was a losing battle. Punk would later come to mean Green Day and Blink-182.

Johnson urged everyone to pick up an instrument and do it themselves. His own K label showed the way forward, before Sub Pop even existed. He seemed to sign anyone with the guts to stand up and pour their hearts out in song whether they could sing or play or not.

It's a nice idea. But what worked for Beat Happening does not work for everyone. Calvin Johnson had a great voice and a magnetic stage presence, and Beat Happening wrote great songs, even if they could barely play their instruments. This does not mean that any indie rocker with an acoustic guitar can do it, too. No, it is difficult to play your instrument badly and still be compelling. But Calvin did it brilliantly.

Marc Alghini of Taang! Records was at the Middle East that afternoon. We had sent our demo cassette to Taang!, and though Curtis Casella, the head of the label, was not impressed, Alghini heard something that he liked. His parents had given him a little seed money to start his own record company, Aurora Records, and he wanted us to be his first signing.

A couple weeks later we were signing a silly little contract that called for us to deliver one single (*Tugboat*), one EP, and one LP to Aurora Records. To celebrate the signing, Marc took us out for buffalo wings.

Life was good. Claudia and I were in love. And someone was paying for my band to make a record. I wasn't going to make a penny, but we didn't care about that. There was no indication that playing in a band could be anything but fun. Our goals were limited—to make a record that we would want to listen to, and to headline at Green Street Station on a Saturday night.

Today

I found another stupid job in the springtime, working eight to five o'clock in the human resources department of a large engineering firm, over near Government Center. I sat in my cubicle entering personnel data and typing letters, while listening to the morning show on WMBR. Mornings they played indie rock, afternoons they played obscure '60s stuff.

I worked all day and rehearsed at night and it seemed like I was on the go from 7:00 A.M. until midnight every day that spring.

The *Tugboat* single arrived in May, on beautiful blue vinyl. Getting the product in hand was a great moment. We took photographs of one another holding the blue vinyl. That blue single was the coolest thing I had ever seen. Alghini had us number all five hundred of the singles. That's what the indie labels liked to do—colored vinyl in small editions. Sub Pop and Taang! did the same thing. They aimed for the collector scum, as they were called. You could press a single in blue vinyl, and then re-press it in yellow vinyl a year later. Real collector scum needed to have both.

I almost feel sorry for kids today. They don't know the thrill of getting a perfect seven-inch single on colored vinyl, with one song on each side. Something you can hold in your hand, put into a protective plastic sleeve with all your other seven-inch singles. They're stuck listening to low-fidelity MP3s on their tiny cell phones.

I took copies of the single around to record stores in New York. The guy at Bleecker Bob's (which by now had moved from MacDougal to West Third) gave it a quick spin. He listened for about fifteen seconds and gave me a snotty look.

"Oh, yeah. What's your favorite Byrds album?"

"I don't have any Byrds albums. I don't like David Crosby."

I later came to appreciate some of the Byrds' albums (even David Crosby's first solo record), but that was how I felt at the time.

He took five copies.

In July we went back to Noise New York to record our LP *Today.* We recorded and mixed the whole album in just three days. The first day, we loaded in at 2:00 P.M., waking Kramer up. We worked on basic tracks for four hours, quit at 6:00, came back and redid a couple of songs the next day. Kramer took an active role this time, really producing instead of looking at us like we were missing something. On "Oblivious," he slowed down the tape so I could hit the high falsetto notes.

Critics later wrote about my "otherwordly wail," suggesting that my voice sounded like I had been beamed in from another planet. Part of that vocal sound was dictated by the recording process. I wasn't entirely comfortable out there in the big recording room, and Kramer generally kept me to one take per song. I didn't have time to experiment, to try getting closer to the microphone and singing in a lower, quieter voice. So I sang high and loud and scared.

He had me play acoustic guitar and slide guitar (something I'd never done) on "Instrumental" and "Song in 3." Don Fleming, the singer in B.A.L.L., stopped by to smoke some weed with Kramer. Fleming lived downstairs with his wife, Margaret Bodde, and they seemed like a great couple.

Kramer sent me out to overdub a lead guitar on our interpretation of Jonathan Richman's "Don't Let Our Youth Go to Waste." The song goes on for a while, and I was completely lost, but when I came into the control room Damon and Naomi gave me the thumbs-up. It sounded great. The guitar had played itself.

On the third day we mixed the entire album, with Kramer adding some piano and synthesized strings as he went.

"You know what would be *hilarious* here?" he would say.

The whole record was made for $750, including sixty minutes' worth of one-inch tape. It is still my favorite Galaxie 500 album.

Kramer did a great job, and we loved being around him. He was funny and charming and seemed to know so much and have such a cool life, being in two bands and producing Half Japanese and having his own record company, and being married to Shannon, who designed wedding gowns and rock T-shirts.

Up to this point it had been smooth sailing within Galaxie 500. We were three friends making music together. But now we had some decisions to make, and we were going to make them democratically. Two issues cropped up after we finished recording *Today.*

The first was which songs we were going to include on the album. We had recorded eleven, but Damon and Naomi only liked nine of them. When we got together to discuss which songs to use, Damon and Naomi formed a voting bloc. They each had the exact same opinion on the subject. I wanted to include a tenth track, "Crazy," but they were both against it. I was out-voted. That's democracy, I suppose. But our democracy had an inherent flaw—two of us had formed a faction that met beforehand in the privacy of their home. This song meeting would be repeated every time we finished an album. Damon and Naomi always showed up with the same opinion, and that opinion would carry the day.

We also argued about songwriting credits. Bands often fight about this stuff. Naomi argued that the songs were a collaboration. Some of them certainly were, but I thought I deserved full songwriting credit on some of them. I was bringing in most of the raw material in terms of what is traditionally called songwriting—the chords, the melodies, the lyrics—so why should they get two-thirds of the songwriting credit?

"But we share everything," they said. Damon pointed out that he had been the one booking all our shows, but he didn't get paid any more for that, so why should I be paid more for writing the lyrics?

I spent a lazy August in New York with Claudia, and Damon and Naomi and I continued our arguments in a series of angry phone calls. Finally, Damon said that he and Naomi would quit if I didn't agree to "Songs written by Galaxie 500," and that I should "find another backing band." Of course I didn't think of them as a backing band. I knew we had created this sound together.

I couldn't stand the thought of the record not even coming out after all this work. I agreed to credit the songs collectively, and Damon said that he would make more of an effort to bring new song ideas to the band.

The moment you make a record, you are in business. It's too bad that we never bothered to sit down with a manager or a lawyer who might have explained that lots of bands fight about this stuff, and that there are common formulas for working out who contributed what. Pete Kember from Spacemen 3, for example, told me that he and Jason Pierce had come to fisticuffs the first time songwriting credits were discussed in a band meeting.

There were no fisticuffs in Galaxie 500. But these arguments had been heated, and I wondered how things would be in the fall when we got back to work. On the one hand I felt lucky to be in a band with Damon and Naomi, who were both brilliant in their own ways. But I had a new taste in my mouth, a taste that never fully disappeared for the rest of our time together as a band.

I think critical incidents like this arise for many bands, and that in those moments your friendship essentially disappears for good. You may still be able to laugh together and have fun, but at the heart of it all something has changed forever. Your friendship has been poisoned.

B-210

When *Today* was released that fall, we were invited down to WBCN to talk to renowned DJ Albert O, who had a Sunday night specialty show. This was my introduction to the Sunday night radio ghetto. All over the country, from MTV to WBCN, they had these slots at midnight on Sunday, where they would actually let the DJs choose which songs to play—when they were sure that no one was listening.

"Albert O loves the record," they said.

"Oedipus loves your album."

Of course, he wasn't allowed to play it before midnight.

My orange VW Beetle (the Chief) was beginning to crap out on me. The rusted driver's-side running board fell off one day. There was a hole in the floor. The mechanic said I needed to spend $600 to get it to pass inspection. I didn't have $600. For $200 I found a Datsun B-210 station wagon stuck in someone's backyard in Sudbury. You always get a better price if the used car won't even start, but my friend John Moore jumpstarted it easy enough. I didn't know it at the time, but the Datsun B-210 handles like a wheelbarrow.

On Friday, October 26, 1988, we had a record release party at the Rat. We were part of a four-band bill—Bitch Magnet, Galaxie 500, Christmas, and Salem 66. Alghini went all out and brought a couple of deli platters. FHB ("family, hold back"), he told us—these assorted meats and cheeses were for the important people. Salem 66 recorded for Gerard Cosloy's Homestead label. They had roadies to carry their equipment in and out of the club for them, like real rock stars. I wondered who was paying the roadies.

We were paid our $70 that night by Mitch, the club manager. Mitch had

had his vocal cords removed. At the end of the night he counted out your money by holding a little microphone in front of his throat. It was intimidating. You can't argue with a guy who sounds like a robot.

Things were happening for Galaxie 500. *Today* quickly became a top seller at Newbury Comics in Boston. In early November we drove down to New York to play the College Music Journal (CMJ) Marathon. We were booked at CBGB's Record Canteen—not CBGB proper, but Hilly Krystal's record store next door, which had a little stage in the back. The Record Canteen wasn't as glamorous as the big club, but at least the toilet stalls had doors on them.

The Chills were playing next door that night, in the big room. We met Ira and Georgia from Yo La Tengo, and Gerard Cosloy, who had booked us at the Canteen and liked our record. I also met an older gentleman named Sandy Bull, who was on the bill with us. He did a really cool set on the electric oud, which he ran through a heavy tremolo setting on his amp. Bull was a little-known legend of the sixties folk scene and had just released his first album in fifteen years.

We came back to New York again a couple weeks later. Todd Abramson said our record was selling well in Hoboken, and gave us a slot opening for Pussy Galore at Maxwell's.

Pussy Galore showed up at Maxwell's with four guitarists and no bass player. Their drummer, Bob Bert, played a homemade drum kit that featured an old gas tank where you would normally find the snare drum. Things seemed a little tense in that band—like maybe they didn't want to be in the same room together. I have since learned that things are tense in every band.

B.A.L.L. didn't seem to get along so well, either. Kramer invited us to open for them at Hampshire College, so long as they could borrow our equipment. This was how Kramer operated. He would find a local band that were fans of his and offer them the opening slot for B.A.L.L. Then he would borrow their drums and amplifiers. This meant he didn't have to bother renting a damn Econoline van and loading it full of equipment. He could just show up at sound check and the opening band would have done all the grunt work. Kramer was a bass player, but I never once saw him bring a bass amp to a gig. He thought that was for suckers.

Don Fleming was pickled that night at Hampshire College, or else he was doing some kind of Dean Martin impression, pretending to be a drunk onstage. He was a master of between-song banter.

"Good evening. We're B.A.L.L. That stands for *Bite My Ass!*"

Kramer yelled, "*Shut up, shut up!*" at him from the other side of the stage. Kramer was so incensed by Fleming's antics that he refused to go back onstage for the encore. The rest of the band took the stage without him.

I n December we all piled into my Datsun (the yellow Fiat was in the shop) and drove down to New York for a big show with Sonic Youth and B.A.L.L.—a benefit for See Hear, the little fanzine shop on East Seventh Street. We drove all the way to New York in a blizzard. Damon insisted on driving. He let me drive for twenty minutes after lunch, but then I had to listen to him tell me what to do from the backseat, so I let him take the wheel again. I remembered this about Damon from high school—that he absolutely refused to ride in a car driven by another high-school student, which was pretty smart of him. But now his behavior struck me as controlling.

CBGB was packed for the big show. Gerard Cosloy was there with a new issue of *Conflict* in his hands. There were lots of fanzines back then, but the ones that mattered were *Forced Exposure*, which employed brilliant writer Byron Coley, and Cosloy's *Conflict*. Cosloy had given us a nice write-up:

> Very low-key, off-center, off-color single . . . a genuinely distant feel to both sides, perhaps 'cause they took precaution to record this somewhere other than the usual 2 or 3 Boston locations. . . . Anything but impersonal, Galaxie 500 risk looking like idiots and they're only stronger for it.
>
> (Conflict 49, winter 1989)

Byron Coley was there, too. Byron used to DJ at WHRB, and occasionally he would come in right after I finished my shift. He wrote us a nice review in *Spin*, where he did the monthly column on underground rock:

> Boston bands have a tendency to run in packs, so it's always notable when a good one comes along that doesn't sound anything like the other stylers on the block. . . . Into the void comes Galaxie 500—a young trio who've been around for about a year. Their live shows are still a bit tentative, but their

album, Today, *is a doozy. . . . It also contains the snazziest Velvet Under-ground revisionism since the Dream Syndicate's debut. . . . The band takes this stuff and tosses it into the blender with a weird lush/stark stance that doesn't not recall the gentle thrippling of the Young Marble Giants. And it may well be that I won't like where these guys end up eventually, but this gorgeous adolescent downstroke is a great snap of a band-in-progress.*

(Spin *magazine, January 1989)*

I asked him what "thrippling" meant.

"If you don't know," he said, "I can't tell you."

Something was going on. People liked Galaxie 500.

This is the great thing about starting a rock-and-roll band. You can make a record and press it up for just a couple thousand dollars. And if it's original, if it does something different, then people will notice. That doesn't mean that you'll be a rock star, or be heard by millions of people. But you'll be heard by some.

Kramer told us that Kim Gordon and Thurston Moore, from Sonic Youth, had been listening to our record on tour and they liked it, too. In 1988, this was already akin to a new cultural award, something you might hear about in the pages of the *NME.* "Thurston Moore's favorite album of the year!" Though Kim and Thurston had championed Das Damen, too, and everyone knew they were crap.

Randy Detroit and
Blue Thunder

In January we received a phone call from Randy Kaye (formerly known by his punk-rock moniker Randy Detroit) at Slash Records. Randy had seen us play one night during CMJ, at Nightingale Bar on Second Avenue at Thirteenth Street. This place was a dump—soon to be known as the dump where the Spin Doctors honed their awful sound. Our gig at Nightingale was not officially part of the CMJ Marathon, but Randy happened to see a flyer that we had put up outside CBGB.

Randy ran his own small label, Genius Records, which had released the Spacemen 3 albums in the United States, but his day job was as an A&R man at Slash. He went back to L.A. and lobbied his boss, Bob Biggs, to listen to our album. It took Bob a month to do so, but when he did, he announced that it was "monumental," and that he wanted us to record some demos for Slash, and set up a gig so he could see us play live.

We immediately went back into the studio with Kramer for a two-and-a-half-day session that yielded eight new songs, "Cold Night," "When Will You Come Home?," "Plastic Bird," "Strange," "Leave the Planet," and a cover of New Order's "Ceremony" among them. We recorded the basic tracks on day one. On day two Damon lobbied Kramer to retrack most of them, but Kramer wouldn't hear of it. He liked to keep things moving forward, which is a good trait in a producer. I spent the day doing guitar overdubs and vocals.

"He's your meal ticket," Kramer told Damon and Naomi during those sessions. "He's your bread and butter."

These comments induced an awkward silence.

On the third day Kramer mixed all eight songs in four hours. That's right—it only took Kramer thirty minutes to mix each song. He was either brilliant or lazy, or a bit of both.

Kramer did a phenomenal job producing our album. Then, the very day after I drove back to Boston, he invited Claudia to the movies and made a pass at her. That was Kramer. He couldn't help himself. Some people might think, I'm working with this band and they're about to get signed and that's a good job for me—so I better not hit on the singer's girlfriend. Not Kramer. He thought more like, Wow, Dean's girlfriend is hot. Maybe she'll fuck me when Dean goes back to Boston. I should have punched Kramer in the nose, but I knew he didn't stand a chance of stealing my girlfriend away from me.

April 28 we were back in New York City, playing the Pyramid Club on Avenue A. We made $280. It was now obvious that we were far more popular in New York than in our adopted hometown of Boston.

The next day I crashed the Datsun, skidding on an exit ramp near Hartford on a rainy Saturday afternoon. I was towed to a gas station, then took a cab to Bradley International Airport, rented a car, and made it to Boston in time for our gig, opening for Eugene Chadbourne at the Rat. Dave Rick jammed with us, and Robyn Hitchcock was in attendance for some reason. He jumped onstage and sang "Rain" with us, the only song we were sure we all knew. The next day we listened to the recording of Galaxie 500 with Robyn Hitchcock. We sounded dreadful, but his voice was great. This little collaboration was mentioned on MTV—we were almost famous.

I retrieved my Datsun from East Hartford. It now handled even worse than before, pulling to the left when I put my foot on the brakes. This would not do. I found new wheels at a trailer park in Dedham—a 1975 Dodge Dart Slant-6, blue with the hard black top, which I bought from an old retiree for $150. I just needed to figure out how to get it started. The battery wouldn't charge, because the alternator was fried. I replaced that alternator myself. It was a filthy afternoon's work of cursing and banging, but I did it.

My new car was so magnificent that it needed its own name: Blue Thunder, for the Roy Scheider film about a special new helicopter designed to pacify the civilian population of Los Angeles.

The Dodge Dart was a whole new world, a world of power steering and power brakes. It also had a few problems of its own. I replaced the radiator with one that I found at a junkyard. Another filthy afternoon's work, and while replacing the radiator I put a hole in the line that circulated the transmission fluid. Because of my clumsiness, the transmission fluid now leaked slowly along the pipes under the car, the hot pipes turning it into foul smoke that entered the car via a hole in the right-rear wheel well.

I loved that car. You can like a Datsun 210, but it's not the same as loving a Dodge Dart. A few years later I bequeathed the Dart to Anthony, when he was living on the Upper West Side of Manhattan. He used it to drive farther uptown and score drugs. A year after I gave it to him, I received a summons declaring that Blue Thunder had been abandoned and towed by the city, with a couple thousand dollars' worth of tickets owed on it. There was no license plate, but the VIN number had been visible on the dashboard. I went to court and explained to the judge that I had sold the car to my brother, the junkie, and that he was the one they needed to talk to. He dismissed the charges and told me to be more careful about who I gave my car to.

I didn't feel good about ratting on my brother again. It reminded me of the Life Savers and the chocolate-coated pink marshmallow fish from when we were kids. But there was no chocolate fish this time.

Spongetunnel

I n March of 1989, during Damon's spring break, Galaxie 500 went on our first tour. Our booking agent was Tom Johnston, who managed Bullet LaVolta and the Cavedogs and later Buffalo Tom and Bettie Serveert. Tom was a workaholic and a truly sweet guy.

Our pal Dave Rick (the amazing guitarist with Bongwater and Phantom Tollbooth) volunteered to be the tour manager. He couldn't do sound, but he had more experience than we did, having been on tour before. He was along to drive and find hotels and teach us the rules and etiquette of life on the road.

Our first show was in New York, at a party organized by Calvin Johnson, at Eighth Street and Avenue B, in a dance studio in the basement. Calvin was dancing wildly when we arrived, high on peanut-butter-and-jelly sandwiches and Tang. Mecca Normal was up first. I found them arty and annoying. She wailed her feminist rants, while he struck guitar poses. We borrowed their shitty equipment and played a fuzzy set for an enthusiastic crowd.

Paleface later immortalized this evening in a song about how he threw up at a Galaxie 500 show. Paleface was Beck's roommate around this time, and one of the originators of the antifolk movement. He later suggested that Beck stole his whole persona, but I don't know about that.

The following night we were back at CBGB, opening for B.A.L.L. and Unrest. A guy named Terry Tolkin, who worked at Caroline Records, had put us on the bill.

Neil Hagerty of Pussy Galore was hanging around during our sound check. I'm not sure what he was doing at CBGB at five in the afternoon, but he seemed to be out of it on smack. His eyes were pinned and he stood by the side of the stage, scratching his legs and telling me about the suede pants that he had picked up on the street for $5. Admittedly, that is a very good price for suede pants.

Monday morning I was at Claudia's place on Bleecker Street, excitedly packing my bag for the trip to Cleveland. I called Tom to get the name and phone number of the club so that we could get directions.

"Bad news. The show at Peabody's is off."

It's a good thing I called. Cleveland was not happening.

The next show would now be in Chicago on Wednesday night. We set out on Tuesday morning, picking up Dave Rick in Brooklyn. He brought a bag, a guitar, and a pillow. Why didn't I think of that? We drove all day through Pennsylvania and Ohio, stopping in the rain outside Toledo to get a $34 room at the Motel 6. Dave and I shared one bed, Damon and Naomi the other.

The first thing we saw when we pulled up to Chicago's Cabaret Metro was GG Allin, hanging out on the street outside. Holy shit! He was wanted by the cops in Boston, something to do with tying his girlfriend up with rope and burning her with cigarettes. He said the whole thing was her idea. GG Allin had some people convinced that he was the essence of rock and roll, a true bad boy, the second coming of Hank Williams. But Hank Williams never took laxatives before his shows so he could strip naked and poop on the stage.

Wednesday was ladies' night at the Cabaret Metro. Ladies got in free, and we had about a hundred people at the start of our set. We were psyched for our first-ever show outside of Massachusetts and New York. We kicked the set off with "Temperature's Rising."

My temperature's rising
My fingers are tingling
I'm starting to shake
I look in the mirror
And everything's funny
I think I'm a fake

Just then, a guy in a black leather jacket who looked like he was probably a musician came and stood directly in front of me, gave me the finger, and loudly denounced me as a faggot. Welcome to the rest of America. What to do? I started the next song. He continued to call me a faggot. Then someone threw a cup of beer at this rude heckler from up in the balcony. This made him furious, and prompted him to throw his beer bottle at me. That was it—the bouncers converged and tossed him out of the club.

The ladies didn't stick around for the rest of our set. They gradually trickled downstairs to the dance club in the basement. Still, it was an exciting night. We were paid $250 and got an entire case of beer. We weren't used to being treated so well by a club.

We still didn't really have enough money to stay in hotels in Chicago. Dave Rick and I spent the night with Dave's friend John, who played in a band called Repulse Kava. John knew the guy who had called me faggot— said he played in a Chicago pigfuck band called Spongetunnel. Apparently there had been a band named Sponge that merged with a band called Fudge-tunnel to form a new Chicago indie supergroup: Spongetunnel. And yet he said I was the nancy boy.

The Top Hat

When the end of the world comes, I want to be in Cincinnati, because it's always twenty years behind the times.

—*Mark Twain*

After a day off in Chicago and a Friday night show in St. Louis, we found ourselves in Cincinnati. There wasn't much fun to be had in Cincinnati. The Saturday night fun for us was actually to be found across the river in Newport, Kentucky. That was where the Top Hat was located. You couldn't even buy a copy of *Hustler* in Cincinnati—you needed to visit Newport. Someone told me that the waitresses at the Top Hat were all hookers. We hit the stage at 1:00 A.M. and played to about thirty customers. For the encore, Dave Rick joined us onstage on "Don't Let Our Youth Go to Waste" and "Tugboat." Dave is a dazzling player, probably the best guitarist I have ever seen in an indie rock band, but he said he had a little trouble with "Tugboat." He wasn't used to having to slowly repeat the same two chords over and over again.

Dave found us lodging for the night with Uncle Dave Lewis, the house soundman. Uncle Dave played with a legendary Cincinnati band called 11,000 Switches, and another called Rasputin Rembrandt. He took us first to White Castle for some late-night burgers, and then to his loft in an old warehouse. He had a huge garage space. We drove the van right into the warehouse and rode the gigantic freight elevator up to his apartment.

Uncle Dave had a massive collection of 78s and very old cartoons, and had spent many hours synching them up. He had a vast knowledge of jazz, cartoons, and Charles Manson. We stayed up late watching his cartoons while he told us all about Charles Manson's recording career. At one point I looked over at Damon and Naomi and they had a look of fear in their eyes. When Uncle Dave went to the bathroom, they suggested that we leave immediately. This Manson talk was scary. Dave Rick told them to chill out.

We woke up at two o'clock on Sunday afternoon. It was pitch-black in the warehouse, so we had overslept. Uncle Dave took us out to Skyline Chili for breakfast. We had the Cincinnati specialty—chili with spaghetti and grated cheese.

We then hit the road again. It was a hop, skip, and a jump to Lexington, Kentucky, where we were scheduled to play at the Wrocklage that night. On the way into town we usually made a stop to find a pay phone and get directions to the club. The club owner had bad news—he wasn't expecting us till Tuesday night. But he said he could make us a deal and put us on Monday night's bill opening for Das Damen.

Dave Rick called his good friends Mark and Khaki, who founded the local college radio station, and they said we could sleep on their floor. Excellent. We checked in at Mark and Khaki's, found some good fried chicken, and then went down to the Wrocklage to check out the bands playing that night— Volcano Suns and Roger Miller. Not the Roger Miller who wrote "King of the Road," this Roger Miller had fronted one of Boston's greatest bands ever, Mission of Burma. I saw Mission of Burma perform at Harvard when I was there, at an outdoor benefit show for CISPES—the Committee in Solidarity with the People of El Salvador. Mission of Burma is today rightly recognized as a band ahead of its time, but back then they weren't so popular, even in Boston. Apparently this is a Boston tradition. The Modern Lovers, for example, were far more popular in New York than in Boston.

That Monday night, the NCAA finals were on TV—Michigan against Seton Hall. They like their college basketball in Lexington, Kentucky. Six people came to our show.

We did better at the Sonic Temple in Pittsburgh, where we had at least eleven in the audience, maybe fifteen. Pittsburgh—City of Bridges—is a beautiful city, not what I was expecting at all. After a seven-hour drive in the rain, we drove through the Fort Pitt Tunnel, which delivers you right to a spectacular view of the Fort Pitt Bridge and the city across the river. They have three rivers there—the Ohio, the Allegheny, and the Monongahela. They must have fifteen or twenty bridges, too, all different colors.

The Sonic Temple was located on the top floor of the old Masonic temple, which had fallen on hard times. Some kids from Carnegie Mellon had been putting on rock shows there. Unfortunately they didn't have a liquor license, and that discourages people from attending rock shows.

The small crowd lay down on the carpeted floor while we played for them. It felt intimate, despite the large and mostly empty room. We spent the night on another floor—this time in the apartment of the kids who had booked the show. They had their own fanzine—*Cubist Pop Manifesto*—and interviewed us that night while we drank Iron City beer in tall cans. It was odd playing to an audience of eleven, and then being interviewed as if anyone cared what we had to say about anything. Such is the world of indie rock.

We now headed straight to D.C., where we stayed with Jay Spiegel, the drummer for B.A.L.L.

The next night we played the 9:30 Club, opening for Throwing Muses, who were just off a tour opening for New Order. We were jealous—we worshipped New Order, while Throwing Muses said they'd barely even heard of them before the tour. The Muses were flying around the country. They wore laminated backstage passes from the New Order tour, and their tour manager carried a gigantic mobile phone, so big it had a special shoulder strap.

The 9:30 Club was sold out, and we sounded awful. I broke a string on the first song, and borrowed Dave Rick's Les Paul Junior, which sounded all wrong. I had a revelation at that moment. I would buy a second guitar, to be used in the event that I broke a string. That's what the pros do.

After the show, we did a fanzine interview with James McNew (who was later to join Yo La Tengo) and John Beers, who was one half of the Virginia duo Happy Flowers. His stage name in the Flowers was Mr. Horribly Charred Infant, while his bandmate called himself Mr. Anus.

The tour ended at Maxwell's in Hoboken, opening for Christmas, the clever Boston band. By this point we were sick of one another's company. This is only natural when you ride around all day in a van and sleep on other people's floors. You get rather sick of everything.

We managed to squeeze in a meeting with Richard Grabel of Grubman, Indursky, and Schindler while we were in New York. They were the big-time music business law firm. Some people called them Grubby Dirty Swindler. Grabel had been contacted by Gary Gersh at Geffen Records, who thought Grabel was already our lawyer. So Grabel gave us a call. Turned out we needed a lawyer.

On Fire

"Gary Gersh at Geffen wants to come see you play," said Richard. "Can you set up a show?"

We set up a New York show for Mr. Gary Gersh, but he called at the last minute and said that he was too busy in the studio with Peter Gabriel, putting the finishing touches on a mix. He was sure we'd understand—this is the kind of attention you'd get if you were signed to Geffen. We didn't understand. We were frightened—we wouldn't want the A&R guy mixing the song. And we didn't like Peter Gabriel.

Mr. Gersh did come to see us a month later, at the Channel in Boston, where we opened for our pals Bullet LaVolta.

Bullet LaVolta was a tremendous live band, and very popular in Boston. If they had been from Seattle, they would have been called grunge. But even though grunge hadn't been widely "identified" yet, it was happening all over the country, a sort of fusion of punk and metal, some of it fast, some of it slow. It was the genius of Sub Pop that they managed to put out some of these records at the same time and give them an identity and a look—which is perhaps a credit to their art department. And of course one of those bands was Nirvana. Still, I refuse to believe that grunge rock was actually invented in Seattle.

The Channel was the biggest rock club in Boston, located near South Street Station. Damon brought confetti and tossed it in the air onstage during one of our songs. The stage manager yelled at us, but it was worth it to watch the little pieces of paper float all over the place. Gersh was in attendance, but he told Damon he didn't have time to talk to us that night—how about we have breakfast in the morning? Then, when Damon got home, there was a message on his machine. Gersh couldn't make it to breakfast after all. He wasn't overly impressed by us. He went on to sign another three-piece band instead—Nirvana.

We did, however, receive an offer from Slash Records—a multirecord deal with an initial advance of $30,000, and they offered to be our music publisher as well. Thirty thousand dollars! That sounded like an awful lot of money to us—we were used to making records for $750 and being paid $75 for two shows. We told Richard Grabel we were ready to do the deal immediately.

But Richard refused to finish the contract negotiations. He stonewalled. He used delaying tactics. He said it wasn't a good deal. They weren't offering us enough money, and they were asking for half of our publishing. That's a big no-no, said Richard. If a record company tries to take your publishing, you walk away.

Bob Biggs was a very charming guy. We had heard a rumor that he used to be a porn star, and that Bob Biggs was his porn name. We weren't sure who started that rumor. Bob had founded *Slash* magazine, which became Slash Records, and he had put out *The Days of Wine and Roses* by the Dream Syndicate, an album that we adored. Bob flew out to see us at the Rat, and he loved us. He told us we should think about a light show. That seemed like a good idea to us. Lights. Since we don't jump around, lights would help create a special mood for our music.

Richard Grabel continued to drag his feet. He insisted that we wait till the New Music Seminar in July, when the A&R people converged on New York City in search of new bands. We were annoyed with him, but agreed to wait.

Things did change at the New Music Seminar. We played Shimmy-Disc night at the Pyramid Club on Avenue A. Shimmy-Disc was Kramer's label. It was hot as hell at the Pyramid and we rocked—slowly. The *Village Voice* likened our set to a long, stoned fuck.

Next day we met with Robin Hurley and Geoff Travis from Rough Trade, who made us the same offer as Slash, but for three records (instead of seven), promising that we would keep our publishing, and that they were going to be hands-off.

Travis said he was doing something special—setting up an independent label and distributor so that no one had to deal with the major labels if they didn't want to.

We met with Bob Biggs again, too, and though we genuinely liked him, he frightened us. He saw Slash Records as his toy, and he wanted to be involved in the whole process, from the choice of producer to the choice of artwork. He said that we were involved with a popular art, not a fine art. Success in a popular art must be defined partially in terms of how many people you can reach. So if your record sells, then you can do whatever you want. But if it doesn't, then he was going to step in and help us find the right producer.

We went back into the studio to record another batch of songs, with Kramer at the helm. That way, we figured we would be able to avoid a discussion with labels about who was going to produce the album. It would be a moot point. We had our new songs ready—"Blue Thunder," which was an ode to my Dodge Dart, "Snowstorm," which was not about a snowstorm per se, but about how excited the weathermen get when a nor'easter hits New England, and "Decomposing Trees," which was about my walk in the woods with windowpane. "When Will You Come Home?" was about a night I watched *Kojak* on TV while waiting for Claudia to come home from a party— this was in the early stages of our relationship, when I was insecure about whether she liked me.

Together with the earlier songs, these were the recordings that formed our *On Fire* LP, our most popular album, which was later ranked number sixteen among the best albums of the '80s by the experts at Pitchfork Media.

Tulse Hill

We signed a worldwide deal with Rough Trade. We also signed with a manager, Craig Taylor, who lived in London and managed the Chills. We thought that if we were going to be signed to a U.K. label, then maybe we should have a manager on that side of the pond to help organize things.

In September we flew to London for our first English shows. It was a whole new world. *Today* got its U.K. release in June, and the reviewers delighted in hyperbole—they loved us. They analyzed us. They asked us questions.

The emergence of what Bob Stanley recently termed the "red-blooded fretwork kings" is the most encouraging trend so far in a year of music otherwise lacking in direction. Reappraising rather than retreading the Sixties, this brave new breed draw inspiration from the past while remaining fully aware of the future. . . . Today, the first album from both Galaxie 500 and Aurora, is an astonishing debut by anyone's standards. . . . It reeks of inspired guitar work, scouring and soaring.

(Everett True, Melody Maker, June 17, 1989)

Galaxie 500 are the soft, sad come-down after the Mudhoney upper: a sleepy sickness of honeycomb guitar, bass lines like the moment when your heart caves in, solos that take their time to linger and loom. A Galaxie 500 song is a fey daze of wistful longing for all that's been lost: for the "sweetest girl," for sure, but also for all the ancient dreams of youth.

(Simon Reynolds, Melody Maker, August 5, 1989)

In England they had these weekly music magazines, which the editors needed to fill with a steady stream of content. They had to get the kids excited. For a little American band that was used to playing to eleven fans in Pittsburgh, it was exciting to be in a magazine like that. You got nice big color pictures in these famous music weeklies, and you felt like a rock star. We didn't stop to ask who actually read these music papers. *We* read them. You could buy all three—*Melody Maker* and the *NME* and *Sounds,* and be entertained for hours.

Maybe they were right. Maybe *Today* was an astonishing debut. It's astonishing because it was recorded in three days and we had no idea what we were doing, and it sounds like it came from another planet.

Our first English gig was at the Institute of Contemporary Arts, a show sponsored by *Time Out London.* A big stage. Lots of people. It was quiet as can be between songs. Does that mean they hated us? No, it means the room was filled with journalists and A&R people and the like.

The reviews were mixed. David Stubbs from *Melody Maker* wasn't so hot on us:

> *Only a rabid rock fanatic could go all the way to extract succour from these remote rock regions. If this is what it takes then I am no longer a rock fan. Dean seems like one more painful misfit sheltering in the sanctioned confines of a guitar band. Perhaps he should have got a paper round instead of lying in bed all morning thinking.*
>
> (Melody Maker, *October 1989*)

Stubbs thought I should be a newspaper delivery boy instead of a singer. But David Cavanagh of *Sounds* loved our show. He wrote some pretty silly things:

> About Damon: *the grooviest and most judicious arbiter of swing, violence, and whatever else armoury a drummer needs.*
>
> Naomi: *I thought she was a bit like early Peter Hook until Galaxie 500 played New Order's "Ceremony" and it was obvious she was far better.*
>
> Me: *Wareham's guitar and vocals make him the focal point, but one to glimpse rather than gawk at. Shyness keeps him at the side of the stage. . . . [Wareham is] in the great guitarists' Bundesliga.*
>
> (Sounds, *October 1989*)

He was right about one thing. I *was* shy. I was frightened. We were used to playing Chet's Last Call and Bunratty's, not the Institute of Contemporary Arts.

S aturday night was Craig Taylor's birthday. He got us a secret gig at his local pub in Tulse Hill. This was akin to playing a secret gig in Ho-Ho-Kus. No stage here. It was much more fun than the ICA show. Craig was tripping on acid. I stayed at his Tulse Hill flat around the corner, sleeping on the floor. I met Tim Gane and his girlfriend, Laetitia Sadier, at this show, and they had a copy of *Today* that they wanted us to sign. Their future band, Stereolab, did not yet exist, but Tim's band McCarthy was still going.

It was cold at Craig's flat and there was never any hot water for a shower. Damon and Naomi had it better—they stayed at rock critic Martin Aston's place in North London. I craved hot water, so Craig moved me to David Boyd's apartment in Clapham. David was a handsome, long-haired Irishman who rode motorcycles and worked in the warehouse at Rough Trade. He loved to come home after work, smoke a big joint, and spin records for hours. It was cozy there in Clapham, and I was much happier. David went on to sign the Verve to Virgin, where he became a music business bigwig, which afforded him the opportunity to buy ever better bikes and sports cars.

David and his girlfriend, Sarah, had a spare room, because their usual flatmate, Martin Phillipps of the Chills, was in the studio—a fancy residential studio in the English countryside. The Chills had signed a *real* record deal with Slash, the kind where you get a big fat advance and go into a studio with tennis courts and a swimming pool. The business affairs people at Slash evidently thought the Chills were worth more than Galaxie 500.

Trains, Planes, and
a Hovercraft

B y the summer of 1989 I was splitting time between Boston and
New York, staying half the time in Roxbury and the other half
with Claudia on Bleecker Street. We booked a gig at CBGB that summer,
but even though the club was two blocks from my Manhattan apartment,
Damon and Naomi asked me to drive up to Boston to rehearse. I said how
about they drive down to New York one night early so we could go into a
rehearsal studio for a couple of hours to run through the set? They countered that they had things to do in Boston and couldn't possibly come down
early.

We argued about this CBGB show for days. Damon became very angry
with me. There was one particularly heated conversation at 3:30 A.M., in a
dorm room at Swarthmore College, where we had just played a gig. I refused
to budge—it seemed absurd that I should have to drive to Boston and back
when the show was just two hundred yards from my apartment. In the end,
they decided to come in a few hours early, and we practiced at a space on
West Fourteenth Street, then played the show.

"That wasn't so bad, was it?" I asked Damon after the show.

"We got by by the skin of our teeth!" he hissed at me. "By the skin of our
teeth!"

O n Fire was released in the fall of 1989. We set out on a five-week tour
of Europe.

Our first gig was in Berlin, at the German equivalent of the New Music
Seminar. We arrived at Flughafen Berlin-Tegel and hopped two taxis to the
Ecstasy in Schöneberg. As we rode into town, I thought about the months

that I had spent in Berlin in 1986, with my girlfriend Eve, who had since moved here permanently.

Just then my Mercedes taxi drove past a supermarket and I turned to my left and there was Eve, the only person I knew in all of Berlin, exiting with a bag of groceries, wearing the same brown coat that she had bought at the flea market in Paris in 1986. It was almost enough to make me believe in God. Instead I chose to believe in poetry and coincidence.

The Ecstasy club in Berlin was run by young people, with a little funding from the government. They had bedrooms for bands to stay in so they didn't have to spend money on hotels. Rough Trade Germany had arranged an afternoon of interviews for us, with *Zitty* magazine and the SFB radio station. One interviewer asked Naomi about her "very unusual" name. Damon found this disturbing—he commented on it later that night.

"Naomi is a Jewish name! It's Jewish!"

"Maybe he meant that Naomi *Yang* was unusual," I said. "To be both Chinese and Jewish . . . that's not something he sees every day in Berlin."

We had barely slept at all on the Lufthansa flight, and were beyond tired. We finally took the stage at 3:00 A.M., right after American Music Club. The club was still jumping—there must have been four hundred people there to see us. They called out for "Oblivious" and "Parking Lot." We couldn't believe that they actually knew our songs. Vivicauldron hit the stage after us, all the way from Detroit. They had smoke machines and were not afraid to use them. They were pissed off about having to play at four in the morning, but that didn't deter them from playing a ninety-minute set. It was difficult to get to sleep in our bunks with Vivicauldron kicking out the jams downstairs, but the music stopped at 5:30 and sleep finally came.

We slept till one that afternoon and rushed over to the Hauptbahnhof Zoologischer Garten, to catch the night train to Paris. We had sleeping cabins, but were separated as *Damen und Herren.* I bunked with Damon, while Naomi roomed with strangers. She came and visited for a few minutes. She was feeling a little claustrophobic. What if the bunk above her should fall?

Rough Trade's French licensee, Virgin, had also set up a day of interviews and photo shoots for us in Paris. Every French interviewer asked us about the Pixies. They figured that since we were from Boston, we must love the Pixies. Nonsense. We had no love for the Pixies.

After Paris we traveled to England, via train and a bumpy channel crossing on a hovercraft. Damon did not want to board that hovercraft, but the ferries weren't running. It was the only way.

Back in London, we had a series of shows that were all within striking distance, so we could return to London each night and save on hotel rooms. I was back sleeping on the floor at Craig Taylor's place in Tulse Hill.

The first gig was a Saturday night at JB's in Dudley, a little town outside of Birmingham. I thought we were going to get the shit kicked out of us. One fellow in the back of the room (which was pretty much empty) called out "Rubbish!" between songs. "Rubbbbb-issssshhhhh!" Still, they paid us five hundred pounds, which was top dollar.

Our next show was at the Polytechnic in Brighton. A reporter from *Melody Maker,* Bob Stanley, rode down to Brighton with us. He was in a band, too. They were called St. Etienne.

"What instrument do you play?" I asked him.

"It's hard to explain."

I went down to the pier at Brighton, which was cold and deserted, and found some fish and chips. People are always saying how bad the food is in England, but for me, English food feels like I have come home.

On Fire was at number six on the *NME*'s indie chart. How they came up with these charts I don't know. Each music paper had its own independent chart, with slightly different chart positions. Except that the Stone Roses were at the top of each chart. Just as Oasis and Blur would become U.K. darlings in the years to come, these were the days of the Stone Roses and the Happy Mondays. The *NME* and *Melody Maker* understood that putting one of those bands on the cover meant that they would sell more magazines. So they featured one band or the other every single issue. STONE ROSES IN PARIS! HAPPY MONDAYS IN THE STUDIO! IAN BROWN BUYS NEW SHIRT! Actually, he wore the same shirt in every photo. It had dollar bills printed on it. He also made the same silly face in every photo, with his lips pursed. He must have looked in the mirror and decided that was how he looked best.

The English music press wrote about the Happy Mondays and the Stone Roses as if they were leading a cultural revolution. In reality, this revolution consisted of wearing baggy pants and taking a lot of ecstasy. Maybe that felt like a revolution after the Thatcher years, but it wasn't. At most, it was a fashion revolution—a fad.

We couldn't complain. *We* were getting nice reviews, too.

. . .

On Thursday we rode the train up to Manchester, now accompanied by Kramer, who had volunteered to be our soundman. Kramer had procured some hash, and he rolled some very skinny, straight hash joints, because he wasn't about to mix it with tobacco like the English do. He thought tobacco companies were the most evil people on Earth. He convinced me to smoke a little hash before our sound check at the International, which I regretted, because I instantly became paranoid. My guitar sounded horribly out of tune, but the guitar tuner said it was fine. I promised myself not to get stoned at sound check ever again.

We had booked actual hotel rooms in Manchester. Damon and Naomi were in one hotel room, while Kramer and I were going to share another. After spending several nights on Craig's floor, I was looking forward to having a real bed. But Kramer rushed back to the hotel immediately after the gig, and when I got to the room he was in there with a girl. He had arranged for an extra folding cot to be put in Damon and Naomi's room for me. What a prick.

Next stop, Holland. For the next couple weeks we were "co-headlining" with Straitjacket Fits, a band from New Zealand. We would take turns headlining, and the audience wouldn't know in advance who would be playing first.

Since we couldn't all fit in the van (which we were renting from the Chills, along with their drum kit and amplifiers), we traveled via train. That suited us just fine. Train travel was glorious.

The first stop in Holland was Deventer, where we played at the Burgerweeshuis. This particular club was housed in an old orphanage that was now an arts center. A crazy-looking old long-haired guy served us our dinner while he coughed and coughed. And then he had the nerve to ask for one of our T-shirts. Clubs always try to take a bunch of your T-shirts. "T-shirts for the guys" is what they say, as if it is somehow our obligation to provide clothes for the stagehands.

After shows in Groningen (at the legendary Vera club) and Haarlem, we arrived in Amsterdam. We were playing at the Melkweg (the Milky Way), and they had put us in a nice hotel and given us our own rooms. I had my own bathtub and a TV set. Things were looking up.

Kramer missed the sound check at the Melkweg. He walked in just as we were finishing and made a little joke about how Amsterdam was the one city in the world where it was perfectly legal to get your dick sucked while smoking a joint. He had a good sense of humor.

Before the show, we hung out backstage and Kramer played John Lennon songs on the guitar. He had a lovely voice. He sang "Mother," which made Naomi sad because Kramer had been adopted at the age of two.

We really got the smoke machine going for the encore at the Melkweg. We bathed the stage in smoke, and Kramer joined us up there, playing extra rhythm guitar. After the show I wandered from coffee shop to coffee shop with my friends Simon and David and Sarah and Justin and Lisa, eating space cake, smoking hash, and drinking Belgian beer. "Coffee shop" is a misnomer—it refers to the bars where you buy hash and weed. We ended the night playing pool while listening to Pink Floyd's *Dark Side of the Moon*. They play bad stoner music in coffee shops.

I used to listen to *Dark Side of the Moon* when I was in tenth grade. Graham and I would go over to our friend Ezra's house to smoke pot and do whippits, and Ezra would put that album on. One day Graham and I decided that Pink Floyd was a total bummer. Why don't you put on some Bob Dylan? Or the Clash? But Ezra stuck to his guns—Pink Floyd and Jethro Tull. We stopped going over to his place.

Our next day in Amsterdam was a day off, and we had to move out of the nice hotel. I checked into a dump called the Euphemia Hotel, with Strait-jacket Fits. Damon and Naomi decided to spend their own money and stay in a nice hotel. Kramer flew home to New York.

I was coming down with a cold, so I ate space cake and rested in the hotel room, watching Dutch TV. I was also coming down with negative thoughts about Galaxie 500.

I started to wonder about how my life would be if I weren't in Galaxie 500. Maybe I was just feeling under the weather. But once you let a thought like that into your head, it's hard to get it out of there. Oh, it may be quiet as a mouse for a couple of days, but just when you think the mouse is gone for good, he's back. He tends to come back on a lonely day in an ugly hotel room.

In Paris we were booked into a two-star hotel in the Pigalle area, the kind where the wallpaper is stained and the beds sag in the middle. The hotels had been provided by the clubs, and since we were on a two-band package tour, that's a lot of beds they needed to provide. So they went for the cheapest hotels they could find. We were starting to realize that this package tour may not have been in our best interest.

Our show was at the New Moon club, at 66 Rue Pigalle. Many years ago it was the Nouvelle Athènes café, and Degas and Matisse and Monet and Manet hung out here. Later it was called Bricktop's and was visited by Picasso and Hemingway and Cole Porter and Josephine Baker and Marlene Dietrich and God knows who else, before it became a real strip club, Le Sphinx, frequented by Nazis and then by American servicemen.

The walls were still painted with beautiful old murals, scenes of naughtiness and debauchery, and we had our photograph taken in front of one of them. Then we went up the street to do a radio interview. The DJ asked us about the Pixies.

We enjoyed the show immensely. The New Moon only held a hundred people, so it's not so hard to sell it out. "More wah-wah!" someone called out, which is better than "Free Bird!"

The three of us traveled in style, riding the high-speed train from Paris to Lausanne, where we played the famous Dolce Vita club and then traveled on to Basel, where we played in an old military barrack.

Monday night we hit Cooky's in Frankfurt, a tacky little place, all mirrored and carpeted. I had a vicious headache, for which I prescribed myself codeine and beer. We played an extraslow set. I shall always remember Cooky's because a lady threw tampons at me onstage while we played "Ceremony." I'm not sure what she meant to say. Maybe she thought I was cute, or tampon worthy. Maybe she wanted to sit on my face. On the other hand, it might have been an insult, a Frankfurter's rotten tomato. And yet the tampons were fresh, unsoiled. I decided to take it as a compliment.

It didn't matter much either way. The only person who approached me after the show was a kid who had started a new band.

"We have started a band, to sound exactly like you. But we're having trouble. It's not going well. . . . I watched you play tonight. I cannot believe how few chords you are actually playing."

In Munich we played a huge club, the Nachtwerk. John Beers from the Happy Flowers was there. He had married a German girl named Sabina, whom he met on tour, and moved to Munich. See, it happens. People meet their future wives on tour. John and Sabina divorced about a year later.

December 1 we were back at the Ecstasy in Berlin. It seemed like we were just here. We *were* just here.

First we made an 11:00 A.M. in-store appearance at the World of Music (WOM) on the Ku'damm. We were supposed to perform a few songs, but the microphone wasn't working. It didn't really matter, because no one had come to see us. Not one person.

I spent the afternoon alone, walking around Nollendorfplatz, Kreuzberg, and the Ku'damm. Tourists had been chipping away at the Berlin Wall, taking little pieces of it home. The wall had become endangered—there was even a campaign afoot to save what was left of it.

The newsstands were packed with East Germans. Helmut Kohl had recently given a little spending money to each East German so that they could buy some cool stuff. They came here to stare at the porno magazines and buy the things you never could get in East Germany, like bananas and cheap gold jewelry. They couldn't believe this shit. They didn't have Silly String in East Germany.

We hung out upstairs at the club and were interviewed by a couple of East German hipsters, up from Leipzig. They were in West Berlin for the very first time in their lives. We had more questions for them than they did for us. These guys had an independent radio show in Leipzig, and they played whatever music they wanted.

"But we won't play fascist music."

I wasn't sure if that meant Carl Orff or Laibach, but I did know you would never hear those words from an American DJ.

Our final German show was at the Kir club in Hamburg. It was a dud. Some nights Galaxie 500 was not a good live band—and this was one of those nights. It was freezing cold onstage, and our guitars were dripping wet from the condensation and nothing sounded right. After the show we went down to the St. Pauli district, where our friends Volcano Suns were doing a gig at 2:30 A.M., in a teensy-tiny basement club that supposedly contained the actual floorboards from the famous Star Club.

Last time we saw Volcano Suns, they were locked out of the Wrocklage in Lexington, Kentucky. We looked around the club. We weren't playing the Sporthalle, but we were doing better than Volcano Suns.

. . .

We said goodbye to Straitjacket Fits, who flew home to New Zealand, and we headed back to Britain for one final week of shows. I was nervous for the London show. We were in the presence of all my friends, and the Rough Trade employees, plus *Snub TV* was filming us and had their cameras right in my face for a few songs, which was distracting. The opening band was Ride. They were roughly seventeen years old, and they were the latest shoegaze phenom.

Sometimes Galaxie 500 got lumped in with this whole shoegaze movement (we were later dubbed protoshoegaze), but we had nothing to do with it. We didn't listen to Ride, Chapterhouse, Lush, Slowdive, Moose, or even the Jesus and Mary Chain (who were derisively known as the Jesus and Money Chain back home in our world).

But no matter. Shoegazing was the new flavor. They stared at their shoes. The guitars were muddy and swirling, and you could rarely hear an actual guitar solo or make out the words to the songs. Compared to these bands, Galaxie 500 was an American band—concrete, not ethereal.

The tour was almost over. It would have been nice to end it in London, but our agent had booked us one last show at the Adelphi Club in Hull. We pleaded with him to cancel it. Can't we go out on a high note, the big London show? He tried to cancel, but the promoter at the Adelphi threatened to go to the music press if we pulled out. I'm not sure what he would have told them. Galaxie 500 canceled their show at the Adelphi? Horrors. We honored our contract in Hull. The promoter ordered us a nice curry from an Indian restaurant and we ate together in the green room.

Back in London the next day, we sat down with Craig in a small office to go over the books. Damon had collected all the money from the shows, and we had averaged $500 per show. Damon had a big ol' pile of cash when the meeting began. But we had to pay Craig for the van that we had rented from the Chills. And for the backline equipment, which also belonged to the Chills. And Craig's management commission, plus the booking agent's commission. After an hour of these calculations, the big pile of money had migrated from our side of the table to Craig's side of the table. We flew home with no money whatsoever. Craig was a nice guy, perfectly honest. But we decided on the flight home that a manager was one luxury we couldn't afford.

The Aerostar

We arrived back in the States on a Sunday, and Karen Schoemer had written a piece on us in the Arts and Leisure section. Our picture was in the *New York Times*. In those days, the *Times* didn't run daily reviews of pop music like they do today, so when they wrote about pop music, you noticed. This was exciting. They referred to me as Mr. Wareham.

Mr. Wareham throws in enough details about his mundane life to drag the listener into his drab, post-Reagan Nowheresville. "I stood in line and ate my Twinkies," he drones in "Strange," then repeats the sentiment—"I stood in line, I had to wait"—drawing out the last word as an exercise in the tedium it describes.

(New York Times, *Sunday, December 3, 1989*)

Why's everybody seem so nasty?
Why's everybody seem so strange?
Why's everybody seem so pretty?
What do I want with all these things?
I went along, down to the drugstore
I went out back, and took a Coke
I stood in line, and ate my Twinkies
I stood line, I had to wai-ai-ai-ait

Bob Lawton, our American booking agent, was pleased with the *Times* review. "This is how you get from point A to point C," he said, "without going to point B."

Sure, I had my photo on the front of the Arts and Leisure section, but I was also broke. I found a temp job at Italian *Vogue* magazine, just for the holiday season. I was one of two administrative assistants in a small office in the Condé Nast building. The other secretary, a Puerto Rican lady, laughed at me.

"You're in a band? Your band must not be so popular, or you wouldn't be working here."

She had not been reading the *NME* or *Melody Maker*.

I n January of 1990 we set out on a short East Coast tour. We rented a Ford Aerostar, the three of us, plus a Belgian graduate student named Frank Albers, who was going to do some of the driving. Damon insisted on driving the first day, the trip from Boston to New York. I sat in the backseat and a chant started inside my head. *Crash, crash, crash. I hope you crash the van.*

I was mad that he wouldn't let me drive. I'm a good driver, I thought, Why can't I drive? *Crash, crash, crash.*

We made it to New York early in the afternoon, and agreed to meet up at six at the Knitting Factory. When I arrived at the club on Houston Street, there was bad news. Damon had crashed the minivan. Holy shit. I was the fire starter. I could make things happen just by thinking about them.

The bummer was that since my name was on the credit card, I had to drive out to Newark airport at 4:00 A.M. to get a replacement minivan.

The Knitting Factory shows (two in one night) were a grand success. We sold out both shows and made $2,000. We sat in Michael Dorf's office while he counted the money. Dorf got a lot of shit in later years from downtown jazz musicians who complained that he didn't pay them enough. I never understood that. Would they rather work with gangsters? The Knitting Factory gave the best deals around, 75 percent of the door. What was there to complain about?

We played Northampton and Washington, D.C., and Columbia, South Carolina, and Atlanta and Richmond. We averaged 150 people a show, and were making enough to get two rooms each night at a Motel 6. We ate well. It was relaxing. There's a nice bootleg tape of our show at the Point in Atlanta. It looked like we were having fun, selling T-shirts from the stage and joking around. These were good times.

In Athens, Georgia, we played at the 40 Watt Club. Peter Buck from R.E.M. came to the show, and he invited us to stay at his big house. He threw us a little party. Mike Mills was there, too, and other people I didn't know. It started to get late, though, and I was pooped. How come they all had so much energy?

A Month of Sundays

Rough Trade landed us a run of shows supporting the Sundays in the U.K. The Sundays was a pop band from Bristol, whose debut album was at number four on the charts—the real charts, not the fake independent ones. They had a bona fide radio hit, an infectious song called "Here's Where the Story Ends." Rough Trade paid our airfares, train fares, hotel rooms, and per diems, and the clubs paid us two hundred pounds a night on top of that. It was a good deal. Of course, tour support is fully recoupable, so our own future royalties were being advanced to us to pay for the trip. But that's the record business. All of this would be moot when Rough Trade filed for bankruptcy the next year. Accounts, royalties, records sold, tour support—it would all be out the window.

A couple of rules were relayed to us by the Sundays' management:

1. They didn't want us getting any press on this tour—apparently their manager was concerned that we were media darlings, and I guess he thought there wasn't room enough in the music papers for both bands. So, no features for us. No talking to journalists.
2. We couldn't play more than forty minutes, because they only had forty minutes of material themselves. We didn't mind.

The Sundays seemed nervous. They had only played about twenty shows in their career, but all of a sudden things had taken off, and they were playing to a thousand people each night. They made sure to sound check for a very long time, which meant that we often got no sound check at all. We didn't mind that either.

The good thing was that they carried our equipment in their truck, and we got to travel by train again. We played Glasgow and Newcastle, and it was good. We rode the train down the coast of Scotland. On the left was the North Sea and a clear sky. On the right there were black clouds. Kramer was with us, and for one day rock critic Everett True came along, too (which we kept secret from the Sundays). Everett had brought a pair of slippers to wear on the train.

I roomed with Kramer. We would smoke a little hash before bed each night and watch old movies. One night he persuaded Damon and Naomi to watch some soft-core porn. It was the first time they had seen such a thing.

Damon and Naomi loved Kramer at this point. We all did. They laughed at all his jokes and tolerated his bullshit. He was well aware of the effect he had on them.

"Are they really huge fans of mine?" he asked me. "What if I do something really fucked up?"

He vowed that he would see how far he could push the envelope that was their devotion to him.

The high point of the Sundays' tour was in Manchester, where Peter Hook of New Order was waiting in our dressing room after the show. We had been doing "Ceremony" every night. Perhaps it was cheeky of us to play a Joy Division song in Manchester, but no more cheeky than Gang of Four's whipping out "Sweet Jane" at the old Ritz in New York City, which I had personally witnessed.

Peter Hook grabbed Naomi's bass and showed her the correct way to play "Ceremony." Then he gave Kramer a ride back to the hotel in his Jaguar XJ12. Apparently he drove Ian Curtis home in his Jaguar the night that Curtis committed suicide. I wondered if it was the same Jag. I wonder what Kramer and Peter Hook talked about. Maybe they talked about bass guitar. Maybe they discussed sports cars. Kramer owned a beautiful old Porsche.

In London, we taped three songs and an interview for MTV. Paul King, who used to sing in a band called King and had appeared on the *Top of the Pops,* conducted the interview. He used to be a pop star. Now he was an MTV VJ—the most despised form of life on the planet. We recorded "Strange" and "Tell Me" and "If She Ever Comes" with Damon on acoustic guitar and me on electric (plus kazoo). It sounded great. Then we did the interview. "Your music has been described as being wimpy," said Mr. King.

Thank you very much, you prick. I must have missed that review.

The final show of the Sundays' tour was to be at the Town and Country

Club in London, to two thousand people. But their singer, Harriet, had a sore throat, and the show was canceled. Instead we played a semisecret last-minute show at the Falcon, a little pub in Camden. The stage smelled of piss, and I was tipsy just the right amount. Kramer joined us onstage for half the set. It was much more fun to play to a small crowd of our fans, Galaxie 500 fans, than to a thousand Sundays fans. That night at the Falcon was absolutely one of the highlights of our time together. We returned to England again later in the year, but things were not the same.

What Else Do You Do?

B y the spring of 1990 I was officially living back in New York City. Damon and Naomi were talking about moving to New York, too, and were checking out some apartments.

Although I was living in New York, I spent most of March, April, and May in Boston, rehearsing new songs for the next Galaxie 500 record. We had just received an advance from Rough Trade to start working on our next album, and it was enough to live on for a few months—I didn't need a job, for once. Things were looking up. But I was getting tired of driving back and forth from Boston to New York. And we were getting on one another's nerves. I was having bad thoughts.

Kramer called me about an acoustic compilation record he was putting out on Shimmy-Disc. It would be titled *What Else Do You Do?* The title was from a clever cartoon by Tuli Kupferberg. The Beatles are playing their songs to a couple of disinterested A&R men, who pose the question.

"You and I should do a song together," said Kramer.

I wrote a song called "Smile" and recorded it at Noise. Kramer added bass and piano. It turned out nicely. But Damon and Naomi were upset that Kramer and I recorded a song together.

"We're struggling here to come up with songs for our next album," said Damon. "I wish you hadn't given one away for this."

"Well," I said, "we can always rerecord it for our album."

But it wasn't really about that.

Mike McGonigal asked if Galaxie 500 would play a benefit for his fanzine, *Chemical Imbalance*. *Chemical Imbalance* had been good to us when we were just starting out, and I thought it would be nice to return the favor, but Damon and Naomi didn't want to drive all the way to New York for a benefit. Fair enough. I told McGonigal no dice. He asked if maybe I could play alone on acoustic guitar. Then Kramer got in on it, too, and we decided to play a thirty-minute acoustic set together.

This opened a can of worms. First Naomi called me and said she was upset that I was playing this benefit without the rest of Galaxie 500. Then Damon got on the phone. He said that since we made the decision, *as a band,* not to play the benefit, it wasn't right for me to then decide to do it on my own. Decisions should be made as a band, not individually.

I told him that I understood his feelings, but I was still going to play the show. After we hung up, he called back again.

"I would really feel more comfortable if you didn't do it."

I started to get angry now. Was I supposed to cancel my appearance at the benefit just to make Damon feel more comfortable? He called again.

"We hope you're not going to play any Galaxie 500 songs."

Damon and Naomi made me feel awful about this benefit, like I was committing a crime by getting onstage without them. Like they were my parents, and I was running away from home.

Kramer and I played the show at CBGB's. It was pretty boring, which is usually the case when two people sit down and run through songs on acoustic guitars. But we helped raise some money. Damon and Naomi drove down from Boston to see us perform. I felt like my disapproving parents were standing in the back of the room.

This Is Our Music was recorded over a period of ten days in June and July. A day in Kramer's studio was six hours, if we were lucky, starting sometime after noon and finishing by 6:00 P.M.

The recording sessions were tense. Kramer wanted to change things up a little. He said there was no reason that all three of us had to be in the studio the entire time, especially when I was singing, or overdubbing guitars. He said he didn't like having Damon and Naomi sitting behind him whispering comments to each other while he recorded me (in fairness to Kramer, there was an exceptionally small control room at Noise New York). He tried to give them errands to run on the days that I was to record my guitars, but this did not sit well with them. They wanted to be there for every second of the process.

On the first day of mixing, Kramer showed us all a review in *CMJ* of his compilation album, *What Else Do You Do?* My song "Smile" was singled out for praise. The writer said that the song was as good as anything by Galaxie 500.

CMJ doesn't give bad reviews. It's a trade paper—the idea is to say something nice and descriptive about every release. I'm not sure if Kramer was trying to play games with us, or set us against one another, but if so, he succeeded. Damon yelled at me in Kramer's kitchen.

"Is that what you wanted? Are you happy now?"

Some days I felt like they were my mommy and daddy and I was a naughty little boy—that they treated me like a child. Other days I felt like I was a member of a cult.

It was a shame that we weren't getting along. Damon knew it, too. Something had happened to our friendship. He wrote a nice song about it—"Sorry," about how everything was business now and we've forgotten that we love each other, and how sorry he was.

"4th of July" was selected to be the single from the new album, and Sergio Huidor, who had directed all our videos, made another great one. As usual, we shot the video in our tiny rehearsal room, which Sergio transformed by hanging sheets of transparent colored Mylar and foil. Sergio rented a gorilla suit for me and a clown suit for Damon. When I wasn't wearing the gorilla suit, Naomi loaned me some of her nice agnès b. clothes to wear, a striped T-shirt and a black shirt with white hearts on it.

Galaxie 500 videos were full of carnage, and this one was no exception. Blood. Aircraft carriers. Explosions. Executions, tanks, guns, stolen video footage. The Stars and Stripes. Lynching footage from Nuremberg. MTV would love it!

The Big Stage

That summer we were invited to play some festivals in Europe. First up was Glastonbury. It rained all week leading up to the Glastonbury Festival, and the field turned to mud. Our shoes were hosed down before we went on, to clean off the mud we had picked up backstage, where the Happy Mondays were kicking a football around. I looked out at people wearing plastic bags on their feet. This was the year they had an outbreak of trenchfoot at Glastonbury, a nasty disease that afflicted soldiers in the trenches during World War I.

We were the first band on the big stage on day one, playing at noon to thirty thousand English people. I should have been terrified, but I wasn't. The people were so far away, and I didn't know any of them personally, except for Kramer, who was out at the mixing board. He was along to do sound again, and had also volunteered to be the tour manager, taking care of getting paid and checking into hotels and organizing car service to the airport.

Kramer wanted to join us for a few songs, like he had done on the last European tour. But Damon and Naomi didn't want him onstage anymore. They now thought it was a bit strange to have the producer jump onstage with us, and maybe they were right. I said I didn't mind if he played on a few songs, but they had made their minds up—from now on it would be just the three of us. They were starting to think that Kramer was a little too involved in our band.

In the middle of our third song I heard a sound behind me—it sounded like someone else was playing guitar. Kramer. He had given the house sound engineer some pointers and had quickly made his way through the crowd to the stage, where he found my spare guitar and a spare amplifier. He couldn't resist—he was Kramer. He wanted to play on the big stage at Glastonbury.

Damon and Naomi were livid, and didn't speak to Kramer for a couple of days. I knew that he had been out of line, but I found his boldness amusing.

Next up was the Lorelei Festival in Germany. High above the Rhine stands the Lorelei rock, which marks the deepest and narrowest part of the river. Legend says that a beautiful young woman named Lorelei plunged to her death in the river, taking her own life because her lover had been unfaithful. She then became a siren, and could be heard singing on the mountain above the river. Sailors would hear her sing, look up, and crash their boats. Heinrich Heine wrote a famous poem on the subject. The Nazis, upset that this popular German poem was written by a Jew, tried to convince the public that it was an old folk song.

An amphitheater had been built on top of the mountain, and the acoustics were great. The backstage area was built on the edge of the mountain, with a spectacular view of the Rhine. It was a world away from the mud of Glastonbury. The promoters had a big barbecue going—they put out a wonderful spread for us, and each band had its own little trailer. Ride was playing the festival—they had gotten pretty big in England since they opened for us at Subterania a year ago. The headliners tonight were The The (which now featured Johnny Marr of the Smiths on guitar) and the Ramones. All the bands hung out in the amazing backstage area, enjoying the barbecue and the sun and scenery. All except the Ramones, who stayed in their trailer and had pizza sent up from town. This was very punk rock of them. The mountain, the cliff, the sunshine, the barbecue—they were against it. Since punk is a celebration of all things ugly, how can punk rockers enjoy the beautiful Rhine Valley?

We played early in the afternoon but stuck around the rest of the day to see the Ramones, and left just as The The were starting—to beat the traffic. A flirtatious German girl struck up a conversation with me by the entrance to the backstage area. There seemed to be some kind of vibe. Then she asked if she could have my backstage pass, because she really wanted to meet Johnny Marr. That hurt my feelings.

We drove back to our hotel, a half hour's drive from the mountain. The hotel lobby was decked out with stuffed animal heads, including a little bunny that had antlers. In the United States that's a jackalope, or deer bunny. In Germany it is the Wolpertinger. These are not real animals, but creatures of folklore. There we were, admiring the Wolpertinger, when

Kramer, our so-called tour manager, remembered that he had forgotten the part of the job where he collects the money. He forgot to get paid.

Our final stop was the Roskilde Festival in Denmark. They had a terrific lineup, spread out over five different stages. I saw the Cramps and the Cure and Nick Cave and Bob Dylan. The first half of Dylan's show was awful. He had that dolt G. E. Smith on lead guitar. G. E. Smith was the bandleader on *Saturday Night Live,* and he was best known for making too many rock faces. Maybe his playing would be tolerable if he put a paper bag over his head.

I am opposed to rock-guitar faces. I am not turned on by guitarists who shake and stick out their tongue and drool during guitar solos. I prefer to let the guitar speak for itself. No need to sell the guitar solo with overly expressive facial expressions.

In the middle of the set, Dylan whipped out the acoustic guitar and did a killer version of "It's Alright, Ma (I'm Only Bleeding)." Kramer and I watched him in awe.

We played on the same stage as Melissa Etheridge, but missed her show. We also missed Lenny Kravitz and Midnight Oil and all kinds of other stupid shit. Rock festivals are celebrations of rock music, and everyone is happy and nice to one another, but the truth is that you hate most of the other bands. Well, you hate their music, and isn't that the same thing?

Kramer and Naomi were just barely speaking by now. Then came the meatball incident. We were having lunch at a little restaurant by the hotel. Naomi ordered some lamb meatballs, and Kramer decided to be offended. He was a vegetarian most of the time.

"Have you ever looked into the eyes of a little lamb?"

Naomi told him to go fuck himself. I had never seen Naomi get angry like this, and I thought it was a good thing.

I made friends at the festival with a beautiful, brown-haired Danish girl who photographed the band standing next to a tree. We walked around together all night, and then we sat down on the grass and talked. I decided I wanted to kiss her. She was offended.

"Is that all you wanted?"

I felt like a jerk. I told Kramer about it, and he was supportive.

"You should have told her you wanted it all. All or nothing." He said I shouldn't be afraid of receiving a slap in the face.

This Is Our Music

This Is Our Music, our final album, was released in October of 1990 in all formats: cassette, LP, and CD. Damon came up with the album title, which he borrowed from Ornette Coleman. Does it sound self-important? It doesn't have the humor of *On Fire.* I guess it was our way of saying, "Fuck you, we play slow and quiet and we're not gonna change." I'm not sure why we felt the need to say "fuck you" to anyone. Maybe we were feeling defensive. Perhaps we felt that we were swimming against the tide. American indie rock was dominated by protogrunge acts, bands who played loud and fast.

This Is Our Music was the weakest album of the three we made. We sat in Geoff Travis's Rough Trade office in King's Cross that summer, and he gently urged us to return to the studio and write a few more songs. We didn't want to hear that, and didn't take his advice, and Geoff was kind enough not to insist. That's not the kind of A&R guy he was. Frankly, we needed the rest of our advance, and couldn't afford to delay that payment by going back into the studio. This is the problem with multirecord deals. Sometimes you find yourself chasing the advance, going into the studio before you are 100 percent ready, because you all need the money.

Geoff Travis was dead right about the record. Half of it is good. The other half is just okay. The best track was probably our cover of Yoko Ono's "Listen, the Snow Is Falling," which John Peel was partial to.

We had one song called "Spook." Its secret title was "Spock," because in fact the song was about the *Star Trek* episode "Operation Annihilate."

When you went blind
Then I nearly lost my mind
It didn't last
'Cause you have another eyelid

Everett True asked me if the song was about a cat, because cats have an extra eyelid, too. Not cat, I said, but Vulcan.

In "Operation Annihilate," Bones makes a terrible error. He accidentally blinds Spock while trying to irradiate a deadly pancakelike creature that has attached itself to Spock's back and attacked his nervous system. Bones is devastated when he learns that Spock will never see again. I was pretty upset myself. But Spock's vision returns—his eyes were protected by a second eyelid, unique to Vulcans.

That fall we did another short run of U.S. dates. It was not the traditional get-in-the-van-and-drive-for-weeks-type tour, with the clubs that treat you like shit. Damon came up with a plan. Instead of hauling our equipment all over the country in a van, we would do a two-week U.S. tour, flying only to the big cities that had important modern-rock radio stations (before the "alternative rock" revolution, they called it modern rock).

Galaxie 500 was not on a mission to play modern-sounding rock, or to create sounds that had never been heard before. We were very much influenced by the past two decades in rock music, and we liked to pick and choose from our heroes, be it the Modern Lovers or the Young Marble Giants. Perhaps we were postmodern. Perhaps we were just old-fashioned.

Jerry Rubino, Rough Trade's radio promo man, tried to set up interviews for us at the modern-rock stations. Only it didn't work out that way. The program directors at those big stations wouldn't return Jerry's phone calls. That was the reality of life on an independent label. You simply did not have access to radio play on commercial radio stations. For that, you needed to hire a different kind of "indie"—the independent radio promoters who worked for major labels, and whose job it was to deliver the key radio stations by whatever means necessary, like repeated phone calls or an envelope stuffed with cash or drugs. The major labels had set up a system they liked, where access to commercial radio was expensive. I'm sure they weren't thrilled about spending the money, but since they could afford it, it wasn't an ineffective way of controlling access to the airwaves.

We started the U.S. tour in Boston, where we played to 210 people at the Paradise—the largest crowd we ever drew in our adopted hometown. The four of us (Chris Xefos of King Missile came along to do sound) flew on to Atlanta, where we ran into Peter Buck in our hotel lobby. Our gig was at the Point, where we shared the bill with Southern Culture on the Skids. We invited Buck to come down to the Point and jam with us. He got onstage for the encore of "Don't Let Our Youth Go to Waste." He made some cool feedback sounds. He also made a couple of rock faces, but nothing truly egregious. He was heckled sarcastically by a kid in the audience, though.

"Rock star!"

Indie kids don't think it's cool to be a rock star. I'm sure Peter Buck wasn't too bothered by it.

The Galaxie 500 tour ended back at the 9:30 Club in Washington, D.C. Before the show, we were interviewed by a young journalist named Jon Wiederhorn, who was profiling the band for the *Boston Phoenix*. We didn't love his questions, and he didn't like our answers.

"Where does your music come from?"

"Our music comes from the air and the sea."

Wiederhorn said we were boring him, and pleaded with us to give him something exciting to print—a manifesto, an explanation, a bold statement of some kind.

"I'll give you a statement," I said. "Boston is a city of maggots. They can all line up outside the Channel and blow me."

I didn't think the *Boston Phoenix* would actually print that, but they did.

These days the Galaxies aren't in the mood to answer journalists' questions either simply or briefly. Usually, they just don't answer. And when they do, they're often evasive, flippant, and sarcastic. Sometimes they're outright obnoxious. . . . Or at least they were before a recent gig at Washington's 9:30 Club. "Boston is a city of maggots. They can all line up outside the Channel and blow me," snaps guiterist/vocalist Dean Wareham. . . . Lyrically, Galaxie 500 make about as much sense as they do in person. Most of their lyrics sound like Dr. Seuss on heroin. "I wrote a poem on a dog biscuit/And your dog refused to look at it/So I got drunk and looked at the Empire State Building/It was no bigger than a nickel," sings Wareham at the beginning of "Fourth of July." It's a typical passage: cryptic, absurdly pained, whimsical.

I liked his "Dr. Seuss on heroin" analogy. That's good rock criticism. Perhaps we were all feeling defensive that evening. We didn't feel particularly great about Boston or the *Boston Phoenix*. You tend to like the places where they like you. They liked us more in Chicago and San Francisco.

The tour was almost fun, though flying to a new city each day is at least as stressful as riding in the van, and flying was expensive, so we didn't make any money. And those modern-rock stations were not about to play Galaxie 500. They played U2 and the Cure and Depeche Mode and the Godfathers. But not Galaxie 500.

Traveling is stressful. And with Damon tour-managing, it seemed like every hotel check-in, every seat assignment, and every rental car was a problem. Damon would argue about what floor his room was on. He would get annoyed if he didn't get the seat he wanted on the flight. I shouldn't have let this bother me. I should have minded my own business. But traveling together highlights your differences.

In New Zealand, if a restaurant brings you the wrong entrée, you might eat it anyway. We are taught not to complain, like that's the highest form of virtue—to silently and stubbornly put up and shut up. My parents always rewarded me with praise if I didn't complain. Which of course was a form of instruction as well, a way of *telling* me not to complain. Fair enough—who wants a bunch of complaining kids?

Damon and Naomi, on the other hand, were born and raised in Manhattan, and were more used to having things just the way they wanted them, and Damon was quite prepared to make a scene if something wasn't to his liking. Maybe that's a better way to be. At least he got his room with a view.

Rock Slip

Our final tour of Europe began like a lost scene from *This Is Spinal Tap*. Chris Stone, our publicist at Rough Trade, was excited—the editors at *Sounds* had promised her that they would put Galaxie 500 on the cover of the magazine. That would be a first for us—a full-page cover photo on one of the three major British weeklies. You couldn't buy that kind of publicity (actually, you could buy it—one common form of payment was a trip to Hawaii for the magazine's editor and his girlfriend).

We sat in the Rough Trade office on a Tuesday afternoon and waited for the music papers to come in. There was good news and bad news. Yes, we were on the cover of *Sounds*. There was a very small photograph of us, inset, on the lower-left corner of the paper. But there was a much larger photograph of another band, the Perfect Disaster, front and center. I had to laugh. Chris didn't think it was so funny.

We had a three-man crew for our European tour: Kramer was back as the sound engineer, Noel Kilbride (from Sheffield, and a member of A.C. Temple) was the tour manager, and Jonny Dawe (who had been in Death by Milkfloat) was the backline technician—or roadie. Johnny liked to open beer bottles with his teeth. I ran into him years later and asked him to open my beer. He flashed me a smile—and a chipped tooth.

"I don't do that anymore."

After our Glasgow show, we went to a party thrown by a friend of the Pastels. Kramer met a girl who was a big Bongwater fan—she and her boyfriend both thought Kramer was a genius. They invited him back to their place, where the boyfriend promptly passed out drunk, and Kramer got it on with his girl. I had the hotel room to myself that night.

In Newcastle the next day, I was having an afternoon cup of tea in our hotel room with Kramer when the phone rang. It was the boyfriend of the Glaswegian girl, and he wanted to speak to Kramer.

"We're connected."

That was all he said. Scary stuff.

Naomi was incensed by Kramer's carrying on.

"I hate him."

He was no longer their hero.

Our very last English show was at the University of London Union (ULU), the biggest venue we ever headlined. Kramer slathered us in reverb and delay, and we sounded huge. The next day we set off for Rennes.

We drove down to Dover, transported the van across the Channel in a ferry, and continued clear across France. We drove into the night and eventually started to get hungry and irritable. There is a critical point on a long drive, soon after the sun goes down, where things can bubble over. The first eight hours of a drive are generally okay, but people start to wig out when night falls. At ten o'clock Noel suggested pulling over and getting some sandwiches at a rest stop, but Damon and Naomi wanted to find a nice restaurant—we were in France. They rolled down the window to ask the people in a car next to us for directions to a restaurant. Damon's French was really quite good. Kramer leaned out the window and yelled at the Frenchies.

"Speak English, damn it!"

Damon and Naomi were mortified. I thought it was funny. There was a childish part of me that enjoyed watching Kramer openly fight with them, talk back to them, and piss them off in a way that I rarely could do myself. I was glad to have him along.

The festival in Rennes was the site of my first "rock slip." That's what Jonny Dawe called it—the rock slip. I went out to a cheesy little dance club with Jonny, and I danced with a girl who had been at the show. We danced to "Rich Girl" by Hall and Oates, and she pushed up against me, and the next thing I knew her tongue was in my mouth. I went back to her place, and she offered me Coca-Cola, which she called *un coca*.

I kept a diary of some of these tours, which is how I remember the names of the hotels and what we ate for breakfast. But there were only three entries in the diary for this last European trip. Here's one:

November 17

Rennes, France

I'm on the verge of cracking today. I can't talk to them anymore.

Everything they said and did was driving me nuts. Why? They weren't bad people. They were good people. So what if Damon is picky about seat assignments? Or if we show up at the hotel in Sheffield after driving all day and they don't like the hotel and want to look for another one, when all I want to do is lie down for half an hour? Why was I finding it so difficult to be with them? As the end of the tour approached, I felt more and more isolated. I had a secret. My secret was that I wanted out of the band. And my secret was creating distance. I had something constantly on my mind, thought about it all the time, but I couldn't talk about it. I stared vacantly out the window. They sensed that I was distant, which in turn created more distance.

I was tired of going up to Boston four days a week to practice, and they had told me that they definitely were not moving to New York. I was mad at Damon and Naomi and I didn't want to be stuck with them in a little rehearsal room, for hours on end, collaborating on new songs.

The tour ended on December 1 in Copenhagen. Wonderful, wonderful Copenhagen. Christmastime in Copenhagen at Barbue. Danmarks Radio recorded the show for later broadcast. A pretty Danish girl made eyes at me from the audience. Perhaps I was imagining it. Maybe she was just watching the band.

After the show, the promoter told me that he wanted to introduce me to some people, and one of those people was Tine, the pretty girl from the show. Tine and her friend invited Kramer and me to a cool party in a squat. It was four floors of partying, with different music on each floor. Then we had coffee with Tine and her friend, and I went home to bed. Tine asked if maybe I would like to go to the movies with her tomorrow.

I avoided Damon and Naomi that day. The phone rang in my Danish Modern room, and I just stared at it. I called Tine and we made a plan to see *Darkman*.

There's nothing better than watching a big dumb Hollywood film when you're in a foreign country. You get to see what kind of odd popcorn they have and enjoy the European commercials. Then, when the movie starts, you feel like you're back home already as the images beam straight to the back of your brain. After the film, we went to a cheap Italian restaurant and drank a bottle of red wine. I was living a Billy Joel song.

Pan American World Airways was in deep trouble. Sometime after our European tour commenced, the airline had filed for bankruptcy, and had promptly begun selling off its European routes. When we arrived at their counter at Copenhagen Airport, we discovered that our flight to New York had been canceled—forever. Damon pleaded with the lone Pan Am agent who still worked at this airport, but to no avail.

Then he threatened to kill him.

"I'm going to kill you if you don't put us on a flight."

That took the cake. It was better than Damon's previous winner, delivered to a customs official on the way in to Holland last year. This customs official had questioned the box of LPs that we were carrying, stating that we were liable to a penalty for traveling with merchandise. "And what is the penalty for assaulting a customs officer?" Damon had asked him.

In Damon's defense, he was functioning as the tour manager, the group leader. Traveling as a group is stressful, and incidents like this can bring out one's more aggressive side. The Pan Am agent did not throw us in jail. He put us on a plane to Berlin, where we spent the night before finally getting a flight back to New York.

The Spotlight

On Christmas Day Claudia and I flew to Wellington, New Zealand, for a two-week vacation. I wanted to allow myself some time to clear my head after the tour. I had seen Kramer quit his band B.A.L.L. on a whim one day, flying home in a snit, in the middle of a tour, and I didn't want to do that. I know that people are generally tired of one another at the end of a tour—it's not a good time to make a major life decision.

But when I came back to New York fourteen days later, I called Damon and Naomi and told them I didn't want to be in Galaxie 500 anymore.

They were very sweet and understanding. They asked me what the problem was. I said something about it just not being fun anymore—which was true. They were so generous that I started to think I was making a terrible mistake. I drove up to Boston to sit down and talk with them. We had lunch and I told them I was tired of traveling to Boston every week to rehearse. I suggested that maybe we should add another guitarist to the band. There were two reasons for this: One, because that would make us a better live band, and two, because it was the very structure of the band—a trio, but with a married voting bloc—that had become irksome for me.

Damon and Naomi said maybe we could practice in New York occasionally. And we could explore adding another guitar player, too—not an official member of the band, but an extra touring musician. It was a good conversation, good enough to make me change my mind and rejoin the band that I had quit. I had been out for twenty-four hours, and now I was back in.

A month later I was back in Boston, rehearsing for an American tour. We had been offered a slot opening for the Cocteau Twins. I soon realized that I had made a mistake by not going through with my earlier decision. Nothing had changed. I was still driving up to Boston. I was still locked in a small rehearsal room with Damon and Naomi. There were three of us in that room, but I was lonely.

The Cocteau Twins' tour kicked off in St. Louis. We got ourselves a professional tour manager and sound engineer named Bill Rahmy, who had just finished a tour with Dokken. Bill was an excellent tour manager—he insisted that we shouldn't have to pack up our equipment, and he would do it for us.

The Cocteau Twins had an elaborate light show. They stood five in a row (Simon, Liz, and Robin, plus additional guitarists Ben and Mitsuo), strumming along to drum tracks that played off of a computer. The lights would sweep out over the audience and they oohed and aahed in delight. After the show, the Cocteau Twins would start in on the case of champagne.

In Los Angeles, I met up with my old college friend Angelo. He was writing a TV pilot, living near Venice Beach, and waiting tables in a sushi restaurant. He was friendly with a couple of sushi chefs, and we went over to their apartment. They had no furniture, just a couple of bare mattresses. Porno magazines were strewn on the parquet floor, and a there was a glass pipe in the center of the living room—for freebasing cocaine. This was their life. Sushi in the daytime, freebasing at night. I smoked a little of their cocaine, but my heart started pounding and my chest felt tight. I didn't like that feeling. I told Angelo I had to get out of there.

The next night Bill Rahmy and I went to the Coconut Teaszer to see a couple of bands: the Dwarves and Hole. Hole was on first, and at this point they were pretty great—Courtney Love was the kind of singer you couldn't take your eyes off of.

The Dwarves took it to another level. The guitarist (who was called He Who Cannot Be Named) wore only a jockstrap and a hockey mask. The singer (Blag Dahlia) wore a pair of fishnet tights and no underwear, so his package was quite visible. After their final song, the drummer knocked over the drum kit, pulled down his pants, and mooned the audience. Then he inserted two fingers in his ass. That was a showstopper. (The Dwarves got in hot water years later, when one stunt proved too much for their record company to handle—the band announced that He Who Cannot Be Named had been stabbed to death in Philadelphia, and had Sub Pop send out a press release announcing it. When the people at Sub Pop discovered that the story was a hoax, they immediately dropped the band from the label.)

After two days off in L.A. came the controversial show at UC Irvine, where I walked downstage during a guitar solo and the spotlight was turned on me.

In retrospect I notice that Dean chose the L.A. show to launch this new trick, when the audience was full of music industry people. We hadn't had any spotlights in Columbus or Dallas!

The University of California at Irvine is to Los Angeles what, say, Rutgers University might be to New York City. But I am quibbling. I remember the night a little differently. I recorded it in my tour diary, which was now a list of petty annoyances and gripes.

Damon said he doesn't like me walking in front of his drum kit—it throws him off. I didn't tell him to go fuck himself.

Anyway, it is true that I stepped downstage front and center during a guitar solo. We were playing theaters and small college arenas—larger stages than we were used to—and I felt a little awkward out there, standing in place in the triangle that was formed by bass, drums, and guitar. At any rate, the singer is generally allowed to stray from the microphone stand.

The lighting director (probably an employee of the Cocteau Twins', but not someone I had ever spoken a word to) turned a spotlight on me. Why Damon thought that this came about because of a secret deal I had made, I don't know. But when I read that interview all those years later, I understood why Damon had been so upset that night in Irvine. It wasn't that I walked in front of his drum kit. It was that someone had shone a big, bright light on me, and not on him.

This can be a problem in a rock-and-roll band. It's probably why they invented the drum riser, a large platform that elevates the entire drum kit, so that the drummer doesn't toil away in darkness and obscurity.

When you're drifting apart, as we were, then the smallest things seem hugely important. A light shone on me, and Damon found this light to be of grave significance. But I was angry, too. This was what our little democracy had come to—the drummer now wanted to tell me where to stand on the stage. Right by the microphone, please—and be sure not to walk in front of the drum kit.

Why didn't I fight? What could I have said? "I'll walk wherever I damn well please"? "I'll stand on top of the drums if I want"? There just didn't seem to be much point in arguing with the Gang of Two.

We could have used some band therapy. That's what R.E.M. did. And Metallica. But they had millions of reasons to go into therapy.

Naomi tried to talk to me. She knew something was up.

"What's wrong? You seemed so relaxed in Boston."

I didn't know what to say. I didn't say that I was still angry about being told not to walk near the drum kit. I didn't say that I couldn't stop thinking about quitting. I didn't tell her that I was having bad dreams. In one dream, I walked into Damon and Naomi's hotel room with a gun. The message was clear—I had to kill Galaxie 500.

I n San Francisco I stayed up partying with Robin and Simon and Ben from the Cocteau Twins—and a coke dealer who worked at the luggage carousel at a national airport, which I guess is a good job for a drug dealer.

Robin was staying up all night an awful lot. But he got through the shows alright. He didn't sing or dance—he just had to run the sequencer and play his guitar by the side of the stage.

In Columbus I went out on the town with Simon and Ben and a graduate student who had a big bag of cocaine and said he knew where the party was. It sounded like fun. Six of us piled into this guy's Datsun 210 sedan (which was smaller than my old 210 wagon) with open beer bottles and a bag of coke, and drove around Columbus. Our new friend drove around in circles for a little while before admitting that he couldn't remember where the party was. He took us to his apartment instead. We could have a party there.

His pad was filthy, the kitchen sink overflowing with dirty plates. "Sorry about the mess. My girlfriend just left me. I'm livin' on the edge right now." He chopped out some lines and shared his opinions on art.

"Advertising is the greatest American art form," he said.

He put on a video, a home movie, in which he could be seen fucking his ex-girlfriend. Nice. This party wasn't turning out so great. We called a cab and returned to the hotel. I lay down on the bed in my nice hotel room. My heart was beating too fast. I was frightened. For a few minutes I thought it might stop beating altogether. I took long, slow breaths and told myself to calm down.

We played the Roseland Ballroom in New York. Peter Shershin from Columbia Records came to the show. He was very interested in Galaxie 500. *On Fire* had sold thirty-seven thousand copies. We were still under contract with Rough Trade, but Rough Trade was in deep financial trouble. Every week brought a new rumor that Rough Trade was going under, or doing a deal with Geffen or Warner Brothers.

The Cocteau Twins' tour ended in Boston, with a show at the Boston University hockey arena. We had one additional show booked for the following night, at Bowdoin College in Maine. April 5, 1991. We were scheduled to go on at nine that night, but the opening band played for an hour and a half while we waited in the green room that the students had set up for us. Being a college band, they didn't know that the opener is supposed to play a short set and then get off the stage. We sat in that green room getting more and more irritated. And that was our final show—an annoying evening at Bowdoin College.

I made it through the set, loaded my amplifier and guitar into the back of my blue '75 Dodge Dart, and drove all the way home to New York City.

Was I being a shit? Should I have told them, as we packed up our cars that night, that we had just played our final show? Should I have told them *before* the show? None of that seemed like a very good idea. I would call them from New York.

Out of the Blue

Here are the dirty facts! What happened was simply that Dean quit, more or less out of the blue, on the telephone one day. We have not seen him since, nor spoken since that week. In fact, he didn't even place the call! It was just after the weekend we had finished what turned out to be our last tour, which was an opening slot for the Cocteau Twins in the States; we had an upcoming tour to Japan (this was something Naomi and I were very much looking forward to, as you can imagine, as was Kramer, we were going to take him with us), and when I opened the paper on Monday I discovered there was a sale on for tickets to Tokyo that was ending at midnight. So I called Dean to say, "Let's buy our tickets," and he said, "no, I quit." No explanation, just "there's nothing more to talk about," and that was it. A lot of years of friendship, not to mention the band, down the drain in a minute flat.

It wasn't entirely out of the blue, as we had already discussed my quitting in January, but other than that Damon got this part right. There was no real explanation. I chickened out. I didn't know what to say. I didn't say, "I quit because I can't be in the same room with you anymore," or, "I quit because I don't like being told where to stand onstage."

The most common reason a guy gives when he breaks up with a girl is no reason at all. You give no reason, or vaguely state that you are confused and unhappy. "No reason" means only one thing—I don't want to be in a relationship with you anymore. It's not me—it's you. I want to lead my life without you in it.

I can see why they were so upset with me. How could a friend do such a thing? But I would counter that we were not quite friends at that point.

We were bandmates. Our friendship didn't go down the drain in a minute flat. Our friendship had been trickling down the drain for a couple of years now.

Was there something wrong with Damon and Naomi? Of course there was—my therapist says there are ten things wrong with every person. There are plenty of things wrong with me, too.

Some of my best friends are crazy. But that's okay, because I don't have to ride in a van with them for five weeks. We're just friends. Damon and Naomi were lovely people, brilliant and artistic and likable. I loved Damon's fluid, jazzy style on the drums, and Naomi's simple and melodic bass parts. I liked Damon's poetry and Naomi's miniature paintings. But they were driving me crazy.

No, you are not just friends when you're in a band together. The band may begin as a pure friendship. You share a love of music, and you start playing together in that spirit. But if the band is at all successful, then it takes on another logic. It becomes a business. Now you are business partners as well as friends and collaborators. You travel together. You spend all your waking hours together. You're a family and a secret society.

Joining a band is like joining a cult. You give your mind and your body and your soul to the cult. You give your money to the cult. If you read interviews with young bands, they say, "*We* think this," "*We* like this," "*We* don't like such and such," "*We* are inspired by," and so on. They have collective opinions. They have a manifesto. This is part of how you define your band as distinct from other bands.

At first, it is fun being in this cult together, this secret society. But you become more involved with one another's lives than you ever anticipated. Instead of being friends, it's more like you are lovers. Only you never really planned to move in together. I loved Damon and Naomi, but I didn't want to marry them. I didn't want us to spend our lives together.

Other artistic collaborators don't really encounter this problem, because people don't work so closely together for so long. Steve McQueen and Yul Brynner did not get along on the set of *The Magnificent Seven.* But then it was over. The rock-and-roll band is a unique construct, one that can last for many years, and one that is subject to many pressures, external and internal.

Since Dean has never told us why he did it we have had to guess, and judg-
ing by his actions we can only assume that he wanted to sign with a major
by himself, instead of as part of the band.

The suggestion is that I broke up Galaxie 500 for the money. No, it was
not the money. There was no money.

I had a hundred reasons, ranging from petty annoyances to major struc-
tural problems in the band. The bottom line is I quit *because I couldn't stop*
thinking about quitting. I thought about it when I went to sleep at night and
then when I woke up in the morning. That's when you know you have to
make a change in your life—when the matter consumes you. The decision
makes itself.

I didn't want to be in a cult anymore. I wanted to be free.

Damon did call me early on a Monday morning to see about booking
flights to Japan. I had been up for about an hour, and was starting to get
that sick, nervous feeling that you get when you have to fire someone or
break up with them—because today was the day.

Damon called first. My heart skipped a beat. The moment was upon me. I
said don't buy the tickets to Japan because I was leaving the band, and this
time it was real.

They weren't so nice and understanding this time. They were furious.
There were three days of angry phone calls. Damon said I was greedy and
irresponsible. The way he saw it, I had an obligation and a responsibility to
keep going with Galaxie 500, this thing that we had created together and
worked so hard on. Naomi got on the phone and told me that I was lazy, had
no ambition, didn't care about anyone except myself and didn't know what
was important in life.

People say mean things about you when you break up with them. Damon
and Naomi had been a couple since high school—I don't think anyone had
ever broken up with either of them, so maybe they took this news extra-
hard. I thought about what Naomi had said. Compared with Damon and
Naomi, perhaps I was lazy. Not so lazy that I wasn't able to write the lyrics
for our songs. But perhaps I was lazy when it came to driving up to Boston every week and working on new songs together. That's because I didn't
really enjoy working on music with them anymore.

Did I have no ambition? I might have been guilty of that, too. I confess that had I never lain awake at night dreaming of being a big rock star.

Did I not care about anyone but myself? I cared about them, but I was fed up. I didn't feel responsible for their lives.

Damon and Naomi said that most of the people they knew in the music business stopped speaking to them after this, and that they were "dismissed as the rhythm section," replaceable I suppose, and "not worth dealing with on our own."

They stayed angry at me for a long time. A couple years after I quit, in an interview with a Spanish magazine, they said I had left Galaxie 500 because of ego and money—that I had a huge ego and I wanted all the money.

I hadn't stolen any money, or cheated them. But that's not how they saw it. They thought that I owed them something after the three years we'd spent together in a band, and they considered my leaving to be a terrible betrayal.

For all the talk of democracy, how members each contribute equally to a band and how bands make decisions as a unit, the ugly fact is that bands are usually dependent on the singer/songwriter.

I'm sure it's not a good feeling to have to lean on someone else, especially when you feel them pulling away. They tried to pull me back in. They expressed their displeasure when I recorded that song with Kramer and laid a guilt trip on me when I took part in the benefit at CBGB. I was scolded when I stepped into the spotlight at UC Irvine. Damon resented my being in that spotlight. For my part, I felt like a lonely prisoner in my own band. I didn't like being told where to stand. And I was tired of being treated like a child.

Moon Dither

Dean Wareham, erstwhile singer and guitarist of Galaxie 500, is sort of a wimp. Not in his personal appearance, good God no; he's really cute actually. No, Dean is a wimp as a counter-cultural revolutionary, making limp, tasteful music in the face of all the bare-chested, impossibly wacko rock gods du jour (viz all the Maker's late spring/early summer covers). . . . "Luna Park" is a thin, colourless wash that drones on without discernable point, other than a few glowering guitar interludes. . . . Now he's signed to Elektra, an entirely carefree, non-careerist move I don't think. . . . A shame and a waste.

(Caren Myers, Melody Maker, August 15, 1992)

It's a fine line between clever and stupid, as Derek Smalls points out in *This Is Spinal Top.* Yesterday I was clever. Beautiful notes floated from my fingers up toward the heavens. Today I was a wimp. Soft. Limp. Tasteful. Where did I go wrong? What were my crimes?

Crime number one: I had broken up Galaxie 500. There was nothing to be done about that, but some fans were upset, particularly in England, where we were most popular.

"You broke up Galaxie 500, you bastard!" one fan hissed at me on the first Luna visit to England.

Crime number two: I wasn't grunge.

I checked out the *Melody Maker* covers for late spring and early summer 1992, to see who those "bare-chested, impossibly wacko rock gods du jour" were. I saw photos of Metallica, L7, Faith No More, Guns N' Roses, Soundgarden, Pearl Jam, Fishbone, and the Red Hot Chili Peppers. Were these the countercultural revolutionaries? Counter to what? Weren't they just the culture? Didn't I see the Red Hot Chili Peppers alongside Andre Agassi doing their "rock-and-roll tennis" TV commercial for the Canon Rebel camera?

But I don't know culture from counterculture. Questions like that confuse me, and they don't help when writing songs. Let the rock critics read Adorno and Althusser. I will study Pops Staples and the Chocolate Watchband.

T hings change quickly in the music business. When you're young and starting a band, you don't realize that. You think it's springtime, when in fact you're on the verge of winter.

The scene changes particularly quickly in England. They have a music press that can identify and champion new trends much faster than the press in the States. You can get your picture on the cover of the *NME* on the basis of a demo cassette that has only been heard by a few A&R guys. They will build you up, and take you down. One week the Clash are the most important band in the world, the only band that matters—but a few months later they are irrelevant corporate sellouts. One week the Strokes and Interpol are the coolest bands ever, but soon all things New York are sneered at.

The U.K. independent rock scene had been dominated by shoegaze bands in 1991. The cover of *Melody Maker* that year featured My Bloody Valentine, Chapterhouse, Swervedriver, Curve, Lush, Ride, and Slowdive. My Bloody Valentine were visionaries, the others not so much.

A year later, grunge was the rage, and all eyes were on Seattle. *Melody Maker* quickly changed its tune, and ran a feature titled "Whatever Happened to Shoegazing?" Grunge happened, that's what.

Nirvana's *Nevermind* was released in September of 1991, as was Pearl Jam's *Ten*. I saw Pearl Jam at a sparsely attended show at CBGB. Eddie Vedder sounded like Cher to me—they both swallow their vowels the same way. He developed the grunge warble that we are still hearing today, parroted by legions of rock singers. A year later we had Stone Temple Pilots. Soon you couldn't get away from grunge. It was in *Time* magazine and in advertisements for a "punk rock" Subaru. Punk, or perhaps more properly some kind of punk/hard-rock fusion, had finally broken in the United States, and Madison Avenue was paying attention.

Crime number three: I had signed to a major label. There had been a shift in the music industry—all the bands were now signing to major labels. Sonic Youth signed to Geffen, which seemed to be a watershed event, leading to Nirvana's being signed at the same label. Suddenly the major labels descended upon the independent scene and signed everything they could get their hands on. Dinosaur Jr., the Flaming Lips, Mazzy Star, the Meat Puppets, the Chills, Firehose, the Afghan Whigs, Screaming Trees, the Butthole Surfers. Even Galaxie 500 had been talking to Columbia Records.

I was ready to try being on a major label. Why? Because major labels were ready to try me. And my experiences with independent labels had been mixed. Soon after Galaxie 500's breakup, Rough Trade filed for bankruptcy. They went out of business, and tens of thousands of dollars in mechanical royalties went with them, along with the catalog itself.

But if everyone was signing to the majors in the States, in the U.K. you were still far better off on an independent label. First of all, the smaller size of the country meant that independent labels could do a perfectly good job. They could get your songs on the radio and your product into the major chains.

Second, there was a certain attitude from the English press about the importance of being indie. Never mind that the "independent" U.K. bands— from the Happy Mondays to Teenage Fan Club to My Bloody Valentine—had licensed their records to Sony and Geffen and Time Warner in the States. That took place on the other side of the pond, away from the eyes of the music critics who thought they knew best how you should run your band's business.

Most of us releasing underground rock records on small independent labels in the late '80s were not on indie labels out of a sense of holiness or indie pride. There was no such thing as being proud to be indie. There was simply no other option at the time. These were the lean years of hair metal and John Cougar Mellencamp. The majors didn't sign bands like Galaxie 500, and we knew it. It wouldn't have occurred to us to send a demo tape to Columbia Records.

Some people who have never been in a band will tell you that the major labels are run by unethical crooks, while small independent labels will deal with you honestly and keep it real.

In 1993, Steve Albini, the man behind Big Black and Rapeman, and the talented engineer and producer of records by the Pixies, Helmet, and Nirvana, wrote an article for the *Baffler,* the Chicago organ that combined cultural criticism with the worship of indie rock.

The article, titled "The Problem with Music," offered Albini's helpful hints to bands who were on the verge of signing to an evil major label. Albini lays out the math for a fictional band that has agreed to a $250,000 deal with a young A&R guy who has them sign a deal memo on the spot after seeing them perform. I've never heard of that happening, because the A&R guy usually needs permission to commit a quarter of a million dollars to a project, but maybe that's how it happens in Chicago.

His math will demonstrate "just how fucked they are." Albini uses some rather bloated figures—$8,000 for recording tape (I am quite sure we never spent more than $2,000 on tape), $10,000 for mastering (the most we ever paid was $4,500—the price charged by top mastering engineers like Bob Ludwig and Greg Calbi). He lists the manager as taking $37,500 off the top of the deal (all the managers I have worked with take their commission *after* recording costs are deducted from the deal, not before). And he has included a $30,000 video budget (in my experience, the video budget does not come out of the artist's advance, though 50 percent of the video cost does get charged against your future royalties). He also includes $7,000 for artwork and photographs (again, these expenses are generally covered by the label, not taken from your advance). But I am quibbling again.

The end result of Albini's math shows that each band member would earn $4,000 after completing their album and first tour, while their manager has earned $51,000, the producer $90,000 (this he probably knows about), and the record company $710,000. Wow.

Things hadn't worked that way in Luna. We managed to save half of our recording advance, so that each of us received $20,000 from the record deal. In addition to that, there was a publishing deal, which was an additional source of income.

Is it only successful people who feel they have the obligation to tell the rest of us how we should do things? Albini was a sought-after producer (and a good one), building his own recording studio and working steadily. He did well from indie rock and also from bands that were signed to major labels.

It is certainly true that a major label deal can bite you. All the money that gets spent on making and promoting your record means that sometimes you are only digging yourself a hole, a deep pit of record company debt. You may get a 14 percent royalty rate, but with all those expenses being charged to your account you are never going to see royalties anyway.

But at least the major labels send out detailed accounting statements, itemizing exactly how you are being overcharged and underpaid. They have a system in place.

Are you safer doing a handshake deal with an upstanding indie guy who doesn't want to bother with the formality of signing a contract? A guy who offers you a 50/50 profit-sharing deal (after expenses), which sounds much better than a 14 percent royalty rate? Of course, he can't give you the $250,000 advance—maybe he can give you $5,000 or $20,000. But you'll keep your costs down and start to see royalties much quicker.

Unless the indie label files for bankruptcy and retains ownership of your record. Or the label boss takes your mechanical royalties and buys a new BMW, while your repeated requests for an accounting statement are ignored.

You pick your poison in the music business. There is a difference between being promised a great royalty and actually receiving it. My own feeling is that you take the money when it is offered—and up front is a good place to start.

Fred vom Jupiter

In 1989, shortly after Galaxie 500 signed there, Rough Trade hired Terry Tolkin to be its new American A&R man. In the words of one of his former boyfriends, Terry was "tall, blond, cute, smart, and very outgoing. He could talk and charm his way around record store people and distributors." Terry wasn't our A&R man—that job fell to Geoff Travis in London, who had signed us, and was the one to give us an opinion on our latest recordings. But Terry was sent down to Noise New York during the mixing sessions for *This Is Our Music,* to take us out to lunch. He walked in just as we were having an argument about the guitar intro to "Fourth of July."

Kramer had asked me to play a little introductory guitar solo, way up high on the guitar's neck, and we both thought it sounded pretty cool. Naomi, however, thought it was harsh and ugly, and wanted me to play something else, something prettier. These are the small things you argue about when you're in a band.

The five of us went out to lunch on Canal Street. Terry spilled his soup on his pants.

"Do I still look cool?"

Terry and Kramer were old friends.

"I knew Terry when he was a different guy. He had long, long hair, and [here Kramer whispered] he lived with a man."

Terry led a new life now, with his hot girlfriend, soon to be his hot wife, Justine Chiara, in an apartment in Jersey City. Justine and Terry shared the same prominent nose, but Justine wore it especially well. She reminded me a little of Nastassja Kinski in *Cat People.*

Terry had grown up in New City, out in Rockland County, but ran away to New York City at age sixteen. He lived for several months on benches in Central Park, and ended up hustling, selling acid behind the Central Park band shell, and having sex for money, operating out of the Fascination game room in Times Square.

From 1978 to 1984 Terry lived with an older boyfriend at Bond Street and the Bowery, right around the corner from CBGB. Initially a Deadhead, he was turned on to punk rock by this boyfriend, who ran a small punk label, and who enlisted Terry to take his records around to the stores. One day Terry talked his way into a job at 99 (pronounced "nine nine") Records on MacDougal Street. 99 Records was a crucial hub of activity in the New York music scene. Out of the record store grew a label, also called 99, which was home to ESG, Liquid Liquid, the Bush Tetras, and Glenn Branca. Thurston Moore used to hang out there, and Terry said he actually introduced Thurston Moore to Kim Gordon.

Terry started booking Rick Rubin's band Hose around town, and then got involved booking shows for the Butthole Surfers and Big Black. To his boyfriend's dismay, he invited the Butthole Surfers to stay at their Bowery loft for weeks at a time.

He briefly moved to Detroit to work with Corey Rusk at Touch and Go Records. But after signing the Butthole Surfers to the label, Terry soon fell out of favor with Rusk and came back to New York, where he worked at Rockpool and Dutch East India and Caroline Records. He claimed to have coined the term "alternative rock." Terry seemed to know everyone in the music scene, from Steve Albini to Captain Beefheart.

I liked Terry instantly. We liked a lot of the same music—Wire, Joy Division, the Comsat Angels, New Order, Lydia Lunch, and Sonic Youth.

A couple months after Terry's studio visit, he asked me to meet him for lunch at Milano's Bar on Houston Street. Lunch consisted of tequila, Rolling Rocks, and menthol cigarettes. Terry was one of two white people I knew who smoked menthols: The other was my brother Anthony—also a recovering Deadhead.

Terry smoked a joint, drank two shots of tequila, and began ranting about his fucking bosses at Rough Trade. He had been courting a Florida band named Rein Sanction, formed by brothers Mark and Brannon Gentry. Terry had become friendly with the brothers, and excitedly offered them a deal with Rough Trade. He was on the verge of signing them, when word came from above—he could not sign the band to Rough Trade.

"Those fucking English bastards! Those fucking English bastards!"

That's how it is at every record company. The A&R guy, even the head of the A&R department, does not have the authority to sign bands on a whim. They have to go upstairs for approval first. It doesn't matter who you are— if it's not your money, if you don't actually *own* the label, then you need to ask for permission.

Terry switched gears after this outburst.

"Things seemed kind of tense when I came down to the studio that day. I want you to know . . . so long as I have a job somewhere, you'll be able to make records, with or without Galaxie 500."

I was touched. And a little tipsy. It was good to know that Terry was on my side. Although I had just heard quite clearly that he didn't have the power to sign a band.

Trouble was brewing at Rough Trade. The U.S. company had always depended on help from the U.K., and when that help dried up (due to financial problems in Europe), Robin Hurley was ordered to make cuts in the United States.

With the losses piling up, they were in no position to sign new bands, and had no need of an A&R guy. Terry was out of a job. We were still with the label, but six months later Rough Trade U.S. was history, too, and so was Galaxie 500.

Terry landed a cushy new job at Elektra Records, courtesy of Vice President Howard Thompson. Howard, then thirty-nine years old, had signed the Psychedelic Furs and 10,000 Maniacs and the Sugarcubes and Adam Ant. He was one of those A&R men who actually made money for the company. There were many others, especially in the '90s, who seemed to fail at one job, only to find themselves with an even better job at another major label. It was a good time to have an A&R job.

Terry wanted me to be his first signing at Elektra. But it wouldn't happen automatically. The new guy doesn't get to sign any old band. There is a process. The first part of the process was that I had to record some demos. They needed to know that I could still write songs.

Terry got me $3,000 to record the demos for Elektra. I booked time at Wharton Tiers's Fun City studio on East Twenty-second Street. Jimmy Chambers of Mercury Rev came into town to play the drums on most of the tracks, with Hamish Kilgour of the Clean doing a few of them, too. I played the guitars and bass and keyboards myself. Seven songs in total, which I delivered to Terry at Elektra, Peter Shershin at Columbia, and Geoff Travis.

Rough Trade had gone under, but Travis was trying to set up a new deal with Capitol Records. He visited me in my New York apartment. I showed him the closet-size room where I recorded my home demos and played him the tracks I had been working on.

"Damon and Naomi told me you were lazy and would never be able to get anything done on your own," he said. "Why would they say that?"

Terry and Howard liked my demos. The three of us went to lunch at Victor's Café on West Fifty-second Street.

"What do you want to do, Dean?"

"I want to make records."

"When I asked Adam Ant that question, he said, 'I want to be a household name.'"

I had given the wrong answer. It never occurred to me to want to be a household name. I did like Ant's album *Kings of the Wild Frontier.* I saw Mr. Ant perform on a pier on the West Side Highway when I was in high school. He had arrived at the pier on a pirate ship that day. I liked his guitar player, Marco Pirroni.

Adam Ant grew out of a different musical environment, and at a time where impresarios like Malcolm McLaren could conjure stars out of nothing (so he would have us believe—the talent did have at least something to do with it). Ant came from the U.K., where bands really did explode on the scene overnight. Those of us in indie rock in the late '80s didn't dream of becoming rock stars or household names. It wasn't an option. Not that we wouldn't have wanted to be rock stars. But everyone knew that the big rock bands were awful and the major labels were a wasteland. College radio and fanzines were the only world we dreamed of conquering.

Howard did not hold my answer against me. He gave Terry his approval to take the deal to the next level—he could now present the proposal to Elektra's chairman, Bob Krasnow.

Krasnow was a legend with a reputation for living large and having a temper, but Elektra had been very profitable on his watch.

He warned Terry that this was not a game and he had better be damn sure of what he was doing. He said they were firing "million-dollar bullets," meaning that each signing to Elektra would probably end up costing the label a million dollars—in advances, video and radio promotion, tour support, and other expenses. Krasnow's assessment turned out to be pretty accurate—today I get royalty statements from Elektra showing that Luna owes them $1.2 million. Which isn't bad, considering we recorded five albums for them. Does this mean that they lost $1.2 million dollars on us? Of course not. That figure does not reflect the money that Elektra made from the sale of our CDs, something like $6 per CD (while they credited our account only that portion that is considered artist royalty—14 percent, or around $2 per CD).

Terry called me with the good news. I went over to his fourth-floor walk-up on East Seventeenth Street, a one-bedroom pad with a roof deck, where Terry and Justine liked to barbecue. Terry had shelves built into the wall to house his large record collection. That afternoon we got stoned and listened to his seven-inch singles, records he had been collecting since his days at 99 Records. He played me the first Dream Syndicate single, their early version of "That's What You Always Say"—when they were still called 15 Minutes. And "Fred vom Jupiter" by Andreas Dorau, a hilarious German synthpop single about an attractive, muscular, and charming extraterrestrial named Fred, who visits Earth in his spaceship. The women fall in love with him, but the men are threatened and force him to leave. The chorus is sung by a small children's choir.

Terry loved music. You meet two kinds of people at major labels—those who live *for* music, and those who live *off* music. Terry lived for music. He liked nothing better than to smoke pot and sit around playing records, and he had managed to parlay this extended adolescence into a high-paying job. In another field, it wouldn't look good on your résumé to be a stoner and a high-school dropout. But the music business doesn't judge you like that. Terry could sit in his office smoking joints or chopping out lines of coke while going through the box of demo cassettes (which they always give to the new guy) and that was okay, so long as he signed a successful act to the label.

Columbia Records also made me an offer—exactly half of what Elektra was dangling. I went with Elektra, which had a better reputation anyway. It's probably a silly thing, but I was enamored of the label that had been home to Television and the Stooges and Love and Nico and the MC5. Peter Shershin called me a few days later to find out why I hadn't gone with Columbia.

"Was it the money?" he asked.

Lunapark

A tremendous weight lifted when I left Galaxie 500. I no longer had to walk around with a secret. I no longer had to drive to Boston and shut myself inside a rehearsal room by the expressway, feeling like a third wheel. I was back in New York City, happily living with my girlfriend, and I felt free.

With the deal in place, I put a band together. I called Justin Harwood in New Zealand. He had recently quit the Chills, without really giving them a reason. They assumed that he was ready to get out of music altogether. The truth was that he was tired of being in the Chills.

Justin jumped at the chance to move to New York City. He arrived two weeks later, and moved into an apartment on East Sixteenth Street.

We had met a few years earlier at a softball game in Islington (North London) arranged by the Chills' manager. Justin grew up in Napier, the sunniest spot in New Zealand, and an important destination for fans of art deco architecture. His father, whom Justin called Rex, was a tour bus driver, and wore a toupee. Justin found this ridiculous. When he started losing his own hair, he went with the shaved head.

Not only did Justin not wear a toupee, he didn't eat vegetables. Nothing green went into his mouth. Sometimes this was explained as a medical condition, the remnant of a sickly childhood—something about a kidney ailment.

"A spear of broccoli could kill me!" he said.

His girlfriend, Lisa, intimated that Justin's mother was to blame—she simply hadn't made him eat his vegetables.

Justin also abstained from drinking or smoking. It is very useful to have a teetotaler in the band. Not only could Justin play the bass and write the set lists, he also was the designated driver whenever we needed one.

Together we auditioned drummers. One guy came by bus, all the way from Baltimore, which maybe explained why he smelled bad.

We settled on Byron Guthrie. Byron was my friend Lisa's boyfriend, and he had recently played with Ultra Vivid Scene. Byron was six years older than I was, but he was boyish and fun loving. He tended bar at Joe's on Sixth Street between A and B, one of our regular hangouts. Byron hailed from Louisiana. He loved country music, had a vast collection of ugly knick-knacks in his apartment on Avenue B, and wore a T-shirt that said I'M WITH STUPID. One day Byron told me that he had written a song.

"It's called 'Stinky Finger.'"

I got a stinky finger
I got a stinky finger

That was as much as he had written thus far.

Byron's friend Louis built a little rehearsal space in the basement of his building on Avenue B and Sixth Street. It was perfect. We would roll around there to rehearse at 2:00 P.M., usually waking Byron up, and go down to the basement.

Although he knew how to play the drums, Byron did not own a drum kit. Perhaps we should have recognized this as a sign, a warning. Instead we combed the classifieds and found some parents on the Upper East Side who were getting rid of their son's drum kit now that he had moved away to college. All Byron needed now was sticks.

In the Chills, the drummer was an eighteen-year-old kid named Jimmy. Justin had been in charge of the rhythm section. He had a good sense of how the rhythm section should play together as one, and he was used to giving pointers to the drummer. Now Justin gave helpful pointers to Byron.

"You need to go to the ride cymbal during Dean's guitar solo. Maybe you need to not play so many kick drum notes, so that you lock in with what the bass is doing." Byron didn't seem to mind. But he had a hell of a time remembering these instructions from one rehearsal to the next. Justin had to remind him.

"You were going to go to the ride cymbal there . . ."

We kept working, and recorded half a dozen new songs at Toxic Shock

Studios on Broadway and Houston. We were getting close to being ready to make our record. But we were a little concerned about Byron.

We booked a show at Bunratty's in Boston, playing with a new band called Come, featuring Thalia Zedek, formerly of Live Skull and before that Dangerous Birds. I had their one and only seven-inch single: *Alfa Romeo b/w Smile on Your Face*. Thalia had dark circles under her eyes.

Terry rented a minivan and drove us to Boston: Terry, Justin, Dean, Byron, and Grasshopper, the guitar player who was on loan to us from Mercury Rev. Terry smoked a big joint before we set out. He was one of those people who insisted that smoking weed makes them a better driver. They can really get in a special zone where they *focus* on the road.

When we arrived at Bunratty's, Byron announced that he had forgotten to bring his sticks. A small thing. He forgot the sticks. It could happen to anyone. But it seemed significant to Justin and me. When we came back from Boston, I called Stanley Demeski, the drummer for the Feelies. The Feelies had broken up within a few months of Galaxie 500's demise. I saw one of their final shows at Town Hall. The Feelies were remarkable for their speed and precision. They seemed to play all their songs at double the recorded tempo, as if fueled by speed and coffee.

Good drummers tend to come from the suburbs. They have a distinct advantage—garages, basements, extra rooms—all things that are in short supply in New York City. Stanley didn't own one drum kit—he owned three. He also owned a leather stick bag, a little case for his sticks and mallets and brushes. Stanley spent hours each day down in the basement of his house in Haledon, New Jersey, playing the drums—because he was a drummer.

Stanley drove into town, and we jammed together in the basement of Byron's apartment building. Perhaps that was cruel of us, but we had paid the rent for the month, so we felt entitled to use the space. Byron was probably asleep anyway.

We played "Slash Your Tires," one of the songs we had been playing with Byron. All of a sudden we sounded ten times better. We were no longer an underpowered old train, struggling to climb a hill. Stanley was like a judicious metronome, a machine. He hit the snare in the same place and the same way each time. His favorite drummers were Ringo Starr, Charlie Watts, Creedence Clearwater Revival's Doug Clifford, and Television's Billy Ficca.

"I do not use the drums as an extension of my penis," he said, explaining why he rarely played drum fills, preferring to keep things steady and metronomic. It was precisely because he played so few fills that when he did play one, you noticed it. It became a special moment in the song.

Our first gig with Stanley was at Maxwell's in Hoboken—Justin, myself, Stanley, and Grasshopper. We sounded good. It was nice to have a solid rhythm section. We recorded *Lunapark,* our first album, named after an amusement park in Sydney, Australia, that I had passed every day on my way to school. Fred Maher produced the record. Fred had recently produced Lou Reed's *New York* album, certainly the best thing Reed had done in years. Fred was a drummer and a would-be preppy. "You know that film *Metropolitan*?" he said. "The one guy who hangs around with all the rich preppy kids, and wants to be one of them? That was me."

Lunapark cost $100,000 to record. Half of that money went to Fred and his engineer Lloyd Puckitt. The rest of it went to RPM Studios, where we spent six weeks working on the record. This was ten times as much money as we ever spent on a Galaxie 500 recording.

Fred did a nice job. Nice enough that the people at Elektra gave him a staff producer/A&R job at the company. The '90s were great that way. It was easy to get an A&R job. All you needed was one job offer, or a rumor of an offer—the right entertainment lawyer could turn this rumor into a high-paying job.

Two Months' Salary

Grasshopper was on loan to us from Mercury Rev, and they were about to get very busy themselves. So we placed a classified ad in the *Village Voice*. LUNA NEEDS GUITAR PLAYER.

We auditioned three guitarists, but it was Sean Eden who got the job. He impressed us with his playing, but I also liked his white Sperry Top-Siders with a hole in the big toe.

Sean was born in Ontario, but his doctor father moved the Eden family to Houston, Texas, where Sean went to high school before studying acting at the North Carolina School of the Arts. Six feet tall and boyishly handsome, Sean moved to New York City to make it as an actor. He also fronted his own rock band, Damp. We asked if we could hear some of Damp's recordings, but Sean wouldn't allow it. He did occasionally sing a line from their song "Guest List": *I'm gonna put you on the guest list!*

Our first recording session with Sean was at Mixolydian Studios in Boonton, New Jersey, where we had gone to record a few B-sides. We recorded and mixed four tracks in two days with Don Sternecker, the engineer who had recorded several albums by the Feelies. Sean immediately stepped up to the plate and played beautiful guitar solos on "Indian Summer," "Ride Into the Sun," and "Egg Nog," our Christmas single. In contrast to our album, which took six weeks to record, this EP was a quick affair—and we were much happier with the results.

The summer that *Lunapark* was released, Claudia and I got engaged.

I went into Tiffany's one July afternoon to investigate engagement rings. I approached the counter where they kept the diamond rings and overheard a conversation between a salesman and a young couple.

"You don't have to spend sixteen thousand dollars," he said. "You can get a perfectly nice ring for eight thousand dollars."

Everyone knows that the diamond business is a racket. The moment you take it out of the store, your diamond is worth half of what you just paid for it. Sure, I've seen those sickening TV commercials from De Beers—"How else can two months' salary last a lifetime?" They want you to think that two months' salary is the yardstick, the accepted standard for what you should spend on a ring.

"Why do those ads upset you so much?" Claudia asked. "I don't see you getting angry at the AT&T ads."

A couple years later, when I was touring the U.K., I saw a film at a cinema in Notting Hill. It was *The Draughtsman's Contract* by Peter Greenaway. Before the film, they ran one of those De Beers ads. Same sickening tone as you watch a perfect gentleman present an expensive ring to his fiancée. And then the tag: "How else can *one* month's salary last a lifetime?"

It's a cultural thing. In some countries you only have to give one month's worth.

Tiffany's also had cute little diamond engagement rings priced at $800.

I left the store and walked around the block, then up Fifth Avenue a couple of blocks, thinking hard. Here I was, making a big decision. Putting down eight hundred dollars—the most I had ever put down for anything. I could have bought the VW, the Datsun, and Blue Thunder for that amount.

I bought the ring and hid it in the sock drawer at home. I would whip it out when the time was right.

C laudia seemed in a testy mood on August 1, my thirtieth birthday. I asked her what the problem was, and she gave me that speech that men get about how they're afraid of commitment, and how it's time to take things to the next level. She was starting to feel that I would never be ready to do that.

I found this all pretty annoying. I was planning on presenting that ring any day now. Maybe today, maybe next Tuesday. I was waiting for the right moment.

"Is that right?" I said. "You don't know what you're talking about."

I retrieved the ring from the sock drawer and tossed it to her angrily.

"Here. What's this?"

Now we were engaged to be married.

Claudia's friend Mary told her it wasn't a good idea to marry a musician in a rock band, because they are always traveling, always onstage, and susceptible to temptation. She was probably right. It's safer to marry someone who works in an office with a pretty secretary.

Double Shot of My Baby's Love

The first Luna tour was six weeks around the United States, opening for Screaming Trees, who had just released their terrific *Sweet Oblivion* LP. Screaming Trees was my favorite Seattle band. I had seen them at the Rat the year before. They were lumped in with the grunge bands, but they were not just another heavy rock band—they were far more melodic than their peers.

It just so happened that they hailed from the Pacific Northwest, and had some of that grunge fashion sense. On bass and guitar were brothers Van and Gary Lee Conner, who were the size of linemen, and who often wore shorts and plaid shirts. Their singer, Mark Lanegan, had a deep rock voice that wasn't so far from Jim Morrison's. Like Morrison, Lanegan was a handsome and charismatic drunk, with long brown hair. He was not always this way—when I first saw them at the Rat, Screaming Trees was cold sober. But a few years on the road had changed that.

Lanegan would stumble into the club for sound check at four in the afternoon, drunk already, often having been awake all night long. Some days he would listen to the Luna sound check, too, and would ask us to play "Don't Let Our Youth Go to Waste."

If you're the singer in a band, you can get away with being just a little drunk. You don't have to keep the beat, or play a dazzling solo. You just need to remember the words. But some nights Lanegan was too far gone to sing the encore, and the rest of the band would go back and do a few songs without him, while he sat sulking in the dressing room, drinking Jägermeister shots.

You get to know one another pretty well after six weeks in a van. Our van was crowded. There were seven of us in total—four band members,

Justin's girlfriend, Lisa, who came along to sell T-shirts, and our New Jersey crew—soundman Rich Saccoliti and driver/tour manager Barry Duryea, who soon became known as the most annoying roadie in the world. Barry so bothered us that he had to make a new rule during the tour—no kicking the driver.

It was Sean who kicked Barry that day. They needled each other all tour long. Barry picked on Sean because he was the new guy, and had never been on tour with a band.

Every day of our tour, Stanley sat in the same seat—the one directly behind the driver, which is the best seat in the van. You get a good view, it's not too bumpy, and there's plenty of legroom.

Once in a while, one of us would take Stanley's seat, just to prove that it didn't belong to him. He could handle it for a couple of hours, but that was it.

He would sit there and read his *Goldmine* magazine, underlining old seven-inch singles that he wanted to buy. And he would buy toys for his two little children at home, and toy trains for himself. By the end of the trip he would have a bunch of toys stuffed under the backseat of the van. We razzed him about the toy trains.

"Neil Young collects toy trains," he said.

Stanley brought along his special mix tapes of material from the '60s and late '70s. Stanley had a talent for making mix tapes. He was a little older than us, and grew up listening to AM radio in the late '60s. He knew more about rock history than we did, and liked to lord that over us.

"What—you don't know 'Double Shot of My Baby's Love'?"

"Double shot of what?"

"It was a hit."

"Maybe it was a regional hit, Stanley—in New Jersey."

Every afternoon Stanley pulled out his practice pad, a special brown rubberized pad that strapped around his leg, so that he could run through his exercises with his drumsticks, exercises he said were necessary for him to stay in that metronomic shape.

This became a fun item for the rest of us to bitch about. Sometimes the pad came out in the dressing room. Other days it was in the van itself. But he never failed to do the exercises. *Rat-a-tat-tat, a-rat-a-tat-tat. Rat-a-tat-tat, a-rat-a-tat-tat. Rat-a-tat-tat, a-rat-a-tat-tat.*

As he was a human metronome, Stanley was intolerant of what he perceived as Sean's sloppiness.

"Do you know the meaning of the word 'ensemble'?" Stanley would ask Sean after some shows.

He also took issue with what he saw as Sean's overuse of the whammy bar on his Jazzmaster, which Stanley said was "a crutch."

"Your solo tonight made me want to bolt the stage. It made me physically ill."

The rest of us were very happy with Sean's playing. And with Stanley's being such a metronome, it was fine for Sean and me to be a little sloppy.

In Long Beach, California, we played a horrid little club called Bogart's, on a triple bill with Screaming Trees and the Celibate Rifles (the excellent Australian punk band whose name was a riff on "Sex Pistols").

Sean loved the dressing room. While the rest of us saw it as the band's room, he saw it as the party room. He had friends scattered around the country, and loved it when they saw him in this environment. On this night in Long Beach, he was busy entertaining friends while we set up our equipment, and was a few minutes late to the stage.

Stanley was annoyed.

"Where the fuck is Sean? It's time to go."

Stanley always wanted to play as early as possible and leave the club as soon as possible, too. He had done this all before with the Feelies, and he wasn't here to party.

When we finally took the stage, a long-haired guy with a mustache stood directly in front of me.

"Kick out the jams!" he yelled, before we had played a note.

And again after our first song, "Come on, motherfuckers! Kick out the jams!"

He was annoyed. Luna didn't rock hard enough for him. He kept his chatter up all set long. After the last song I told him to go fuck himself, and he challenged me to a fight right then and there. Luckily for him, Stanley pulled me away.

I felt like a wimp. But Screaming Trees hit the stage and the heckling started anew.

"What the fuck do you call that? Kick out the jams!"

He had come out tonight to stand in the front row and insult the bands.

At the end of the Screaming Trees tour Claudia and I were married in front of twenty friends and family members at her parents' Park Avenue apartment. Judge Shirley Fingerhood presided.

My father is an excellent public speaker. I would say he had a natural gift for this, but the truth is that he grew up with a stutter and it was only by hard work that he overcame his fear of speaking in public. He gave a swell toast that night.

"I think it was George Bernard Shaw who said that marriage is like a castle under siege—everyone on the outside wants to get in, and everyone on the inside wants to get out. Welcome to the castle!"

My brother Anthony came to my wedding, too. He had returned to New York City in the early '80s, taken some classes at Columbia University's extension school, become a coke addict, been a guest at the Hazelden clinic, and even stayed straight for a time. But 1992 was one of the dark years. It had been months since I had seen him, and he looked awful. He had dropped about twenty pounds and his skin was stretched tightly across his cheekbones. He looked like a thief—a junkie thief with a $200-a-day habit.

When we were kids, Anthony had always told me that he was going to be very wealthy when he grew up. It hadn't happened yet, but he hadn't really grown up, either.

Back to the Old House

Galaxie 500 had done well in England. I figured Luna should go over well, too. But it wasn't the same. The cucumber sandwiches were still delicious, but the situation was different. I was starting over.

According to the terms of our Elektra deal, we were licensed to WEA (the Warner-Elektra-Atlantic label) in Europe. I never realized that this was tantamount to committing career suicide in Europe. WEA was good at selling records by Prince and R.E.M. and Madonna and Natalie Merchant. But Luna meant nothing to them—ours was just another CD that had been tossed on their desks.

Without the support of the weekly papers and national radio, and without any help from our record company, touring England was a drag.

In September of 1992 we played a gig at the Tivoli, in Buckley, which is in northeast Wales. Buckley is a small town in the middle of nowhere, though not far from Liverpool. People come from nearby Chester to see shows there. Somehow the Tivoli had attained pseudolegendary status. Led Zeppelin had played there, and Black Sabbath. And now Luna.

After the show, I was approached by a mousy Japanese fan, who introduced herself as S. She had sent me a couple of nice postcards over the last year, written in strange English. I remember the one she sent right after Galaxie 500 broke up.

Please. Don't go so far alone!
—*S.*

The postcards were cute.

Tonight she was in a pickle. She had come all the way from Japan to see Luna, took the train from London, and arrived just in time for the show. But she had neglected to book a hotel room, and the trains had stopped running.

"What can I do?" she asked.

It's annoying when people ask you to solve their problems for them, but we gave S. a lift to our Travelodge out on the highway. She could get herself a cheap room there.

At four in the morning there came a knock on my door. S. stood there in tears. She needed to talk. She wasn't happy with her boyfriend back home.

"My boyfriend—he wants me to be his secretary!"

"Ssh! Stanley is trying to sleep!"

She pressed herself against me. I thought about it for a tiny moment—because when a girl presses her body against you, well, you feel it. But I wasn't interested. I told her to go away.

Maybe her boyfriend really does treat her like a secretary, I thought. That would be very Japanese of him.

I tried to sneak out of the hotel without having to see S. again, getting up bright and early. But she was up even earlier, and was sitting in the lobby, writing in her journal.

I walked quickly to the van.

"Let's go!"

S. came running out of the lobby.

We screeched out of the parking lot with S. chasing after us, waving and gesticulating, trying to tell us something important. Two minutes later we realized what she had been trying to say—we were speeding down the highway with the back doors of the van wide open. Fortunately, our guitars and suitcases were intact.

I was hoping never to see S. again, but she showed up repeatedly at Luna shows over the next year, in Tokyo and Birmingham and London.

In Sheffield, she gave me her diary and asked me to read it.

"Why you are writing all your songs to me?" she demanded angrily.

I couldn't read her diary—it was eighty pages in Japanese, broken occasionally only by a quote from one of my songs, in English.

I told her to see a psychiatrist.

She came back six months later.

"My psychiatrist says I have two minds."

"That's not good."

I last saw S. two years later, in the lobby of the ULU. She slapped me in the face and demanded that I return her diary.

Penthouse

With some bands, their first album is perfect, the best thing they will ever do. The Strokes will never top *Is This It?* Television never improved on *Marquee Moon.* (The genius of the Velvet Underground is demonstrated in how they made a perfect first record, and then followed it with three more perfect, yet different, statements.)

Lunapark was nice enough, but we weren't really a band when we recorded it, rather we were three musicians recording songs that I had written.

The second Luna album, *Bewitched,* was better, and became our best seller. Justin and I wrote several songs (like "Bewitched" and "Tiger Lily") as a team—he would give me a little demo and I would figure out a melody and lyrics. *Bewitched* had some nice moments, like the stellar guitar playing of Sterling Morrison, who guested on two songs and played an amazing guitar solo on "Friendly Advice."

We had met Sterling on the Velvet Underground European tour in 1993. Lou Reed had picked us to be the opening act. This I heard from our new manager, Renée Lehman. Renée was twenty-eight, lived in Hoboken, and had just quit her job working for Gary Kurfirst, who managed the Ramones, Talking Heads, B-52s, and Big Audio Dynamite.

Getting the call to open for the Velvet Underground was weird. I thought I might have been dreaming. But weeks later I found myself in a dressing room at the Edinburgh Playhouse, listening to Lou Reed, John Cale, Moe Tucker, and Sterling Morrison run through "Venus in Furs."

That tour was grueling. We ate cheese sandwiches for dinner every night, and while the band was good to us, their English crew was not. It didn't matter—I knew I was lucky to be able to see the entire Velvet Underground tour from my spot on the side of the stage.

In Berlin we went out drinking with Sterling Morrison at the Obst und

Gemüse (fruit and vegetable) bar. Our soundman, Gordon, scored some ecstasy in the bathroom there, which made the night even more special. I will always remember riding home in a Mercedes taxicab that night, listening, incredibly, to a live Velvets bootleg on German radio, enjoying the strange confluence of events, thinking how lucky I was to be on that tour.

I t was on our third album, *Penthouse,* that Luna really hit its stride musically. We had now been touring together for a couple of years, and we had learned to appreciate the subtleties of one another's playing (as well as how to get on one another's nerves).

We eased into the third album by recording "Chinatown" and "Bonnie and Clyde" at Sorcerer Sound on Mercer Street, with engineer Mario Salvati.

Terry Tolkin had recently signed Stereolab to Elektra. He suggested that Laetitia Sadier and I sing a duet together—something by Serge Gainsbourg. Laetitia picked "Bonnie and Clyde," and helped me with my French pronunciation. Jane Scarpantoni came in to add some frantic cello parts. We played the song fast, and we played it slow, and it worked both ways.

Not only that, it seemed to help our profile in England, where we released an EP containing "Chinatown," the two very different recordings of "Bonnie and Clyde," and Talking Heads' "Thank You for Sending Me an Angel." All of a sudden, we started getting good reviews in England. *Melody Maker* called the EP the single of the week.

B onnie and Clyde" was not a hit at radio. I'm sure the people at Elektra wondered what the hell Terry was doing—why was the A&R guy suggesting that we record a song in French? But ten years later our recording of "Bonnie and Clyde" was licensed for use in a Cadillac commercial and the Warner Music Group made a quick $120,000. The fee from licensing a song to a movie or TV commercial is split 50/50 with the band, but the artist doesn't get their 50 percent until the record company has recouped the whole deal. Since we were still in debt to the label, they collected the entire fee. They credited the Luna account $60,000. So instead of owing them $1.2 million, we only owed them $1.14 million. If we got nineteen more Cadillac commercials, we might actually see some royalties.

Another of Terry's ideas was to have his wife, Justine, manage Luna. She had worked for a management company that handled 10,000 Maniacs and the Waterboys and Electronic, but was itching to set up her own company. I liked Justine, but it seemed obvious that our manager should not sleep in the same bed with our A&R guy. This was a recipe for trouble. What if she needs to yell at his boss? What if we need to get out of the contract and move to another label? We said no, thanks.

The Afghan Whigs had heard the same spiel from Terry and Justine, and they went for it. Justine became their manager, and trouble followed.

Terry and Justine were freethinkers. They both told me that affairs were healthy in any relationship, because they helped to keep things interesting. Just before we went in the studio, Terry dropped a bombshell. Justine had left him.

I should have seen it coming.

Justine had stopped coming to dinner with us, because she was always working late, often till midnight. And she was boning up on Eastern philosophy, which is often the first sign of trouble. Something was not right in her world.

Terry confessed that Justine had caught him with another girl's phone number in his wallet.

"I've never really been faithful to her," he said.

He had more shocking news. He suspected that Justine was sleeping with their mutual client, Greg Dulli, his "best friend" and lead singer of the Afghan Whigs.

Justine and Greg denied the story, but she moved out of their apartment. I didn't know what to believe.

Terry ratcheted up the level of his partying when Justine moved out. He took ecstasy every weekend and went out clubbing every night. He started hanging out at the Tunnel, where he met a new friend, Richard the exterminator. Richard was just twenty years old, a kid who had moved down from Albany and landed a job killing rats and roaches.

Terry was a generous person. Some days he could hardly believe that a stoner, a high-school dropout who used to sell acid and sex in Central Park, was now earning a nice six-figure salary and sitting in a fancy office at 75 Rockefeller Plaza.

"Look at these leather tiles," he'd say. Elektra's offices, three floors at 75 Rock, were covered in green leather tiles.

He loved sharing his good fortune and treating his friends to the good things in life, with his expense account. He took Claudia and me out for dinner once a week, to Rolf's on Third Avenue, Ecco on Chambers Street, Periyali, and his favorite, Kin Khao, on Spring Street, where Terry would order expensive drinks and ogle the waitresses.

"Wow. She's got an ass like a twelve-year-old boy."

Some people say you should be careful with record company dinners. You think you're being treated when in fact the dinner is being charged back to your own account, against your future royalties. Terry always insisted that Metallica was paying for dinner, or the Eagles—the bands that kept the label afloat. Sometimes he wrote Richard Nixon's name down as the dinner guest on the expense report.

If Terry was devastated by Justine's leaving him, he managed to hide it. He enjoyed his new life. He drank and partied and showed up late to work most days, or worked from home. His new life inspired the lyrics I wrote for "Chinatown":

You're out all night
Chasing girlies
You're late to work
And you go home earlies

Looking lost in Chinatown
Why are we hiding from our friends?
Rushing round in taxicabs
Is it time to make amends?
You'll get yours and I'll get mine
Can't be lucky all the time

Chinatown" and "Bonnie and Clyde" were better than anything we had ever done. We decided right then to track the whole record with Mario, producing it ourselves, bringing in a separate mixing engineer to finish it (the label likes you to have a mixer who has mixed a few hits). Pat McCarthy was the mixing engineer on Counting Crows' "Mr. Jones"—another one of those universally loathed songs that pays the bills for years to come.

The B-room at Sorcerer, accessed by a freight elevator to the top of a rickety old loft building, was a strange, dark, handmade studio. They had spiders and snakes in glass cages. There was an automatic toilet paper dispenser. The bathroom was rigged so that the radio switched on when you opened the door.

Mario Salvati looked like a greasy biker dude from upstate, with long hair and a handlebar mustache. He smoked two packs of generic cigarettes a day. Brian Eno he was not, but Mario had a good ear for guitar sounds.

Sean was still the new guy when we made our second album, *Bewitched.* Having now been in the band for two years, though, he decided to express his opinions more this time around.

"I will not be silenced," he said. I'm not sure who he thought was trying to silence him, but that's the way he felt.

He brought in three ideas of his own, for which I wrote lyrics—"Tracy, I Love You," "Sideshow by the Seashore," and "Roll in the Sand." These three songs proved difficult to record.

Sean didn't like Justin's bass line on "Tracy, I Love You," or my rhythm guitar on "Roll in the Sand."

We decided to give Sean a whole day in the studio by himself to work out the guitar parts on those songs and get them just how he wanted them. On "Sideshow by the Seashore" he recorded about eight different guitar tracks.

"Okay," we said. "You should decide which tracks you want to use before the mixing engineer arrives. You don't want to just hand the whole mess over to him and make him fix it."

Sean couldn't decide which tracks to keep. There were good things in each track.

This was a difficult process for Sean. He had these pieces that he had recorded at home, with all the guitar parts worked out, like a little concerto. But they didn't have melodies or lyrics. And then he brought these little gems to the band, and the thing about being in a band is that you have to let other people have their way with your ideas. You have to share. You have to let go. You have to accept that things won't turn out just like your home demos—because you're in a band. Of course, all bands wrestle with this problem. The guitarist writes something pretty, but he hates the lyrics that the singer comes up with (see the Smiths, for example).

Pat, our mixing engineer, cleaned up "Sideshow by the Seashore" for Sean. He removed all the guitar tracks except the ones that contained the signature riff. This did not sit well with Sean.

"Did you listen to all those slide guitar tracks I did?" he asked. "They are very evocative, if you put reverb on them and have them in the back of the mix."

Instead of putting the guitars back in, Pat rented a theremin, and had Justin play it all through the song. We all thought that Pat made the song sound ten times better. Even Stanley said so.

"Sean, he took that riff and turned it into a song," Stanley said.

But Sean did not agree. He made a cassette of his home demo, and pleaded with Justin and me to listen to it. He kept talking about it, even after the record was finished and mastered. He argued that we should go back and remix "Sideshow by the Seashore," and "Chinatown," too, before the record went to the presses.

P at McCarthy was an Irishman living in Los Angeles. At twenty-eight, he was just a bit younger than us, but he made it clear that he was in charge. Pat had worked with R.E.M. and the Butthole Surfers and U2, but he usually worked under a producer, someone who made many of the mixing decisions for him.

One requirement of a producer is that he be decisive. When everyone else is saying, "I don't know," the producer has to know. Even if he's wrong, at least he can point the way forward.

Pat smoked a good amount of weed, and I don't blame him for that. If I had to spend every day of my life in a recording studio, I'd probably smoke weed, too.

He and Justin didn't always see eye to eye. Justin liked to insult people that he hardly knew, as a way of showing that he was your friend—it's a New Zealand thing. But Pat didn't always see the humor.

"Just mix the damn song," Justin would say.

"I *am* mixing the song," Pat would answer incredulously. "What do you think I'm doing?"

"Just mix it."

"I am."

"Mix it, then."

Pat was meticulous in his mixing. He could spend hours adjusting the level of the vocals so it was just right on each syllable. Each mix took at least a day and a half to complete. In the middle of what was supposed to be our final week in the studio, Pat put "Double Feature" up on the Studer two-inch-tape machine.

Pat didn't like Stanley's drum track, so he had him come back and redo it. And he didn't particularly like Justin's bass part. So Sean picked up the bass and tried some ideas in the chorus section. Pat still wasn't thrilled. I picked it up and ran it through a fuzz pedal, which made the bass sound like a fat trumpet.

After an afternoon of each of us trying to play a new bass line, we gave up. We had gigs in Providence and Boston that weekend, and had to leave Pat alone.

We came into the studio Friday morning to pick up our amplifiers and guitars.

"We'll be back on Sunday."

"I'll have this one mixed, and probably two more," he said.

We returned from Boston Sunday night and "Double Feature" was still up. We were annoyed that he was still working on it, but we sat and listened. All of our bass parts were in there. In addition, he had created "chimpanzee noises" to accompany the words

I have seen the chimpanzees
In the afternoon sun

"Do you hear the chimpanzees?" he asked. We applauded. Pat had taken our song and turned it into something very groovy. So what if we went a little crazy getting there?

This was the first somewhat *difficult* album that Luna had made, where we fought and were set against one another. Where things took longer than they should have. Where we went over budget. But it was also clearly our best album.

"You have to go a bit mad to make a record," Pat said.

We compiled the mixes on the final day, and Pat brought them down to my apartment, where we all took ecstasy and listened to the entire record. Perhaps we were cheating, but the album sounded outstanding that way.

I chanced upon a show for the photography of Ted Croner at a gallery in SoHo. Croner had taken magnificent shots of New York City in the 1950s. Our album title, *Penthouse,* was already set, and Croner's images of an Upper West Side skyline seemed perfect.

He was alive and well and living in a huge, messy loft in the Flatiron District. I visited him there several times. He seemed lonely, and quite excited that someone half his age was interested in his photographs. He bought me a copy of the *Harvard Concise Dictionary of Music.*

"I probably slept with more women than I should have," he told me.

Terry took Ted and Claudia and me out to dinner at a nice Italian restaurant on Irving Place. Ted explained how he had come to take his signature images of the New York skyline, with the blurred vertical lines of light. He had been photographing the skyline from Central Park one wintry evening. It was so cold that his hands shook—he couldn't keep the camera steady. When he got the pictures back, the results were unusual. His shaking hands had created pretty strips of white light. Thus one of his more famous images was born.

"Kids today don't know their history," he said. "They're ignorant. Can you tell me the name of the British general who surrendered to Washington, to end the Revolutionary War?"

"Lord Cornwallis," said Terry.

Terry hadn't graduated from high school, but he was an avid watcher of documentaries, and some things did stick in his brain.

We used another famous Croner photograph, of a speeding taxicab, for a special *Chinatown* single. Bob Dylan later borrowed this same image for the cover of his *Modern Times* disc. This borrowing caused a very small stir, and was mentioned in a few magazines. Dylan had already been accused of borrowing chunks of his lyrics from Henry Timrod, an obscure nineteenth-century poet. This followed an earlier episode where some people thought he borrowed too closely from Junichi Saga's *Confessions of a Yakuza.* Jon Pareles came to his defense in the *New York Times.* According to Pareles, this was not plagiarism so much as "cultural collage."

I've borrowed things, too. I borrowed "give me a slug from the wonderful jug" ("Moon Palace") from an old song by the Ink Spots. I borrowed the chord progression to "Double Feature" from "Miss You" by the Rolling Stones.

Folk singers are allowed to borrow from folk singers. You just say it's part of the tradition of writing songs, and you generally get away with it.

The crux of this matter: songwriting royalties. If a folk singer has merely adapted an old American classic, then the record company doesn't have to pay him a mechanical royalty on that song. They can pass the savings along to themselves. The songwriter must claim *authorship* in order to pick up that extra nickel (per song, per record pressed), which is a very important nickel to get.

P enthouse was released in August 1995.

Kim France wrote a piece on *Penthouse* for *New York* magazine (August 28, 1995), explaining exactly how Luna did not fit on the radio:

> *Luna's softly delivered blows don't even register on the radar of most of today's alternative fans, whose taste runs more to the likes of Eddie Vedder, Trent Reznor, and Courtney Love. . . . Luna stands only a slightly better chance of fitting in on Adult Album Alternative–station playlists. This relatively new format (which VH1 is betting the farm on) is for baby-boomer listeners whose tastes are too sophisticated for soft rock. But many of its typical artists—Counting Crows, the Cranberries, [Melissa] Etheridge— have personae just as overdramatic as (if less desperate than) their MTV counterparts. And the happy quotient in triple-A music is much higher. In this context, sandwiched between Sheryl Crow and Hootie and the Blowfish, Luna would be, like, a real downer.*

She was right. "Chinatown" did nothing at commercial alternative radio. Not only were we competing against Everclear and Green Day and the Smashing Pumpkins and Alanis Morissette and Garbage, but the radio playlists were shrinking, too. Many of these stations had only twenty-odd songs in rotation—the songs their listeners liked best. The music directors' job was to identify those songs and play them again and again.

Didn't it all get better when Nirvana came along? Weren't the airwaves filled with great alternative rock? No, it got worse—because alternative or modern-rock radio became a much bigger business. You could make a case that Nirvana ruined everything.

When you're signed to a major label, you don't compete just against other labels but also against the other "alternative" artists at your own label. Every Monday morning at Elektra they scheduled meetings with the important VPs and radio promotion people and sales people, and came up with priority lists for the week, in each genre.

Luna was never at the top of the label's priority alternative list—those slots were reserved for the big sellers: Natalie Merchant, Third Eye Blind, Better than Ezra, Björk. It was understood that when the head of alternative radio called the program director at KROQ each week to pressure the station into playing Elektra artists, he could maybe convince them to play one or two Elektra artists, but not all of them. So he was instructed to make sure that at least the priority acts were added to the radio playlists.

The same was true at MTV. The channel had come a long way from its early days on the air, when it actually helped break new artists like Devo and the Human League, who were not previously getting radio play. But in order for your video to be in the "Buzz Bin," MTV now wanted to see that you were charting at radio first. That way the Buzz Bin was guaranteed to be a success.

Since "Chinatown" had flopped, the radio department was given the choice of a second single from *Penthouse.*

Nancy Jeffries, the new head of A&R at Elektra, had been in A&R since the 1970s—at RCA and Virgin before Elektra. Before that she was in a folk band herself—the Insect Trust—along with Robert Palmer, who later became a music critic for the *New York Times.*

"It's always the song that you like the *least*," she said, "that will be picked as the single."

The smart guys in the alternative radio department chose "Hedgehog," track nine. It's not that we didn't like the song. We just thought it was the worst of the ten on our album. We had buried it at track nine, where you put the weakest song (the final track on an album should be a good one). They identified "Hedgehog" as the most alternative-sounding song on the record, being that it was short and slightly aggressive. Maybe the program directors would think that Luna was grunge.

It's no fun, it's no fun

Reading fortune cookies to yourself

Are you a fox or a hedgehog?

Do you care anymore?

Wasting time, wasting time, wasting time all the while

I don't know what they're sayin', but I hate it anyway

I borrowed that fox/hedgehog opposition from Isaiah Berlin's famous essay, feeling pretty sure he wouldn't come after me.

"The fox knows many things," wrote Berlin, "but the hedgehog knows one big thing." Some artists are foxes. Aristotle, Pushkin, Goethe, Picasso, Paul McCartney, Beck—they can do all kinds of dazzling things. But others are hedgehogs—Hegel, Nietzsche, Dostoyevsky, Jackson Pollock, and Keith Richards. They stick with one idea.

Willie Nelson's Bus

In September 1995 we set out on tour. For the first week, we traveled in two Chevrolet Astro vans—one for the band, the other for the crew and equipment.

Bill Caulfield was our tour manager, a big, grumpy, pipe-smoking vegetarian preppy/Buddhist from San Francisco. Our guitar tech was Stephen Joyce, who had worked with Dinosaur Jr. and My Bloody Valentine. Stephen hailed from Newcastle, and was the hardest-working tech we had ever seen. He told us how great the mad-cow scare was, because beef was suddenly cheap and plentiful in the U.K. He and his family ate steak every night. The bus driver was Richard Kimball, who looked to be about sixty-seven years old. We called him the Fugitive.

Our first date was at the Black Cat in Washington, D.C. On the way back to the hotel after our show, Stanley announced that we had to stop at the 7-Eleven to buy some milk. He had brought a box of cereal on tour, because he wanted to cut back on the greasy breakfasts that upset his stomach on our last outing.

This was perfect. We would have to stop for milk every night, which gave us something new to razz Stanley about on a daily basis.

Stanley always made it quite clear that he did not like touring—he would rather be at home with the kids. None of us could understand this, because none of us had children. We thought that being on tour was grand.

We had recently bought Stanley a shiny new Ludwig drum kit, with money provided by Elektra for an equipment upgrade. Stanley loved the new Ludwig kit, but Justin liked to remind him that it belonged to the band, not to him personally.

"It's my drum kit, Stanley, just as much as yours."

Riding in a van all day would turn all of us into children. We had some interesting discussions on our long, rainy drive to Atlanta. We played a game called Who Would You Fuck?

It had started out as Who Would You Open For? As in, which bands is it worth going out on tour in front of? Opening for other bands is a thankless job. It's more fun to play to a hundred of your own fans than two thousand of someone else's. But it seems to be a necessary evil. The record company doesn't want you playing to your own fans. What's the point of that? Your own fans will already buy your CD. You need new fans to buy it, other people's fans.

Sean was firmly of the opinion that you shouldn't open for uncool people.

"Sean, would you open for David Bowie?" I asked.

"I guess so."

"Bush?"(The much maligned U.K. grunge band—hated in England, but loved in the States—who happened to be Luna fans, and who had offered us some dates opening for them in Europe.)

"No."

"Smashing Pumpkins?"

"Yes."

I was surprised that Sean said yes to that one. He didn't really like the Pumpkins. We all thought Billy Corgan was a major asshole. In fact, Sean did a brilliant mocking impression of Corgan, singing "despite all my rage, I am still just a rat in a cage."

"Natalie Merchant?" (Renée had once suggested that maybe we could get on the Natalie Merchant tour.)

"No!"

"Let me ask you this, Sean—would you fuck Natalie Merchant?"

"Yes."

"But you wouldn't open for her?"

"No, she's awful. I would fuck her because she's famous and it would make a good story. I could tell people that I fucked Natalie Merchant."

"Would you fuck Courtney Love?"

"Yes."

"Tipper Gore?"

"Yes."

"Helen Hunt?"

"Yes."

"Paula Jones."

"No."

"Would you fuck David Bowie?"

"I would let David Bowie fuck me for one hundred thousand dollars."

"How about for ten thousand dollars?"

"No."

"How about twenty-five?"

"Maybe."

Stanley had a little joke he liked to play when we arrived in a new town. If he saw a nasty-looking hooker out the window, or a sad homeless lady, he would pretend to call out to Sean's mother.

"Mrs. Eden! Mrs. Eden!"

Sean countered by suggesting that Stanley's mother was obese. He called her the HMS *Demeski*.

When you're on the road every day, you sometimes come across a truck that is hauling a house. On the back of the house you see a sign: EXTRA WIDE LOAD.

"Look, Stanley," Sean would say, "it's your mother."

O ur rooms at the Travelodge in Atlanta smelled dank and musty. Sean and I rushed off to WRAS for a taped performance, then to a special dinner—two lucky radio contestants had won a free meal with Luna at a Jamaican restaurant near the Point, where we were playing that night. One of the winners was my old friend John Beers, aka Horribly Charred Infant.

I had played at the Point with Galaxie 500 and Peter Buck all those years ago. The club was still tiny, and it was packed, and we had a great show. Matthew Buzzell was in town, and took us to an after-hours club where a band played a great version of "Moon River."

When I got back to the hotel at 3:00 A.M., Justin had a girl in his bed, Alison, who worked at the radio station. They were fully clothed, and nothing was going on—she had merely missed the last bus home, and he said she could stay in our room. They lay there whispering as I tried to sleep.

Justin had broken the cardinal rule, which is that you don't bring a girl back to your room if you are sharing that room with another band member.

It was Stanley who taught us that rule. He knew, because he'd been on tour before, and he didn't like it if someone brought a girl to the room. Sean tried it once, but Stanley told Sean and his date to get lost.

S ome days we would discuss who was gay or who was short.

Eddie Vedder was short.

Prince was, too. It was top secret. His publicists were not allowed to disclose his height.

Bono. Bono was short. And he looked ridiculous—why did he never take those shades off?

And what about the Edge? What was he, ten years old, calling himself the Edge?

What if I decided I wanted to be called Cool Breeze?

"The Edge is cool," said Sean.

"The Edge is not cool," I said. I don't think U2 is cool. Remember that awful video from Red Rocks, where Bono prances around with a big flag, singing, "All I have is this red guitar, three chords, and the truth"? I have not forgotten.

But it takes all kinds to make a band. Sean's style of guitar playing was certainly indebted to the Edge, but it worked with Luna. It's good to have two distinct guitar styles, and it was the way that Sean and I played together that came to define the Luna sound.

S ay what you will about the records, but Luna was a much better live band than Galaxie 500. Galaxie 500 shows sometimes felt like they were on the verge of falling apart.

Luna shows felt much more solid. Justin and Stanley formed a completely tight rhythm section, a section that rocked and rolled. While I played the earthy, clumsier guitar solos, Sean added atmosphere and beautiful textures. He had impeccable tone—the sound coming off his Matchless amp was always perfect.

By the time we reached Boston on the *Penthouse* tour, it felt like we had turned a corner. We had built a live following—people were now excited to see Luna, instead of just coming out to see the guy who used to be in Galaxie 500. We could hear it in the roar of applause that greeted us as we took the stage.

T hat Friday found us in Providence, Rhode Island, at a birthday party for WBRU, the big commercial alternative station there. Birthday party my ass. That's how stations got bands to play for free. It would be understandable if WBRU was actually playing our record, but they were not. Still, we had to suck up to them anyway. Radio was king, the only surefire way to sell massive amounts of records. When a commercial radio station asked you to do something, you did it.

We returned to New York City for a triumphant show at Tramps, and then received the delivery of our first tour bus, the bus that would take us from New York all the way to San Francisco. We were looking forward to it.

Renée initially priced a bus out at $400 a day, but the head of business affairs at Elektra ordered her to find a cheaper one. There was a bus in Florida that could be ours for $225 a day. Apparently it used to belong to Willie Nelson.

We asked the driver about the Willie Nelson connection. Yep, it had been Willie's bus—about twenty-five years ago. This explained why it had a manual transmission, and smelled of diesel fumes and other things. We would later learn that it had a little trouble climbing hills. We called it the Little Engine That Could.

Still, we were happy to be riding in a bus—this was a step up. We left at midnight for Montreal. This is how you make a bus pay off—you travel at night and save money that would otherwise be spent on hotel rooms. And when you arrive in town, you get one hotel room for the driver, and another room for the band to share, to shower and shave and take care of other business.

I woke up early in the morning—we were no longer moving. I was excited, thinking that we must have arrived in Montreal. I pulled on my pants and climbed out of my bunk. It was dark. It was dark because we were not in Montreal. It was six in the morning and we were stuck inside a garage in North Plattsburgh, New York, an hour from the Canadian border. The bus had broken down.

We waited all day for replacement brakes to be brought in from Burlington. The brakes were coming on the ferry.

This sucked. Something always goes wrong on tour, but you don't like it to be on the first day.

At the Canadian border the customs guys (Mounties) found a box of undeclared T-shirts. See, you're supposed to declare your T-shirts, so the Canadian government can take a cut, but frankly it's such a pain in the ass that sometimes you just hide them. The Mounties confiscated all our shirts, and made us sit at the border for two hours.

Somehow we made it to the famous Foufounes Electriques in Montreal an hour before showtime. There was no time for a sound check, but at least there would be a show.

Sean and I went drinking after the show with two nice sisters, who showed us around Montreal. It's a lovely city. One of the sisters took me to her studio and showed me her artwork, and then it was time for me to go and get back into Willie Nelson's bus. The bus pulled out of town at 4:00 A.M., with me drunk in my bunk.

The next day, Justin argued with Bill about what time the bus should leave.

"The bus should leave right after the show. Why do we have to wait around till four A.M.?"

But Bill wouldn't budge. He was the tour manager, and he made the rules.

Also, there would be no smoking cigarettes on the bus, according to Bill. But if you happened to be a pipe smoker, like Bill, then you were in luck, because he had designated the lounge in the back of the bus the pipe-smoking lounge.

We all thought this rule was bullshit, but he refused to change it. I didn't mind so much—the pipe smoke reminded me of my grandfather. Short of firing Bill, it looked like we were stuck with that rule.

Sunday we drove on to Cleveland, where Sean and Justin and I went to see *Showgirls*. It was bad alright. The next day we ran lines from the film.

"Baby, you got low self-esteem."

"You're a great lay!"

We had a new opening band for this leg of the tour—my old friends Mercury Rev. I played on their best song ever, "Car Wash Hair (the Bee's Chasing Me)," shortly after Galaxie 500 broke up. Mercury Rev was much bigger than us in England, but in the States they weren't so well known. They had too much equipment for an opening band, which is poor etiquette. They also played too loud, as if they were involved in a competition with one another to see who could be the loudest. The result was that you couldn't really hear the songs.

Mercury Rev had a strange touring van. It looked like one of those little courtesy vans that takes you to the car rental at the airport. I've seen other bands make the mistake of buying a courtesy van. You can pick them up dirt cheap, but you pay later.

This one had an electrical problem. If they switched the engine off, they couldn't get it started again. So they had to keep it running at all times. All night long.

Before our show at the Grog Shop, Justin and I ran over to the Agora Ballroom to catch Fugazi. Ian MacKaye had put us on the guest list, which was nice of him. At the show, Ian was heckled by one of his fans after trying to stop him from slam dancing.

"You suck, Ian!"

"Right, I suck. That's good."

Fugazi was a great live band, and I loved their *13 Songs* LP. They did things their own way, insisting on all-ages venues, keeping admission to their shows at $5, and putting the records out on their own label, Dischord.

There are people who will extrapolate from their model and insist that this is how it *should* be done—bands should operate outside the mainstream music business, sleep on people's floors, and stay in filthy squats. I think people should mind their own business. That approach worked for Fugazi and Ani DiFranco, who had a built-in hard-core following—fans with a religious zeal. But that business model doesn't work for everyone.

I t was raining when I woke up at noon in Cincinnati. I had a 1:00 P.M. interview scheduled at a radio station—the exact same time they were scheduled to announce the O. J. Simpson verdict. Surely someone's ass deserved to be kicked for this blunder.

Sudsy Malone's was a bar, a rock club, and a laundry. You got a discount on the ticket to see the band if you brought your laundry as well. We were able to wash our clothes, and the club was packed. But it was a bit depressing to play at a laundry, no matter how punk rock it was. You could smell the fabric softener from the stage, and it didn't smell like rock and roll.

After the show, Sean and I were invited to a strange and pathetic party at some kids' apartment. There was no music, because the record player was broken. The kids were smoking pot and making grilled-cheese sandwiches with Cheez Whiz and Wonder Bread, and talking about moving to L.A., which was probably a good idea.

At about three in the morning I asked myself, What the fuck am I doing here, eating Cheez Whiz and Wonder Bread? I was talking to a girl who was making me a sandwich, that's what.

Being on tour with a rock-and-roll band is a whole alternate reality, a parallel life. You are no longer yourself—you are now a musician in a band. You have no bed and no home and there is no way to get ahold of you and you have every opportunity to do something stupid. I retreated to my bunk in Willie Nelson's bus.

Thursday found us in Detroit. It was still raining—it had been raining for days. But even though it was a rainy Thursday night, we managed to sell out Alvin's, and we were happy.

We pulled out a new cover song that night, "Walk on the Wild Side," which we were doing ironically. Since we always got compared to Lou Reed, we figured why not perform his biggest hit, but with a new twist—I played the saxophone solo on a kazoo. People loved our version of the song. They liked it a little too much. It was embarassing somehow.

Richard Kimball got lost leaving Detroit. He often got lost, usually when entering or leaving big cities. You can tell there's a problem when the bus keeps making U-turns while you're trying to get to sleep. Richard was not so good with directions. Or cleaning the bus. He was a nice man, though. He told us he carried a little gun in his boot, and he liked to flirt with waitresses when we stopped for breakfast.

"Hungry?"

"For love."

We sold out the Cabaret Metro (1,100 people) despite the fact that we were getting no radio play on the alternative-rock stations in Chicago. Visits to radio stations had been few and far between, which was a mixed blessing. It may have been bad for sales, but it meant less work on tour, and we were working plenty hard already.

In Minneapolis we actually did get played on the radio—on REV 105, one of the few stations that seemed to play by their own rules. We had a big crowd at the First Avenue club, and a treat awaited us after the show. Our label rep took us over to Paisley Park, where Prince was shooting a video for his new song "Gold." I never did see the final cut, but it is possible that Luna is in that Prince video (except for Stanley, who had gone straight to his hotel room).

There we were, with a few hundred other partyers. There was gold everywhere. Gold floating down from the ceilings, golden statues all around the soundstage, gold gold gold. After they got all the shots they needed for the video, Prince came out and played a few songs for us all. Yes, he was short, but so was his hot featured dancer (and soon-to-be wife), Mayte Garcia.

Prince is an astoundingly good guitarist. He never gets his due as such, perhaps because genius guitar gods (other than Hendrix) are supposed to be white. Or because he's so good at singing and dancing and writing songs that his guitar playing is overlooked.

Minneapolis to Boulder, Colorado, is a two-day drive. We made it as far as Kearney, Nebraska. We pulled into town around ten o'clock in the morning and found a strip of cheap motels.

"Let's stop here," we told Bill. "There's a Super 8 and an IHOP. It's perfect."

We were hungry. But Bill wanted to find a cappuccino, and he had the bus drive us all over town looking for one.

"You're not in San Francisco, Bill!" we said. "You won't find a cappuccino in Kearney, Nebraska!"

That was the truth. Starbucks had not yet conquered the nation. We drove around Kearney for half an hour, then finally rented a room a mile outside of town and went to Perkins for lunch. Perkins is like Denny's, with an added emphasis on pies and other desserts.

The waiter who served our lunch at Perkins recognized us.

"Are you guys Luna? No way!"

He ran home to get his *Bewitched* CD and had us all sign it over pancakes and bacon. Years later we would run into our waiter at Luna shows around the country. He always identified himself as the dude from Perkins.

Sean was not with us for this two-day drive. He had flown straight to Boulder to go skiing with a couple of girlfriends. He called them the hot sisters. It was quiet in the bus without Sean there.

By the time we caught up with him in Boulder, he had developed a medi-cal problem—a rash in his crotch. He saw a doctor, afraid that he might have caught something from one of the hot sisters, but the doctor said that he probably had some kind of mite—an invisible insect that was biting him. The doc gave him a special cream, and said he had to apply it all over his body, from his toes to his neck. Bummer.

Sean was excited that night in Boulder. He had a special friend hang-ing out in the green room before the show, an attractive girl who played the cello.

"Sean," said Stanley, in front of the girl, "did you tell her about the rash?"

"What?"

"The rash. You went to the doctor yesterday. Did you tell her about the rash?"

Sean yelled at Stanley as we walked onstage, "You're an asshole, Stanley!"

I t was on to the Town Pump in Vancouver next, another long haul.

"Vancouver is a naval town," said Stanley. "There'll be a lot of seamen on the dance floor."

Before the show, Bill took Justin and me to the Cecil—a strip club. Bill said it was the most famous strip club in all of Vancouver. This was my first time in a strip club—at age thirty-two. We sat in the VIP section, where a woman took all her clothes off and danced slowly on a big, round table. I found it odd to be that close to a woman's private parts when you don't even know her name. One guy stood up and put his face a bit too close to her crotch. She told him to stop doing that or she would have him removed.

"But it's so beautiful," he said. "If I had that, I'd never leave the house."

Guys are creepy. I looked around. Maybe we were creepy, too.

T he coffee was good in Seattle, but the music was not. Yet there was a general attitude you sensed there, as if they really thought they had saved rock and roll. Bands had moved here from all over the country to be part of the grunge revolution, to learn the Seattle sound.

We laughed and pointed when we saw a kid in a brown suede jacket or a flannel shirt.

"Look! Grunge!"

One good thing did come out of grunge—Jason Reynolds of Sub Pop signed Luna to a publishing deal. These publishing deals are important, as they allow us all to earn a monthly wage. You get a fat advance on your songs, and in return the publisher owns a quarter of your songs, and collects all your songwriting royalties from the record company. And if you sell a song to a film or a TV commercial, they collect these royalties on your behalf until their advance is recouped. Which may be never.

We weren't so popular in Seattle. Maybe that's why we made fun of them, to make ourselves feel better. Never mind, we were off to Portland now, playing at La Luna.

Last time at La Luna a hippie acidhead chick (who earned her living by braiding people's hair downtown) jumped up on a table in the green room and hiked up her skirt to show me her tattoo. She wasn't wearing any undies. She invited me to come back to her place with her girlfriend.

"We have a really big bed. There's room for three."

I said no, so they took one of our crew guys home instead.

We asked him about it the next day in the van.

"Did she want it?"

"Did you do it?"

"Did they sit on your face?"

He wouldn't tell.

"I have a private life." That's all he would say.

We were sharing the bill in Portland with Buffalo Tom, whom I knew from my days in Boston. Technically they were the headlining act, but we didn't quite see it that way. Buffalo Tom had actually made us an offer to be the opening band for their whole tour, but we weren't that stupid. We didn't open up for just anybody. We wouldn't open for them, and we wouldn't fuck them, either.

Buffalo Tom had a big, shiny new Prevost bus. They let us take a tour of the inside. They had little individual TV screens in each bunk. Nice. This was a *real* bus.

We had bus envy. They also had a bigger crew than we did—in addition to the soundman and guitar tech, they had someone along to do lights and another guy doing monitors. But apparently their tour wasn't going so well.

We took a small amount of pleasure in hearing this. It's always good to hear that some other band isn't doing well. It makes you feel better about yourself. Both bands went out together for Chinese food. Things seemed a little tense in Buffalo Tom, like they were sick of talking to one another.

I n San Francisco we bid farewell to the Little Engine That Could. Richard Kimball drove her back to Florida. We had two nights at the Phoenix Hotel, in the Tenderloin.

Life was good in San Francisco. Claudia came out to visit, and Justin's girlfriend, Lisa, and Renée were there, and so was Terry, with Richard the exterminator. The gang was all here.

That second night, we played the Great Amercian Musical Hall. We had scored some ecstasy from a friend at the Fillmore. I had a hard time concentrating on the show that night, distracted as I was by the hit of E waiting in my shirt pocket.

We gobbled the pills immediately after the show—Terry and Claudia and Renée and Stephen and I—and went back to Terry's swank suite at the Hotel Nikko.

Richard was just getting dressed when we arrived at Terry's room, and so was the Asian waitress he had befriended at dinner earlier that evening. Terry loved to tell us about the girls Richard was fucking. We couldn't see what Terry saw in Richard. I thought he was dumb as a chair, a cheap hustler from upstate New York, with bad teeth and a stupid smile. When he opened his mouth to speak, we all groaned. But Terry thought he was adorable. Perhaps he saw something of himself in Richard—the kid who ran away to the big city and got by the only way he knew how.

Terry had an idea at 4:00 A.M., just when the E was starting to wear off. How about a limo ride to the Golden Gate Bridge, his treat? He called for a big stretch limo, and we rode out to the bridge, listening to *Avalon* by Roxy Music and watching the city lights speed by. Soon the driver announced that we had reached the bridge, and we gingerly stepped out of the limo to take a look. Unfortunately a thick San Francisco fog had rolled in, and we couldn't see twenty feet in front of our noses. For all we knew, the bridge had fallen into the bay.

Two days later we were at the Roxy in Los Angeles, on a bill with Air Miami and Spectrum.

Terry threw another little party, this time at his suite at the Chateau Marmont. We were staying at the cheaper Roosevelt Hotel, down on Hollywood Boulevard. Terry's suite was stocked with wine, liquor, candy, and condoms wrapped in faux gold coin. Terry offered me another hit of ecstasy, but I declined. We had another show to do the following night, and I hadn't fully recovered from the late night in San Francisco.

I couldn't keep up with Terry. I had to perform, to remember words and patterns and keep up appearances. I didn't want to be canceling shows due to "nervous exhaustion" (which I always figure means excessive drug use).

We never brought drugs on the road. The drugs only showed up when someone from the record company showed up—they were the ones who could afford to party every night.

The *Penthouse* tour ended in a small room at Cal State Fullerton, in front of 150 college students. Terry was tripping again. He had dropped a hit of acid that afternoon, which he washed down with a bottle of wine and another hit of ecstasy. When you're on LSD, you can take vast quantities of other drugs and hardly even feel them. The acid trumps them all. It makes you superhuman.

Terry asked if he could introduce the band. He jumped onstage, grabbed the mike, and delivered an impassioned sermon on behalf of Luna, lamenting the sorry state of radio in America.

"Listen to me! This is very important! If you love Luna . . . if you love music . . . this music is in great danger. You need to pick up the phone and call KROQ, and tell them to play Luna!"

"Fuck KROQ!"

It's never a good idea to introduce a band, unless you like being abused. How many times have I seen some guy from a radio station get up there and talk in his stupid DJ voice and get heckled?

I'm not sure that Luna's music was in great danger. Perhaps I was just tired of hearing it, how I had to deliver a radio hit or my career in rock would be over.

Terry's career, however, *was* in danger. He was making a lot of money, and though his bands were critical successes, none of us were making gold records. His wife had left him, and he was spiraling out of control.

Sean drove Terry's rental car back to L.A. after the Fullerton gig, and Terry gave us each a hit of E. Terry and Renée and Sean and I were off to a party at Timothy Leary's house. It was just like the parties you see in the movies. Up in the hills. A swimming pool. A view of the twinkling lights in the distance. Hundreds of people. But they were out of beer, and there was no sign of Timothy Leary.

"Maybe he dropped out," said Sean.

It's a little-known chapter in the life of Timothy Leary that this counter-cultural icon became an informant for the CIA and named all the names he could—and he could name some. He turned on the Weathermen, who had helped him escape from jail after his arrest for possession of marijuana and transported him all the way to Algeria.

We stayed at Leary's house for twenty minutes before returning to Terry's room at the Chateau Marmont. Terry plunked down his Elektra Amex card and got an extra room for Sean and me. We got about two hours' sleep, and somehow made it to LAX the following morning.

On mornings like this, after a long night of partying at the end of a tour, we relied on Justin to check us in. We would stand in line, half alive, leaning on the luggage carts, and hand the tickets to Justin. He would take care of it. Justin could always be counted on.

I popped an Ambien and slept the whole flight home, with my head on the foldout tray. It was not a good sleep. It was one of those postecstasy sleeps, where your mind is stuck on a horrible loop. Your mind plays the same twenty seconds over and over and over again, and you say to yourself, "I can stop this," but you can't stop it. You keep going back to the beginning, and saying "I can stop this" over and over.

Goodbye Terry

If the war is over
And the monsters have won
If the war is over
I'm gonna have some fun
And as the sun peeks in
On an afternoon drunk
All the green green bottles
But it won't last forever

—*"Kalamazoo"*

D oes anyone else see it?"

Terry was shouting. He was excited.

"Does anyone else see it? It's made of red silk but it has these little golden tassels and it's floating over the table. It's hovering. It's rotating. Does anybody else see it?"

We couldn't see it. Only Terry could.

It was 4:30 A.M. and there were eight of us sitting around the glass coffee table in my living room, loaded with dirty ashtrays and vodka tonics, plastic wrap, cigarette box foil, bottle caps, beer bottles, and scratched jewel cases. We were flying. Flying at a lower altitude now than an hour ago, perhaps— we were on the slow ride down from the ecstasy peak, in the extra hours where you are still high but no longer feeling quite so euphoric or fuzzy, and your jaw is starting to ache from all the clenching you weren't even aware of and your eyes are drooping at the corners and your face looks like it's melting and you need to pee but you can't pee.

We had been listening to Lee and Nancy's *Fairytales and Fantasies.* They do the most amazing version of "You've Lost That Lovin' Feeling." Lee's voice comes in first, and it sounds like the voice of God, with luxurious strings swirling behind it. Then Nancy and Lee sing together, and with the gentle brushes on the snare and the tic-tac bass and Nashville-tuned acoustic and tinkly pianos—well, it's beautiful, especially on ecstasy.

I met Lee Hazlewood years later, and asked him how he got his great vocal sound. He said you put echo on the reverb (or was it reverb on the echo?), instead of on the voice itself, so that the voice retains its presence while still having a huge echo sound . . . like the voice of God.

"No one takes the time to do that anymore," he said.

We all listened to Gainsbourg's *Histoire de Melody Nelson* and Mazzy Star and New Order and the Beach Boys and the Velvet Underground and Petula Clark and Dusty Springfield and Spacemen 3 and side two of *Tattoo You* and "Moon Palace" and "23 Minutes in Brussels." It was a good night.

We smoked cigarettes. We lay on the floor. We ventured outside for a quick walk around the block and listened to the sound of the taxis' rubber tires cruising up Lafayette Street. Even traffic sounds are beautiful when you're on E.

Terry's favorite activity on these nights was taking Polaroid photographs with his SX-70 or with the Land Camera. I still have a box of photos from those nights. The best spot for the photographer's subject was on top of the radiator. Not only did it keep your ass warm, but there was just enough light in that spot for the shot. Except that the photographer's hands invariably shook from the ecstasy, so half the photos came out blurry. I have a dozen shots of Terry on the radiator. In some he sports sunglasses, in others it's a cowboy hat.

Terry's most recent signings to Elektra had been two fiascos—Research and Vaganza. Research was the brainchild of Kenn Richards, one of Terry's best friends through that last crazy year. Kenn never seemed to have any money, but he always had the latest gadget, like the Apple Newton. He didn't have a performing band, either—Research was more of a laptop-and-turntable-type thing. All he had was a handful of demos, but Terry convinced Sylvia Rhone to sign him.

Soon after their record was finished, Research played a gig at Brownie's on

Avenue A. Elektra sent a few of their honchos down to check it out. It being their first-ever show, the performance was a little shaky. A band should play a few anonymous shows before presenting themselves to the record company, because it always takes a few shows to figure out how to play the songs.

The following week Terry got the news—Elektra was not going to release the album. Word had filtered up that Research was not a good live act. They were dropped before anyone ever heard their record.

Terry was furious. He started raging against his ignorant employers. He was especially angry with Sylvia Rhone, the first African American woman to chair a major label. They used to argue about Kenn Richards. Rhone objected to Terry's calling him black.

"He's an African American, Terry."

"He's a black man. He prefers to be called black."

Vaganza, Terry's other new signing, was going to be huge—Terry was sure of it. But they, too, were a "band" that didn't really exist—they had never played a live show. They had the concept and the songs, but they were not a band. And their record cost a small fortune to make.

Renée kept telling Terry that he really should go in to work—she was hearing rumors.

"Fuck that shit!" he said.

Terry hated it at work. He missed his friend and ally Howard Thompson, who had been pushed out of the company in 1993. When Bob Krasnow departed the next year, following a corporate realignment at Time Warner, he was replaced by Sylvia Rhone, and Elektra Records was merged with EastWest and Sire into the Elektra Entertainment Group. Terry thought Elektra was ruined. Krasnow's philosophy had been "small but beautiful"—he deliberately kept a small roster at Elektra, thinking of it as a boutique major label. Krasnow listened to the A&R people, said Terry. Under Rhone, who came from a radio background, power shifted to the radio department. If they weren't going to listen to his opinion or support his bands, Terry said, why should he show up at the office? He told them he was out in New Jersey each day, working on the Vaganza album.

One day Terry was called in to a meeting and was warned that he needed to show up on time for work in the mornings. But Terry came prepared. He brought along all his time sheets obligingly signed by one of his superiors, which he said proved that he had been working regular hours.

One last incident precipitated Terry's firing. Terry had posted some highly insulting comments about Sylvia Rhone on the Velvet Rope, a music industry chat page. Terry felt secure behind the anonymity of the Internet, but he left enough clues that the honchos at Elektra figured out who was behind the posting.

They printed out the offending comments and left them on Terry's desk before summoning him to a final meeting. They offered to put Terry in rehab, knowing full well that he had developed a drug problem. Perhaps this was a legal maneuver—offering rehab before firing someone. Terry declined, and was ordered to clear out of his office immediately.

Renée heard stories about why they had fired Terry. They didn't mind his sitting in his office getting stoned. They didn't really mind his being late to work and going home early and charging liquor and limo rides to the company credit card. But they said that Terry was a liar, and this they found intolerable.

The lying might have done it. But record companies are full of pathological liars, drug addicts, and assholes. Terry's chief failing was that he wasn't generating money for the label. If he had signed just one platinum act, all would have been forgiven. Instead he gave them Luna, Stereolab, and the Afghan Whigs. Elektra didn't lose money on these bands, but they didn't get rich, either.

Terry had lost his wife, which he pretended not to care about. Now he had lost his job.

He did have a lovely new girlfriend, Ann, but said he wasn't in love with her. And he still had his own independent label, Number 6 Records.

He developed a heroin problem. He broke up with Ann, who then ran off with Terry's new best friend (and recent signing to Number 6), Bill Whitten.

A month later, Terry's apartment building on East Seventeenth Street fell down. The back wall collapsed, taking Terry's record collection and his expensive telescope with it. His cats ran away, and he was devastated.

Six months later he was working at a gas station in New Jersey, changing oil and brake liners by day, snorting heroin by night.

From New Jersey he moved to Wichita, Kansas, where he had family, then on to Florida, where his sister lived. He worked in a scuba shop, where he once rented a boat to Gene Hackman. He pumped gas at the airport in Fort Lauderdale, before finding work on a tramp steamer, hauling stuff from the Bahamas to Florida.

I miss Terry. I wish I could go over to his apartment on Seventeenth Street and climb out on his fire escape and take Polaroid photos, posing as a gargoyle. I wish I could listen to his seven-inch singles and hear about the old days at 99 Records, or how many men it took to build the Holland Tunnel and how many of them died building it. What was it that I liked about Terry? He was generous and outgoing and fun to be around. Maybe I need to have someone like Terry in my life. He was like the older brother that I had always had—only I couldn't have a drink with my older brother, because he had a drug problem.

Terry and Anthony both smoked menthol cigarettes. They were both recovering Deadheads, potheads, cokeheads, smackheads, music fans, and charmers.

I was not a rock star. Terry was the rock star. Waking and baking, doing lines of coke at work. Fucking girls and boys. Terry didn't think of himself as gay or straight—he just liked sex. Showing up late, telling lies, getting fucked up all the time, living a crazy life that couldn't go on anymore. Taking drugs and going onstage. Going to the liquor store and charging it all to the label. Cleaning out the hotel minibar. Riding around in limousines. He lived the life.

For years I heard nothing from Terry. I had been the last person we all knew who was still in touch with him. And then nothing. I started to think that he might be dead.

Terry wrote to me in 2006 after three years of being out of touch. The boat that he lived on had been sold to pay a docking fee that was long overdue, and he found himself living for a couple of weeks in a shelter up in central Florida. I sent him some cash and a copy of Luna's *Best Of* and *Lunafied* (a collection of all the cover versions we recorded). He sent me this e-mail:

Hey Dean,

I was just listening to the Lunafied CD (and thanks for the player too). The Wire track "Outdoor Miner" came on and I had to jump on the shelter bike and peddle on down to this library to dash off a quick note of thanks to you, um, er, thanks for knowing you.

I'm holding back the tears as i write this trying to stop the flood of evaporating (and indeed, superfreaky) memories that just can't wait. I think that the Wire track really brought back alot of my great life experiences. You see, I was living in a loft at 51 Bond St. (now Joey Ramone Alley) from 1976 until 1983. They are one of my favorite bands of all time and their three albums reflected my musical maturation exactly. From the unabashed intellectual punk of Pink Flag to the diabolical skewing of that same genre of Chairs Missing and culminating in the inscrutable 154. I owned all of their recorded output by the time they played across the street at CBGB's in the winter of 1980. Joy Division, A Certain Ratio, Liquid Liquid, Bush Tetras, Lydia Lunch, Comsat Angels, Glenn Branca and the burgeoning Sonic Youth were all of my life.

So I'm lying on my bunk at the shelter in the central part of a red state swampland listening to this golden nugget wondering how the fuck my life got into this sordid mess? I sit here holding nothing but useless memories of a life nobody around me could contemplate. I AM AN ALIEN. I have lost everything and have nowhere to go. What major malfunction did I induce to cause the karma wheel to crush me so thoroughly into the earth's topsoil? Why hasn't it just finished the job and tilled me six feet under? I would much prefer that to this. I really tortured myself the other day by renting Woody Allen's Manhattan.

Even our friendship seems at times like a fantasy I made up as some deranged fan. As I watched the Sean Eden documentary and Justin mentioned my name in his "telegram" and I saw your lips form the word, I almost had a panic attack. I have had some inexplicable Tony Soprano style blackouts from jail. Yes, Chinatown was really written with me in mind, um, I think that was me at least. JP Sartre couldn't have come up with this shit my friend, no way in hell. He had it easy. He had plagues and world wars as an impetus. I just grew up loving music. When

I was 9 years old my parents went on a cruise and left us at home. I took their record collection and filed it the only way that made sense to me at the time; by record label and then by catalogue number. They were most perplexed when they had a coming home from the tropics party and their Frank Sinatra records were in three different places!

Well, the library is timing me out of my half hour time limit. Gotta Go. I need confirmation that mine is, has been and will be a worthwhile life.

Your friend—Terry

Don't You Like
Making Records?

When five people live in close proximity, in a residential recording studio or on a tour bus, they start making rules. I suggested a new rule during the making of *Pup Tent,* Luna's difficult fourth album—no Ping-Pong matches after 4:00 A.M.

The table, you see, was right outside my bedroom door, and the games were noisy, with the bouncing balls and the overhand slams and the curses and cries of disappointment.

We played Ping-Pong to help us unwind from a long, tense evening in the studio. But Ping-Pong is not a sedative. It gets you sweaty and keyed up. The games were heated. Our frustrations from a bad day in the studio were played out on the table.

We created an official Ping-Pong ladder. Small strips of paper bearing our names were affixed to the wood-paneled wall with pieces of masking tape. Each of us had an alias. I was the Cowboy, because I had showed up in Cannon Falls wearing a cowboy hat. Justin was the Bald Eagle. Our new drummer, Lee (more on this later), was the Stealth Bomber. Sean called himself Canadian Bacon. And our Irish producer, Pat McCarthy, was the Dublin Dynamo. If you listen carefully to the end of "Pup Tent," you can hear me mumbling about the Cowboy and the Dynamo and the Bald Eagle. I was short on lyrics.

The Dublin Dynamo was always at the top of the ladder. Pat was better than the rest of us, probably from years of working in expensive residential recording studios. I thought I had him beat once, and I smiled a small, nervous smile. I tried not to let Pat see my excitement. But the Dublin Dynamo reeled off eight straight points to take the game, and I went to bed frustrated. I lay there thinking about how many lyrics I still had to write and how many guitar tracks we had yet to record.

. . .

After *Penthouse*, we should have all been happy, right? It was our best album. We got good reviews in England and in the States. The album went to number one on the college radio charts—which apparently has little impact on actual record sales.

From Elektra's point of view, the album had been a failure. Sales were down slightly from *Bewitched*. We did not get played on alternative radio, alongside Tool and Nine Inch Nails and the Smashing Pumpkins. We did not get played on adult alternative, alongside Natalie Merchant and Paula Cole and Counting Crows. So what if we got great reviews? Reviews don't shift units.

I was friendly with Jim McGuinn, the program director of WDRE, the big commercial alternative station in Philadelphia. Jim came to all our shows— he said that Luna was his favorite band. Since he was the program director, you might think that would have translated into radio play for Luna. But he explained to me why he couldn't put Luna into the rotation. He was a music fan, but he also had an M.B.A., which was why they had brought him in to run the station. And he said he would lose his job if he started just playing the music he liked. We have all heard stories of a DJ in Cincinnati liking a song, putting it into heavy rotation, and then the rest of the country follows suit and you have a hit on your hands—all because one DJ took a chance. It doesn't work that way anymore. Radio is big business—the business of delivering young minds to advertisers. The listener is the true commodity. The radio stations tried to be scientific about it. The playlists were not based on hunches. Jim's job was to find the twenty songs that their listeners liked the most, and then play those songs constantly. We all know about payola, the system by which major labels encourage the radio stations to play their records. Such encouragement comes in many forms. It is expensive, but they like it because it gives them guaranteed access.

But the radio stations were starting to do their own research in addition to taking bribes from the labels. They paid close attention to telephone calls from listeners. They set up special focus groups, hiring researchers to test the listeners' responses to songs that were in their playlist. The researcher played a seven-second snippet of your song to radio listeners, and their responses helped the program director decide whether or not to put the song into rotation. You can make a case that this system is even worse than payola.

"Unlike Britain," writes Simon Reynolds, "with its national, state-run pop station Radio One, American radio was a Balkanized welter of city-based and regional stations, further fragmented by formats that were precisely geared to please audience demographics defined by age, taste and race. . . . American radio resembles a gigantic machine for ensuring that people almost never encounter any music they're not already predisposed to like. The motor fear of radio programmers is the fickleness of listeners, whom it's believed will instantly flip to another channel if they hear something that offends them."

Radio stations are in a constant state of flux. They try this format and that. Their owners couldn't care less what kind of music they play. They'll try alternative rock, but if they don't sell enough advertising, they'll switch to country in a second. WDRE in Philadelphia, for example, was bought by Radio One, who converted it to a hip-hop station in 1997. Many of the DJs went over to rival station Y100, which was then also bought by Radio One and converted to hip-hop.

We needed a producer for our fourth record. We met Steve Lillywhite for drinks at the Columbia Hotel in London. He was a charming guy.

"You know that single the record company is always asking you for—the perfect pop song? You can't write it. You can't do it. That's my job—that's why you hire a producer."

That sounded good. We would just show up, like we always did, and he would craft the hit for us. But Lillywhite went off to make a record with Morrissey, and we put on our thinking caps.

We came back to Pat McCarthy. He had made *Penthouse* sound great. Sure, the mixing took two weeks longer than we had anticipated, but that's not a big deal. Sean and Justin and Renée and I all agreed—Pat was the best option. We told Stanley about it on the way to our next gig. Stanley didn't take part in band meetings, partly because he lived out in Haledon, New Jersey, and partly because he didn't consider himself a member of the band.

"I won't work with Pat McCarthy," said Stanley. "He's too crazy."

Stanley had always had one foot in the band, and one foot out. We had offered to make him an official band member, part of the legal partnership, but he preferred being a hired hand, receiving a guaranteed salary, doing things on his terms.

And Stanley had plenty of power anyway. He had the power to say no. There were times I had to plead with him to go on tour. We were offered three weeks of support for Lou Reed on his Hooky Wooky tour. But Stanley had already opened for Lou Reed, when he was in the Feelies. He didn't want to do it again.

"I'll do it for the drum kit," he said, referring to the Ludwig drums we had just bought, the ones that Justin said belonged to all of us.

In order to convince Stanley to do the Lou Reed tour, we gave him the drum kit, on top of his regular weekly salary. Now Stanley had put his foot down again by declining to work with Pat on the next record. We decided to hire someone else to kick the kick drum.

Stanley's penultimate show was on July 21, 1996, at the Central Park SummerStage. For the first time in his four years with Luna, Stanley's wife came to a show, with his two little kids in tow. I felt awful knowing that we were about to let him go. We had one last gig with Stanley the following night, at the Mercury Lounge on Houston Street. Then Justin and I made the unpleasant conference call.

Stanley was a wonderful drummer. He was a stylist—that is, he had his own very recognizable style of playing—and a man with impeccable taste in music. I was very fond of him, but he had too much control over my life. That's the curse and the beauty of being in a band—you are bound together. You all have to want to do it. Stanley was at a different point in his life. He had a family and a house in the suburbs. You can't fully commit to a band in that situation, because you're a grown man with responsibilities.

It was time for a new drummer, a drummer who wanted to be in Luna and fly to Japan and Paris, someone who wanted to tour the world in a rock-and-roll band instead of stay home in Haledon.

I saw Stanley at Maxwell's six years later—Yung Wu, a Feelies offshoot, had reunited for one night, and I didn't want to miss that. I nervously approached Stanley to say hello.

He told me he never liked being in Luna anyway, that he had only done it for the money. I don't really like to believe that, but perhaps it was true. Maybe he only made those records for the money—but I enjoyed his playing anyway.

One particular Luna fan—Nate, aka the "City Kitty" guy because he always called out for "City Kitty," reported his own (possibly drunk) encounter with Stanley that night at Maxwell's. Nate said he approached Stanley to tell him what a big fan he was, and how he missed Stanley's drumming in Luna, but Stanley's response was "Fuck that . . . Fuck that and fuck you."

Sean recommended his friend Lee Wall to take over on the drummer's throne. Like Sean, Lee had attended the North Carolina School of the Arts. Sean had studied acting, while Lee had actually studied music. Lee was an excellent drummer. He was also agreeable and soft-spoken and dressed nicely—and he liked the idea of being in a band. He wanted to fly to Spain and drive to Baltimore, and he wanted to make records.

Pat McCarthy was excited about making a whole album with us.

"We'll produce it together," he said. He laid out his plan. We would start in New York City with a week at Sear Sound. You could call it preproduction, but the tape would be rolling at all times. Maybe we would get some basic tracks (bass and drums) completed there, if we were lucky. Then we would break for Thanksgiving, and reconvene in December at Pachyderm Studio in Cannon Falls, Minnesota, for three weeks of serious recording. Next we would fly to Los Angeles to finish overdubs and mix the album, either at Ocean Way or at Sunset Recording. He hadn't decided which one, but they were both fabulous studios, rich in history.

Sear Sound was located on West Forty-eighth Street. We started out in Studio A, where John and Yoko once recorded. One little room was kept just as John and Yoko had liked it—it had been their lounge. Pat decided to set the drums up there, instead of in the big live room.

The first order of business was shopping for toys. Pat gave us a wad of cash and sent us to Toys "R" Us. We arrived at the studio with a toy drum kit, a toy sampling keyboard, a toy megaphone that made a sound like a car whizzing by, and an official *Toy Story* toy-robot cassette player, with a little microphone attached.

The toy robot became my alter ego for the album's title song, "Pup Tent." The rest of the band tracked this one as I lay on the sofa, mumbling vague nothings through the toy robot, which made me sound like a voyeur making an obscene phone call.

We all liked the way my vocal sounded through the robot—small and distorted. Except for Sean, who lobbied for me to sing it through an expensive, nice-sounding microphone. We took a vote, and it went four to one (Pat voted, too) in favor of the robot. But that didn't stop Sean from bringing this point up again. And again. Until Justin yelled at him.

"We already voted on that! Why are we still talking about it?"

That's part of being a band in the recording studio—endless discussions and arguments about small things that no one else would ever notice, yet seem so very important at the time.

It was a productive week at Sear Sound. We recorded drum tracks for nine songs, and left in good spirits. We went our separate ways for Thanksgiving. I was off to Guadalajara for a vacation with my wife and the in-laws.

From Guadalajara I flew directly to Minneapolis. I was tanned and rested, and wore the aforementioned cowboy hat, which I had picked up at a flea market. Brent Sigmeth, our engineer on the Pachyderm sessions, met me at the airport and drove me to the studio, thirty-five miles south of Minneapolis, in Cannon Falls. Population 3,700. The ground was covered in snow.

The studio brochure described a "Frank Lloyd Wright–inspired 6,000 square foot house overlooking a spring-fed trout stream winding through old growth woods teeming with wildlife. . . . The recording studio is naturally lit by large picture windows that frame the landscape. . . . It is an entirely unique and peaceful work environment that is extraordinarily conducive to creativity." That must be why Nirvana came to Pachyderm to record *In Utero*.

That's exactly what Pat was thinking, how good it would be for us to get away from New York City and isolate ourselves from the distractions of our home lives. In Cannon Falls there was nothing to do but concentrate on making a record.

"Making a record!" Pat would exclaim excitedly when a song started to sound good. He rubbed his hands together as he said it. "We're making a record!"

The house and studio were fantastic. We each had our own bedroom. Pat had the deluxe producer's room, which had a queen-size bed and its own bathroom. He had brought a supply of ginseng and his trusty tan suede Birkenstocks (which he always wore with socks—he was years ahead on this one). My bedroom was downstairs by the Ping-Pong table and the indoor swimming pool. The studio manager offered to hire a cook to prepare our lunch and dinner for $100 a day, but we decided to save the money and that we would each take turns cooking dinner for the group. We came to regret that decision.

I didn't much like the hours we kept at Pachyderm. I was the first to wake every morning, at eleven, which didn't seem early to me. I would jump out of bed, ready to make a record, only to find that everyone else was still asleep. I would bang around in the kitchen, making a pot of coffee in the hopes that the aroma would wake the rest of the band. Lee and Justin and Sean would slowly drift out of their rooms. But Pat had come to Minnesota from Los Angeles, and never really left the Pacific time zone. He rose around one o'clock, showered, and cooked himself a good breakfast. He was as meticulous a cook as he was a producer.

Around three o'clock each day we took the short walk from the house over to the annex that contained the studio itself. The main recording room had glass walls, affording a beautiful view of snow-covered trees and the stream that Pachyderm overlooked, but by three there wasn't much daylight left. So instead of peering out at nature, we soon saw our own reflections in the glass, and were acutely aware of how dark and wintry it was.

From three to six we procrastinated. We tinkered. We played with the toy drum kit and the toy keyboard. We put paper clips on the piano strings for "Bobby Peru"—they call that a treated piano. Lee attached two kick drums together to make one extralong kick drum, which we called the extralong kick drum. We were making a record, but some days we spent an equal amount of time avoiding recording. For "Pup Tent," Pat and Justin spent hours turning the main guitar riff into a faux sample, complete with vinyl-scratch noise, so that it sounded like the riff had been stolen from an old record. Nice.

We usually broke for dinner around six or seven, having accomplished very little.

Sean said he made a delicious macaroni and cheese. If you consider Kraft mac and cheese from the box to be delicious, then he was right. I prefer it baked, maybe with some cottage cheese and milk to bind it together, and bread crumbs on top.

After one week, Pat rearranged the main recording room, dragging the sofa and chairs and coffee table in there and declaring it the Scrabble corner. We would now follow dinner with a relaxing hour of Scrabble and Cuban cigars. Like Ping-Pong, Scrabble isn't a particularly relaxing game. It can get testy. I was certainly testy. I didn't come all the way to Minnesota to play Scrabble.

The longer a band has been together, the longer they will take to make a record. The second record takes longer than the first. The difficult third album takes even longer. On the fourth album you start experimenting, questioning, scrutinizing. On it goes, till you get to the album where you go "back to basics" and make the record the way you used to, recording everything live with minimal overdubs (which is what Luna did for *Rendezvous,* our seventh and final album). *Pup Tent* was our experimental album, which meant toys and Scrabble and avoidance.

Things really got going between the hours of 10:00 P.M. and 3:00 A.M., when we actually recorded some bass and drums and guitars. We had recorded most of the drum tracks back at Sear Sound, but we still had four new songs to track.

On the previous Luna albums, we generally kept the live bass track that Justin had recorded with the drums—perhaps doing a couple of punch-ins if he had made a mistake. But Pat didn't do it that way. He and Justin would sit down to record the bass track together, section by section, measure by measure. Pat would query Justin—"What other note might you play there?" Three hours later we would have a bass track to go with the drum track, a solid foundation on which to build the song.

Each successive track was done the same way, and each track took at least three hours, whether it was piano or guitar or finger snaps. Everything had to be perfect. If you had a little section of eight bars, they all had to be just so. You would play the eight bars and Pat would look at you.

"Let's go back and get two, seven, and eight."

So you would fix two, seven, and eight.

"And five and six."

You would do that, too.

"You're playing it so much better now. Why don't we get one to four again?"

Eventually you would have done them all again. Every single instrument on the record was agonized over in this way, every guitar lick or tambourine hit or handclap meticulously studied for any signs of deviation or "flamminess."

"That's flammy," Pat would say.

"Flam" is a term that properly applies to the snare drum: a deliberate stroke on the drum, "a short grace note preceding a main note" (according to the *Harvard Concise Dictionary of Music.* But Pat used it in a different sense. It meant that your playing was sloppy and you had to do it again till there was no flam.

Some days we would object.

"Listen to *Unknown Pleasures,*" we would say. "Joy Division's master-piece. It's very flammy. Or *Exile on Main Street*—full of flams, yet still a great album."

Pat wasn't having it.

Around three in the morning we'd trudge back over to the house and play a few Ping-Pong matches before bed. Next thing I knew it was 4:00 A.M. I needed to be asleep. I lay in bed trying to sleep. At five, I would break down and take an Ambien.

Ambien stays in your body for six hours, and then you wake up. You don't wake up drowsy like you do with some other sleeping pills. But you don't wake up happy like in the TV advertisements, where the guy wakes with a smile and his dog jumps on the bed and everything is great. In my case, I would wake up cranky. The first word out of my mouth would be "Fuck!" I would sit bolt upright and immediately think angry and impatient thoughts, spending the next couple of hours waiting for Pat to wake up and stewing in my anger. The day would begin all over again, a cycle of procrastination, Scrabble, bad food, arguments, painstaking recording, and Ping-Pong.

After a couple of weeks of this, I decided that I was suffering from polar hysteria, SAD (seasonal affective disorder), Ambien snarkiness, and writer's block. We weren't getting anywhere. We would spend whole days working on something and then decide that we had nothing.

Then came the incident. We hadn't yet decided where we were going to mix the record. Every day Pat would bring it up. He had those two Los Ange-les studios in mind.

"Shall we go to Sunset? Or Ocean Way?"

We could do a week at Sunset and then a week at Ocean Way. We could do the whole thing at Sunset. We could do it all at Ocean Way. Which studio had a Ping-Pong table? Every day we pondered the options. One afternoon, cranky from the Ambien, I snapped at Pat.

"Make up your fucking mind! Make a decision!"

Pat and I didn't speak for forty-eight hours after this incident, and the tension in the studio was extrathick. Finally Pat suggested that he and I go for a walk. We put on our parkas and hats—a beanie for me, an Irish tweed cap for him—and walked down the road, looking out at a snowy field.

How could we finish the record if we weren't speaking to each other? We patched things up. We agreed that Pat would take care of booking the studio, and I didn't need to worry about it. It was a decision best left to the producer. We were friends again.

"Making a record!"

The toy Casio keyboard had some interesting little preset patterns in it. There was one little sample that we called the hemiola. A hemiola is two bars in triple time that you play as if they are three bars in double time. When Pat heard that little pattern, he thought it would be cool if we used it as a click track, to track "Beggar's Bliss." We recorded that song together, all of us playing along to a pattern that was neither in the right time signature nor the right key. It was a good exercise, though, to see if we could concentrate on the song while a strange loop played in our headphones. We did it.

It was "Tracy, I Love You" that gave us the most trouble. This composition was left over from the *Penthouse* sessions. I had written the lyrics, but the chords and guitar riffs were Sean's. The whole band spent a couple days rewriting the chord progression in the bridge, trying many different permutations. Then we recorded fifteen takes till we had a drum track worth keeping. But neither Sean nor I could record a rhythm guitar track that Pat was happy with. Sean kept hearing a tuning problem, so he removed one string from my Gibson ES-335. It didn't help. We spent all day trying to get that rhythm guitar right, but it wasn't sounding so great—not on its own, anyway. I suggested that maybe we should just move on and come back to it later. I said the rhythm guitar track wasn't the most important element anyway, as we were going to smother the song in synthesizers and lead guitar. But Pat didn't buy it.

"I'm very worried about the guitars on this record," he said.

"I'm going to put that in the Pat McCarthy quote library," said Sean.

Some days, we had a hard time figuring out what this Irishman wanted from us. Pat spoke in riddles. He asked rhetorical questions. His own answers were evasive. He answered questions with questions. He didn't tell us what to play, he told us what *not* to play. He was a taskmaster, but he also wanted to collaborate. He invented new descriptions for our music.

"It's urban prairie music, that's what it is!"

"It's an electric Mardi Gras."

If Pat was in a cranky mood, then we knew we were in for a long day. If I was cranky, he would jokingly accuse me of being "the bad-vibe merchant."

"Are you the bad-vibe merchant? Are you waving the flag of doubt?"

After three weeks in Cannon Falls, we broke for Christmas and headed back to New York. We were happy to be escaping the lovely residential studio that felt more like a stylish and comfortable prison.

Things had gone backward after that first week at Sear Sound. We had more to do now than before. Flying to L.A. to finish the record was no longer an option. It made more sense for Pat to fly to New York. We reconvened in January at Baby Monster Studios on West Fourteenth Street for two weeks of overdubbing. Not a fancy place, but at least we could order decent food. My favorite spot was the Chinese Cuban restaurant, La Nueva Rampa, where they made a mean beef stew and the best café con leche on Fourteenth Street.

The first decision made at Baby Monster was to retrack "Tracy, I Love You" yet again, this time with a different chord progression in the bridge. We worked on the new chord progression all day long, recording take after take till finally we had it.

Since we still had so much work to do, Pat suggested that we set up a workstation in the back of the studio, so that the whole band could be working on various aspects of the record simultaneously.

"The notes won't magically float onto the tape," said Pat.

I wondered about that. Sometimes I thought that the notes could magically float onto the tape—if we only let them.

Justin set up the workstation in a vocal booth and started on "Fuzzy Wuzzy." The song had started as a shuffle along the lines of "Spirit in the Sky." Our initial demo was an easygoing extended guitar jam, but Pat said that it was boring, and he was probably right. He told Justin to sequence a synthesizer track, which we would then play on top of. This would give the song a machinelike quality. Justin worked at the workstation for two days before presenting us with the synthesizer tracks.

"That sounds cheesy," said Sean.

But we were just getting started. We added the drums and the guitars, and then Justin wrote a cool string arrangement, note by note, with Pat prodding him each step of the way.

"What other note could you play? Higher. Lower. That one . . ."

The strings sounded Scottish. We danced around the control room, wearing invisible kilts. The song sounded great.

"Making a record!" said Pat.

"Fuzzy Wuzzy" refers to a lady's private parts. I came across the phrase in Don DeLillo's novel *Ratner's Star*. The young math wiz in the book asks to see a woman's fuzzy wuzzy.

Loose joints, loose joints
Symphonic Vaseline
Tight jeans, tight jeans
Say exactly what you mean
Daddy run through the forest
See the goblins all around
Daddy run through the forest
Daddy doesn't make a sound

I stayed up late working on these lyrics, sitting on the sofa drinking aquavit and smoking cigarettes—to get in the mood. I stole a couple of lines from a women's fashion magazine, always a good source for florid and silly descriptions. The magazine said that sexy long sweater dresses were a must-have for the season.

Sexy long sweater dresses
Chocolate knee-high leather boots
Maybe tonight will be the night
I can see your fuzzy wuzzy

A fan in Ohio later wrote me a letter. He and his girlfriend had stayed up all night on acid, listening to "Fuzzy Wuzzy" over and over. They decided that the song was about a female orgasm, and that it was structured like a female orgasm, and they were sure that this was all intentional, the way it builds to a crescendo and then slowly falls apart. Was that our intention, to simulate orgasm?

Things were coming along, but we still had a lot of guitars and vocals and other bits to get down. We ran out of time at Baby Monster, and moved on to Big House on Forty-second Street. After ten days at Big House we moved to the Magic Shop on Crosby Street, and then on to RPM Studios on Twelfth Street.

A few months ago, we said that we would never go back to RPM, where we had recorded the bulk of our first three albums. It was a great studio, but the owner drove us crazy, and so did the elevator—the slowest elevator in New York City. But there we were, and it felt good to be back. We ordered sushi from Japonica and banana cream pie from Coffee Shop on Union Square.

The days at RPM turned into weeks. We worked six days a week because we had so much to do that Pat said we couldn't possibly take the weekend off.

One morning I came into the studio and Sean and Pat told me that we needed to retrack "Beggar's Bliss," the other Eden composition on the album. I yelled at Sean about this, and then apologized for yelling at him. But I was still pissed off about it. Why were both of Sean's songs being rerecorded?

I don't like retracking songs. My first studio experiences, with Galaxie 500, were superquick. Kramer generally insisted that the first take was just right. He didn't have all day to record one vocal.

Pat McCarthy was a teenager when he started assisting on U2 records—he had worked on *The Joshua Tree*. U2 routinely spent a year in the studio. I don't know if they played Scrabble or Ping-Pong while they were there, but they were millionaires—they could afford to let the days tick by, experimenting to their hearts' content. Trying this, trying that—essentially writing the record in the studio with the aid of Daniel Lanois and Brian Eno and Steve Lillywhite. I have a theory: If you put four monkeys in the studio for a year with Lanois and Eno and Lillywhite, they would make a pretty good record, too.

Some days, Pat wouldn't let us play the guitar. He didn't love long guitar jams, which had always been a part of the Luna sound. He was more interested in "soundscaping." He pushed us to create deep layers of sonic texture. This was called making the bed. Before we could record our gui-tars, we needed to "make the bed," the sonic bed on which the song would rest. Before we could play the guitar, he wanted us to have fun with a mel-lotron or an Optigan.

In the past we would record the basic tracks and vocals, and then add whatever ear candy was needed. Candy—or gravy—depending on your point of view. It's good to have candy, but you don't want too much gravy on the meat.

Pat liked to *start* with the gravy.

We turned our attention once again to "Tracy, I Love You." Justin played some great keyboard parts on a Roland Jupiter synthesizer. Sean said they sounded cheesy, just like the keyboard parts on "Fuzzy Wuzzy." We added more bits and bobs, like a strange "bubble" sound from the toy keyboard. I added a vaguely Duane Eddy guitar part that we called the cowboy guitar. I sang "ooh oohs" that I borrowed from "Final Solution" by Pere Ubu.

The time had now come for Sean to play the lead guitar. "Tracy, I Love You" was very important to Sean, and he wanted his guitar tracks to be outstanding.

Pat and Sean spent five days recording the lead guitar tracks on "Tracy, I Love You." Pat sat in the control room, Sean out in the live room, and they argued about the guitar solo.

"That sounds kind of cool," I would say.

"No," said Pat, "it's rubbish."

He offered to write the guitar solo for Sean. "I'll write a hundred guitar solos for you," he said.

He came up with two new nicknames for Sean during this five-day period: Empty-Faced Eden, because he didn't know what he wanted to do, and Meanderthal, because he never played the same thing twice in a row.

At the end of each day of abuse, around three o'clock in the morning, Pat and Sean would go out for a nightcap.

After five days, at a cost of about $10,000, we had a lead guitar track for that song. Sean never forgot this week in the studio. He saw it as five days of psychological abuse.

It was time to record the vocals, and once again, "Tracy, I Love You" proved difficult. I sang it fifty times at three different studios. Pat liked to record five vocal takes in a row, then comp them together—syllable by syllable—to build the perfect vocal track. Then I would sing it four more times, and he would comp it again. We would listen to the comped track the next day, and Pat would ask me to sing it with more energy. He wanted me to belt it out. I tried belting it out, but it sounded phony. It wasn't me.

One night Seymour Stein took us out to dinner at the Gotham Bar and Grill, next door to RPM. He had recently been installed as president at Elektra (under Sylvia Rhone, the chairman), apparently to give the label some rock-and-roll cred. I ordered lamb chops, which were just right. Seymour Stein sent his pasta back to the kitchen.

"It should have more tomatoes," he said, in his soft, lisping voice. He told us what was wrong with the music business today.

"There are too many small boats in the harbor. They're all trying to get out to sea. But it's crowded—so many little boats, the big boats can't get out to sea. It's terrible."

Seymour was right. The music business had exploded in the '90s. Bands were signed left and right and stores were selling a ton of CDs. There were ten times more records released each week in 1997 than there were in 1987. Reviewers and DJs were inundated by new releases. Now there were too many bands and too many records—but it would soon get much worse.

We finished mixing our record a month later, at six o'clock on a Tuesday morning, at Room with a View studios in the Flatiron District. The last song to be mixed was "Tracy, I Love You." A bad note had been discovered in Sean's guitar solo. The offending guitar track was routed to the Eventide Harmonizer, which had a pitch-shifting feature. When the bad note came along, it was Lee Wall's job to push a button and activate the pitch shift, just for a second. Today they have software that will just change a note for you.

Pup Tent was not our best record, but it was our best-sounding record, containing all kinds of sonic textures that we would never have discovered alone. This was Pat's gift to us—a shimmering, psychedelic swirl of sound that enveloped each song. He had done a great job. Half the time we didn't understand what he was talking about or where he was leading us, but we got there eventually, and we had to admit that "Pup Tent" and "Tracy, I Love You" sounded magnificent. So what if we could barely speak to one another after nearly four months of recording? We would get over it, wouldn't we? So what if we had gone way over budget? They wouldn't mind, would they? After four albums, we were already $700,000 in debt to Elektra. It might as well have been a million dollars. It was all funny money, after all. We didn't have to pay it back.

We turned the record in to Elektra. The radio department chose the unlikely "IHOP" as the first single. The song didn't sound like typical Luna, but it was up-tempo and in a major key, and it had hooks and some catchy lyrics. One thing it lacked was a chorus. I mentioned this to Nancy Jeffries, who was now our A&R woman.

"The single they picked . . . there's no chorus—"

"Why don't you write a chorus, then?"

Damn. Now I had to write a chorus. I had patched the "IHOP" lyrics together from an episode of *Wheel of Fortune,* my own readings on André Breton, and an article about the Khmer Rouge in the *New York Times.* They seemed to make sense. The song was about a cad.

At the weekly meeting
Of anonymous cads
You shuffle your feet
And whistle out aloud
Listen what they're saying
What a load of crap
You ain't no Cary Grant
But then again,
Who is?

Verses are easy. The verse can meander and linger and tell a story or make clever and inconsequential observations. Writing a chorus is more difficult. The chorus has to be repeatable and catchy without being stupid. It was especially difficult to write a chorus for "IHOP," because there were only fifteen seconds between each verse, and that's where it would have to go.

I went to the movies. When you need to write something new, you can lock yourself in a room with a pad of paper and pray that the words will magically appear on the page. Or you can look at something you haven't seen before, read an old book of poetry (like Bob Dylan did), or study the titles of paintings or descriptions of ladies' clothing. That week I saw the documentary about Mohammad Ali and George Foreman, *When We Were Kings*. Ali and Howard Cosell had a special relationship. Ali called Cosell a phony, and said that his hairpiece had been stolen from the tail of a pony. Maybe that could be the chorus for "IHOP."

> *Your hair is a phony*
> *You stole from a pony*
> *You're going through changes, yeah!*

We booked another day at Room with a View to record the new chorus. Pat flew back into town. Before I could sing, he spent eight hours playing with the mix, making little tweaks here and there, turning up the percussion and then turning it back down. At midnight, Pat finally let me sing. We knew immediately that it was rubbish, that the song was better without the chorus.

What were we thinking anyway? They weren't going to play this song on commercial alternative radio stations, next to Pearl Jam and the Smashing Pumpkins and the Cranberries. When have you ever heard someone rap about the Khmer Rouge and Cary Grant and English cigarettes on the radio?

> *You stand accused*
> *Of smoking English cigarettes*
> *That's a provocation*
> *If ever one was*
> *Brother Number One*
> *Brother Number Two*
> *Why are we fighting?*
> *What are you gonna do?*

"IHOP" would be the first single, despite the lack of a chorus. We turned our attention to the second single.

How about "Bobby Peru"—didn't that have a catchy chorus? Didn't it have a connecting lyric?

S is for Sorry
For all that I did
Now is the time to turn it all around
I really don't mind you keeping secrets from me
But please don't keep them from yourself

The radio department guys agreed that "Bobby Peru" would be the second single, but recommended that we first do a special radio-friendly mix, to pump it up and make it ready for the airwaves. Renée called the famous producer and mixer Bob Clearmountain. He had produced some amazing records—he mixed *Avalon* by Roxy Music, and *Tattoo You,* the last great Stones album. *Tattoo You* is only half great (side two), but I'll take five or six great Stones songs any day.

The multitrack tapes for "Bobby Peru" were sent out to Clearmountain in California, and for about seven thousand dollars he punched it up, adding a little extra compression and turning up the drums and the vocals. Now the radio department people felt a lot better about delivering it to radio stations, because it had been mixed by Bob Clearmountain, who knew a thing or two about hit records. Another seven thousand dollars added to the Luna tab. What was the difference? Renée had already told us that this was a make-or-break album. Either we would have a hit record, or Elektra would cut us loose. The ride on the major-label gravy train would be over.

Rock on the Road

There is a sense of optimism on the first day of a tour. We show up at the airport in good moods, ready for action and happy to see one another. Day one begins with show-and-tell. Who has a new pair of Pumas? Sunglasses. Headphones. A new suitcase is always a good topic of conversation. Hard case versus soft case. Wheels or no wheels. I showed up with a large, ugly, khaki-colored soft case. Lee dubbed it Grandpa, because he said it looked like an old man's suitcase. I pointed out the retractable handle and extralarge wheels for smooth pulling.

"Yes, Grandpa."

We sat in the British Airways lounge at 8:00 A.M. in good spirits, looking forward to the tour—Lee's first full European tour. *Pup Tent* had just been released. *Rolling Stone* gave it a nice review and said that Luna was the world's greatest rock-and-roll band no one's heard of. This was a good thing to send around the Elektra offices.

We were still on Elektra in the United States, but were signed to Beggar's Banquet throughout Europe—Elektra had agreed to let us out of our worldwide deal, in exchange for lowering our advance. Our previous releases on WEA were generally invisible in Europe. Things were going to be better on Beggar's Banquet. They had already paid for Sean and me to do a one-week promotional trip a few months before the tour, hitting Paris, London, Hamburg, Cologne, Brussels, Madrid, and Stockholm. They were actually working on our record.

The good vibes disappeared quickly on the first day of this tour. Our plane had a mechanical problem and the flight was rescheduled for six o'clock in the evening.

"How much are we getting paid on this trip?" Sean asked.

"Didn't Renée talk to you about this?"

"No."

No one was being paid, aside from a $25 per diem for each member plus whatever we might earn selling T-shirts. There were salaries for the sound-man and the driver and the guitar tech, but not for the band members.

When we toured the States, we managed to put some money in the budget toward musicians' salaries. The business affairs people at Elektra didn't mind. Tour support was fully recoupable out of artist royalties, so they were only advancing us our own money. But Beggar's Banquet was an independent label, and they didn't throw their money around so easily. That was how they stayed in business. They had already paid for Sean and me to do that little promotional trip. And they had committed to paying more than $20,000 in tour support—to pay for our flights and hotels, the salaries for the sound engineer, the guitar tech, and the driver, and our per diems. But the official Beggar's policy was that they were not responsible for paying musicians' salaries.

Sean was pissed off that he wasn't going to make a salary, and that no one had bothered to tell him. Unlike Justin and me, who had been on independent labels, had done time sleeping on floors, and didn't necessarily expect to be paid a salary, Sean had only known the major-label experience, having joined Luna after we were already signed to Elektra.

We checked into our rooms at the Columbia Hotel on a rainy London day. I was rooming with Justin on this tour, while Sean and Lee would share another room.

The Luna show was at the London Astoria, and we had sold it out. Maybe this had something to do with the opening band, Cornershop, which was on the verge of bigness.

After the show it was on to a club in Soho, where our booking agent, Russell, was the guest DJ. Russell didn't play hard. He played soft music—like *Beach Samba* by Astrud Gilberto. This was fun, but I left the party early to do something more fun than listen to Astrud Gilberto.

We had a week of shows in England before heading to the Continent proper. Our sound engineer was Matthew Kettle, a Canadian living in London, and the guitar tech was Hoppy, whom we called Mr. Hoppy. Mr. Hoppy wore the same pair of jeans for four weeks, stiff Levi's that were eight inches too long, so he folded the cuffs. It was a good look.

We were going to travel around Europe in an almost-bus. It wasn't quite a bus, but it was bigger than a van. It came with a fifty-ish driver and owner named Mick, who hailed from the Yorkshire town of Doncaster. He told us that he used to be a mod but he never liked the Who. Mick called his company Rock on the Road. He would be doing all the driving, helping us load and unload our equipment, and also selling T-shirts during the shows. The bus had five little bunks to crawl into if you needed to take a nap, and a toilet, a busted television, and a little table where we could play cards or something.

The Venue in Edinburgh was a cool club. I had played there with Galaxie 500. Tonight, an obnoxious, drunk Scotswoman barged into our dressing room and told us what was wrong with America.

"Have you been to America?" we countered.

"Don't need to. It's rubbish!"

Sure, there is plenty wrong with the United States of America, but I didn't need to hear it from this drunk lady. I was coming down with something. I went back to the hotel with Justin and drank some Night Nurse (the English equivalent of NyQuil). It tastes much the same, but it's more poetic. Justin and I stayed up late watching *In the Heat of the Night* on our TV set.

"It's going to sound *horrible* tonight," said Matthew Kettle the next day.

He's Canadian, so he says "horrible" the same way that Sean says "sorry."

He was quite wrong. We had a great show at the Market Bar in Nottingham. This often happens. The shows that should suck, like a Sunday night in a tiny basement club in Nottingham, turn out to be exciting. Roger Trust, our U.K. A&R man, came up from London for the show and took us out to dinner. He liked seeing us play in these little spaces. Roger gets in there— he is one of those A&R people who actually likes to listen to music for the sheer pleasure of it.

The Chunnel is a wonderful invention. We rode Le Shuttle. You stay inside your vehicle, which is loaded onto a train that takes you under the English Channel to Calais in a mere twenty minutes. No waves. No seasickness. No white cliffs of Dover.

"What if we came out of the Chunnel and landed in the twenty-second century?" Sean asked.

We didn't. We came out in Calais and then drove to Brussels.

Brussels was not our favorite city. It might be a perfectly nice place to live, but I've always had a rotten time there, stayed in cheap hotels, played to small crowds on cold, rainy nights. The Botanique was a small, seated circular room located right in the middle of the botanical gardens. Since it was a seated show, the small crowd was extraquiet. We received polite smatterings of applause after each song, followed by a deadly silence. We went back to the hotel right after the show, in poor spirits, wondering why we ever bothered playing Brussels anyway. Belgians didn't care for Luna.

We had ten paying customers at the Paradiso in Amsterdam. We were playing in the small room upstairs, opening for the Welsh trio Stereophonics. They used to be called the Tragic Love Company, but no one loved them till they changed their name to Stereophonics, and after that they became real popular. You wouldn't know it tonight, though—they had about twenty in their audience. The promoter said that there was a big football game on TV.

We got up at the crack of dawn the next day to drive all the way to Copenhagen, a thirteen-hour trip including the ferry between Germany and Denmark. It was cold up on the top deck of the boat, but it felt great to be out there on the Ostsee (the Baltic).

The Loppen in Copenhagen sits in the middle of the Christiania neighborhood, a special enclave famous for hashish and hippies. We loaded our equipment into the club via a special cage on a hydraulic pulley, which hauled the cage up to the second floor. Sean bought a chunk of hash, which the hippies sell right out in the open on wooden tables.

The people at the club cooked us chicken stew with mushrooms and rice for dinner. Sean smoked some hash before dinner, and was still stoned when showtime rolled around. He thought he was going to faint onstage, but he made it through the show without falling down.

Tine approached me after the gig.

"Tine?"

I wasn't sure it was her. It had been seven years and her face was thinner. Still, how could I not recognize her? We went out for a quick drink and caught up on the seven years that had passed since the day we went to see *Darkman* together. We were both married now. Tine met her husband the week after that Galaxie 500 show, and they had two children and she now worked for a large book publisher. I was still playing in a rock-and-roll band.

I took a taxi back through the rainy Copenhagen streets to the Cosmopol (where I had also stayed with Galaxie 500) and the room I was sharing with Justin.

Touring was an eternal return. We played at a club and stayed in the hotel where they put the rock-and-roll bands. Seven years later we were back at the same hotel and our lives had changed. Or they hadn't changed at all. But other people—their lives changed. They were getting on with their lives, while we were on a treadmill, a cycle of making records and touring and then making more records.

I became morose. For some ridiculous reason I was sad about a life that was never going to be mine. What if I had stayed in Copenhagen after that Galaxie 500 show? Maybe Tine and I would have fallen in love and been married and had two little blond children—half Danish, half Dean. I would drive a Saab and enjoy the socialized health care and generous paternity leave.

I must have been tired. A week of poorly attended shows will make you wonder about the direction your life is taking. And my own life was just fine, wasn't it?

Friday night at the KB in Malmö brightened my perspective. The KB holds seven hundred people, and it was packed. Who knew? I had never played in Sweden before. The opening band, First Floor Power, featured two pretty sisters, and closed their set with a rendition of Luna's "City Kitty." No one had ever done that before. That night in Malmö felt like the greatest show of my life.

At eleven o'clock the club turned into a disco. The club manager let us stay and party in the spacious upstairs dressing room, with all our new Swedish friends, a crate of beer, and a bottle of Jägermeister. I got stuck in the corner talking to an annoying drunk guy. He kept asking why I didn't like him.

"Why don't you like me?"

"I don't *not* like you. I don't know you."

"Why don't you like me?"

After he asked me for the tenth time, I started not to like him. I had the feeling that he might try to punch me.

"Why don't you like me?"

A light snow was falling as we pulled into Stockholm on Saturday afternoon. What a gorgeous city. Water, water everywhere.

The show there was tremendous. It was hard to fathom after a miserable run from England through the Benelux that people liked Luna in Sweden. A handful of girls in the front row sang all the words to "Tiger Lily" and "California." What were the odds of that?

After the show the same girls crashed the backstage area to talk to us. They were four friends who had just spent a year in Long Island, where they had discovered Luna.

"What were you doing in Long Island?" I asked.

"Partying!"

They said this in unison, with one big Long Island accent. They looked Swedish, but they sounded Long Island. It was deflating. Still, we all went out drinking downtown with these girls and with Oskar from the record company. At 2:00 A.M. downtown Stockholm was filled with beautiful Swedish people, all out partying. Kramer once told me that God decided to put all the beautiful women in this one country. At four, I found myself in a Long Island girl's apartment, on the outskirts of town, with my hand down her pants. She was drunk, a little too drunk.

"You're drunk."

"Yes!"

I decided to leave. I had no idea where I was, but fortunately my hotel key contained all the information I needed. I showed it to a taxi driver and was able to pay for the cab with a credit card, something we still couldn't do in New York City.

The Herbertstrasse

We arrived in Hamburg at eleven o'clock on Sunday night, only to find that the clerk at the Hotel Monopol on the Reeperbahn had given away our rooms. They had the reservation in the computer, but the rooms themselves were now occupied. Shit. Luckily we found rooms at the Ibis Hamburg Altona, just down the street. Justin and I splurged on an extra hotel room so that we would have our own rooms all the next day. We did that once in a while. Sometimes Lee would beat me to the punch, making a secret deal with Justin to split an extra room, and then they each had their own rooms and I bunked with Sean, who was not in the mood to splurge because he had been expecting to get paid on this trip but now knew he was getting nothing.

Since we were here in St. Pauli, and right on the Reeperbahn, we thought we might as well pay a visit to the famous Herbertstrasse, a short street, around the corner from the police station, that was reserved for ladies of the night and their customers. Entrances on each side of the street are blocked by large metal gates, signposted ENTRY FOR MEN UNDER 18 AND WOMEN PROHIBITED. You go through the gates and on either side of the street stands a row of buildings with ladies sitting in the windows, scantily clad in the sexiest undergarments. As you walk by the buildings, the girls open the windows and ask how you are doing.

I stopped in front of a German girl with short blond hair.

"*Wieviel nimmst du?*" I asked. It's handy to speak a little German.

"Fifty deutsche marks."

Hmm. I was too scared to ask any other important questions, like what would I get for the DM 50. I was acting like a fifteen-year-old boy, old enough to have sex but not mature enough to talk about it. It would be rude to come right out and ask if she was going to fuck me for that price.

I said goodbye to Lee, Justin, and Sean, and followed my new friend upstairs. She took me to her little rented room and told me to take off all my clothes and sit on the bed while she put on some music—the Spice Girls' "Spice Up Your Life." She left me alone for a minute. I sat there feeling naked and vulnerable. My friend returned wearing only panties and a bra and said that for another DM 50 she would take her clothes off, too, and wouldn't that be nicer? She was being very gentle with me.

She knelt on the bed next to me and applied the condom. What happened next happened too quickly. I was very excited, and the motion of her hands applying the condom was enough to make me come immediately. *Scheisse.* Premature.

"*Schade,*" she said, which translates, "It's a shame."

That was that. I got dressed quickly.

The whole experience was disappointing. Sex isn't much fun when you have to pay for it. There was no sweet kiss, no lingering over the moment. I'm not sure if that encounter qualified as sex at all. I felt like I had just paid too much for a falafel sandwich, a disappointing meal at a tourist trap.

Lee and Justin and Sean were waiting for me outside the gates.

"All you got was a hand job?"

I had to admit that there might have been more to it, but that I had ejaculated too quickly, before I could find out.

Justin was pretty sure it sounded as if something more exciting was coming, the way I described her kneeling on the bed.

I was just glad that no one seized on this incident and decided to give me a hideous nickname. The Early Ejaculator. Sperminator. Early Man.

I would have been better off sitting in my room alone. Then I wouldn't have cheated on my wife, which is what I had done. Or had I? Paying a German hooker, who didn't even tell me her name, to give me a hand job—was that cheating? It didn't feel like it. I know, I had cheated before, and it felt bad. It stays with you for days and weeks and more. But this incident—well, it felt hollow and a little sordid, but it quickly disappeared from my conscience. I didn't think about it much. It was almost like it never happened.

The next day I woke up and did my laundry again. I wondered if I had brought enough underpants. Lee brought seventeen pair. He hadn't done his laundry yet. Sean had six pair. It hadn't been long since Brussels, but it was important to do your laundry when you could, not when you had to. Or you ended up like Justin, with a bag full of dirty clothes. Justin often *started* the tour with a bag of dirty clothes because he didn't get around to washing them before the tour began. We'd be in the van for only an hour and already he would say, "I need to do my wash."

After washing my clothes, I wandered around the inner harbor, ate a bratwurst and a Berliner, looked at the ruined spires of Hamburg, and thought about the terrible and senseless burning of the city during World War II. I got in touch with my sensitive side again. I hadn't lost it.

The Germans are barely allowed to talk about what happened to Hamburg, how their civilian population suffered through terrifying aerial bombardments. They are supposed to understand that they deserved it, as punishment for the crimes committed by the Nazi regime.

I wandered into the WOM and picked up some German music—a collection by Andreas Dorau (of "Fred vom Jupiter" fame), and a disc by Donna Regina. She lives in Cologne, sings in English and French, and is popular in Japan.

We played at the Logo to one hundred people who demanded three encores. Birgit from Beggar's Banquet Germany bought us all shots of a particularly revolting green liqueur. It was a Hamburg specialty, and we pretended to like it.

By the time we reached Munich, I had developed a nasty cough. I'd had the cough for days, but now it was nasty. The cold, damp weather did not help. Nor did the cigarettes and the beer and the singing every night and not getting enough sleep.

We played a cool little lounge called the Atomic Café. They didn't have a stage, so it was one of those shows where you are literally standing right next to your audience. In that audience I spied Armin from the Bartlebees—my favorite German band.

"Are you in the Bartlebees?" I asked.

"*Ja.*"

The next day I called the hotel doctor. She looked into my throat and said say "ahh" and diagnosed bronchitis.

"You must stay warm, and rest."

No time for that—I had plans. I spent the day wandering around Hamburg with Armin. He worked as a mail carrier for the post office, but today was his day off. He recommended Jägermeister—he said that's how the hunters keep warm. It did feel warm going down.

Armin invited me to eat with him and his girlfriend. We drank beer from large brown bottles, and he showed me his collection of Donald Duck toys (he owned three hundred). He was not only a drummer and a postman but also a Donaldist. He belonged to an organization called DONALD—an acronym for Deutsche Organisation Nichtkommerzieller Anhänger des Lauteren Donaldismus (the German Organization of Non-commercial Devotees of True Donaldism).

Armin also had a huge collection of seven-inch singles—he owned about seven thousand of those. He played me some great music—La Düsseldorf (who were once part of Neu!), Jimmy Tenor, and Kaleidoscope (the English psychedelic band, not to be confused with the American psychedelic band of the same era). We sat and listened to their eight-minute epic, "The Sky Children."

The sky children flew in a chariot of silver and gold to a future land of sunshine and flowers. They came to a village where turtles in caves made pies and lemonade, and a king came down from his castle and gave them a gift of tiny silver bells. The children traveled farther, in a boat with a porcupine captain wearing a coat of black needles, and his crew of six rabbits with fluffy ears, till they came to another dark cave, where they met Neptune, who gave them magic musical pink seashells to put to their ears. And then, sadly, it was time for the children to leave. It was time for me to stumble home, too, but it had been nice to have a day off.

Russell called to tell us that our Prague show was canceled. We now had three days in Dresden, a city undergoing major renovations, as the German government attempted to return it to its former glory. Once known as the Florence of the North, it was now alternately beautiful and ugly. Germany may have unified, but the two halves of this country felt about as similar as the United States and Mexico.

I got in trouble with Mick after the show. He caught me selling a T-shirt out of the back of the van, to a poor fan who was a few dollars short of the official selling price.

"Never let the band near the T-shirts," he said.

He was right about that. That's the problem with selling the shirts yourselves from the stage, which we had done on occasion. You have to deal with the desperate, pleading kids who only have five dollars but really, really need a shirt.

"Please. Please. I've only got four quid."

You wind up giving shirts away.

Berlin, too, was a giant construction zone. We stayed on Greifswalder-strasse, in the former East Berlin. I rode the S-Bahn from Savignyplatz to Alexanderplatz, and then walked down Unter Den Linden, another address being restored to its prewar capitalist splendor. Signs everywhere—that's the first thing you notice about the new Berlin. They didn't have much advertising in East Germany.

After the Berlin show we said goodbye to Uli, the promoter's rep who had been traveling with us for a few days. German promoters like to send someone out to look after you. It always seemed like a waste of money to me. We're not children—we could get from Hamburg to Munich. But maybe some bands have trouble showing up on time. At any rate, the promoters were likely losing money on this Luna tour, and we were losing money, too. This had been a most unproductive couple of weeks. The entire last week saw us play to a total of about 250 people—in Dresden, Berlin, and Karlsruhe—at a cost of many thousands of dollars in hotel bills and crew salaries.

We finally got out of Germany, only to land in Switzerland. In Fribourg and Geneva we opened for another American band—16 Horsepower. They were touring in a big white bus. I'd never heard of them, and I confess I didn't like them. I mean, I didn't know them personally, but I didn't like their music or their instruments or their porkpie hats.

In Fribourg, our record company rep showed up with Swiss Army knives for each of us.

The Geneva hotel was a dump, but I didn't spend much time there. I met a beautiful dark-haired dancer at the show, who invited me out for a drink at an illegal bar where they served only wine in very small glasses. She had ridden her bicycle to the show and she asked me to walk her home at 2:00 A.M., and then she invited me upstairs and asked if I wanted to take a shower.

Yes, I did want to take a shower.

I walked back to my hotel at five o'clock, through the quiet Geneva streets. I saw the white 16 Horsepower bus, just now pulling out of town. I was glad not to be on that bus. I was glad to be alive and walking through Geneva early in the morning. That night washed away all the frustrations of the previous week—the poor attendances, the cold weather, the bronchitis, and the traffic jams. It was nice, after two weeks of being cooped up in a van with a bunch of guys, to spend some time in the company of a woman. It was nice to have someone be nice to me. And now we were heading for Paris.

When we last played in Paris, back in 1995, the city was in the midst of a transportation strike—there were no buses or subways operating, which is a bummer when you're trying to get people to your show. The transportation workers were back at work now, but the truckers were on strike. They shut down the French highways and crippled road travel. Mick was worried. He was considering driving his bus straight back to Doncaster.

We went to plan B. Each of us packed two days' worth of clothes and our guitars and boarded the high-speed train from Geneva to Paris. Having slept two hours the previous night, I was now feeling slightly wretched—a combination of exhaustion and remorse. I collapsed in my seat and slept all the way to Paris. Years later, I used poetic license and turned this day into a song, "Swedish Fish":

So tired, I did it again
The trucks are on strike and I slept on the train
There's evil in Sweden
And evil in Spain
Drinking my lunch
All over again

On a gorgeous, sunny Saturday in Paris, we rode two taxis to the FNAC in Montparnasse, where we performed for a roomful of Luna fans. I still had a touch of bronchitis, and had to turn my back to the audience when I felt a cough coming on. A green piece of phlegm flew out of my mouth and landed on Lee's ride cymbal. Fortunately, the drum kit was a rental.

That night's sold-out show at Le Divan du Monde was part of the *Les Inrockuptibles* festival. *Les Inrockuptibles* (a clever play on Robespierre and his "incorruptibles") was the leading French rock magazine. Our set was a bit rushed, because that's how it is when six bands are playing the same stage.

Strangelove took the stage after us. They could only come from England. They in fact hailed from Bristol, and sounded a bit like Suede or Radiohead. The songs were alright, but their singer, Patrick Duff, made a fool of himself. He wore makeup and rambled in between songs. He had a reputation for being a complete drunk onstage, and tonight he showed why. I was a bit drunk, too, but I wasn't onstage anymore. Russell was here, too, and he was also drunk.

"This is a song about waking up in the park and you're still so drunk . . . that the wind knocks you over!" said Patrick.

Russell and I started heckling.

"Rub-bish!" I said.

"You're a clown!" said Russell. "You're bumming me out!"

"Asshole!" someone yelled from the balcony in a French accent. The crowd was joining in.

A couple of days later we were in sunny Valencia. There was a furniture convention in town, so we were booked at the two-star Hotel Sol Playa, miles from the Roxy.

"That means 'sun and beach,'" said Mr. Hoppy.

The location was swell, but the rooms were tiny and the beds were about three feet wide and bolted to the floor right next to each other. It was almost like Justin and I were sharing a bed. There was a dirty little shower stall in the room.

Oh well, we had seen worse. Right next door was a gigantic seafood restaurant, brightly lit, a family sort of place, where we ate fresh fish pulled straight from the sea.

Tomorrow came and it was sunny again. I hand-washed some underpants and socks in the sink. Justin's term for that is "doing a small load by hand." I walked on the beach. Lee sat on the roof and worked on his tan. It was too cold to swim, but hanging out on the beach sure beat riding in the van.

We had been here on the Mediterranean coast of Spain the previous summer, to perform at the Festival Internacional de Benicassim, an hour north of Valencia. It was a great festival in a great location. Claudia was there, too—we had planned a week's vacation in Catalonia after the show. Dinosaur Jr. played, and Pavement, and Suede. We were scheduled for an early show on Saturday night, following Urusei Yatsura, the Scottish band with the Japanese name, and before Veruca Salt, the Chicago band with the Willy Wonka name. It was a warm and muggy afternoon, and it rained for a while, but then the rain abruptly stopped.

This was the proverbial calm before the storm, a storm that roared in off the Mediterranean. I was standing at the back of the stage, starting to take my guitar out of its case and get my pedals ready, when I noticed the extraordinary wind. I looked up at the huge metal scaffolding that held the lights above the stage, and the big canvas sign with all the sponsors' names on it blowing in the wind. It didn't look quite right to me. I thought of Curtis Mayfield, who was paralyzed in 1990 when a lighting rig fell on him at an outdoor gig in Brooklyn.

Then came the rain. It came in horizontally, and Urusei Yatsura's drum kit started to move. Those brave/stupid Scottish kids kept playing their song even as the wind blew the drum kit clean off the stage. Ten seconds later I saw the entire scaffolding come crashing down, and the stage collapsed and everyone was running and screaming. And that was the end of the rock festival that year.

Veruca Salt's roadie came running into the backstage area.

"It's okay. Everything is okay. Our equipment is safe."

Now we were back. During our show at the Roxy, I made a comment about Benicassim and everyone cheered. Yay Luna! Yay freak storm! Yay Friday night at the Roxy! We weren't in Belgium anymore. Valencia is famed as a hard-partying town where people dance all night long and take tons of drugs. There is an unwritten code about parking your car in Valencia on a weekend night. People double-park everywhere, and they leave their car doors unlocked so that other motorists can release the hand brake and push the cars aside to get their own cars out. It's an honor system, and the police do not issue parking tickets on those nights.

We went out drinking after the show. One girl cornered me outside the bathroom and said she wanted to talk to me.

"I am not a groupie," she said. "I am a poet."

She had written some poems and wanted me to hear them. Sigh. I wasn't in the mood for poetry.

Justin was busy trying to talk to the very hot blond barmaid from the Roxy, but she didn't speak English. He soon gave up.

He and I shared a cab back to the hotel by the beach.

"No one ever goes home with the chick behind the bar," said Justin. "Ever."

Lee told us all about it the next day, and he had a letter for me. Right after Justin and I left, the bar had shut down, and Lee found himself standing outside with the hot barmaid. They couldn't really converse, but they just looked each other in the eyes and she took him back to her place. Her roommate, the poetess, was there, too, and while Lee and the hot barmaid made out on the sofa, the poetess composed a letter to me, reading it aloud to Lee.

"Do you think Dean would like this?"

Justin had to eat his words. And we got to tease him about how he had talked to her all night but then gave up and Lee swooped in, silently, and went home with the girl.

The end of the tour was approaching and that was a good feeling. We played Madrid and Barcelona and stayed out all night partying with our friends at the record company. Thank God we had little bunks in the van— these bunks saved us that week. But we were off to Majorca now, and Mick was leaving for Yorkshire.

"If ever you're in Doncaster," he said, "you're welcome to stay at my house."

Majorca was a blast. We each had our own little suites on the beach, much appreciated after five weeks of sharing rooms.

The show was chaotic. Some kids stole our set lists from the front of the stage. Usually they had the courtesy to wait till *after* we played. Lee still had his set list, so he called out the songs for us.

The stage lights kept going on and off, not in time with the music, but because there was an electrical problem. So what?

We went to the Mala Fama bar later that night. It was incredibly, deafeningly loud—they were playing Luna on the sound system as we walked in. We stayed for half an hour before heading back to the hotel. One of the record company employees poured out a huge pile of cocaine. The very sight of it made my heart race. I decided I didn't want to stay up till eight in the morning doing blow, and excused myself.

. . .

We made it to the Southern Hemisphere that year, playing shows in Sydney, Melbourne, and Brisbane. Spring came to Sydney the week we were there, and it was glorious. We stayed right on Bondi Beach. I rode the ferries all across the harbor and wondered why my parents had ever left this paradise.

Our shows in Sydney were not well attended, but we did much better in Melbourne, which some say is the more cultured city (the people in Melbourne say that). From Melbourne we flew to Brisbane, where we played the Livid Festival. The headliners at the festival were Sonic Youth and Public Enemy.

The Dandy Warhols were also on our early afternoon flight to Brisbane, but I was lucky enough to sit next to Flava Flav, who sat down in the empty seat next to me after being kicked out of first class, where he had tried to sneak in.

Flava Flav wouldn't put his seat-back in the upright position for takeoff. The gentleman sitting behind us gave him an earful.

"Excuse me! Excuse me! If we have an accident, my daughter will hit her head on the back of your seat."

Flava Flav stood up and turned around to face his accuser.

"Man, you got to think positive! Me, and you, and your daughter—we're all gonna get there just fine. High five!"

He proceeded to get loaded on gin and tonics, and told me about the big plastic clock he was wearing around his neck, which was set to six o'clock because it's "straight up and down, just like I'm being with you right now." He told me about the many children he had fathered, and his apartment on the Grand Concourse in the Bronx, right by Yankee Stadium. The gin soon worked its magic, and he snored for the rest of our trip.

I ran into him later that evening, backstage at the festival. He was wearing a rubber mask and rambling around with his friends. He recognized me, sitting alone having a beer.

"Man, where's your posse?" he asked.

The Days of Our Nights

The '90s were salad days for those in the music business. Every year set a new record for CD sales. The record companies not only sold new music, but they also convinced us to throw out that scratchy vinyl and repurchase our LP collections on compact discs, which they said would provide perfect sound forever (it has now been proven that vinyl LPs deliver a more accurate and pleasurable listening experience).

After many successive years of solid growth, 1999 was the most lucrative year for the record companies. The Backstreet Boys, Britney Spears, Ricky Martin, 'N Sync, and Shania Twain were among the top sellers that year. In 1999, 939 million compact discs were shipped, and the RIAA put the overall value of the U.S. recording industry at over $14 billion (up from $6.5 billion just ten years earlier). But the alternative-rock movement was on the wane. Labels were no longer looking for the next Nirvana. They were looking for the next Britney.

Nineteen ninety-nine was not a good year for Luna. We were dropped by our record company (Elektra), our publisher (Polygram), and our accountant (Siegel, Feldstein, and Duffin).

It began with the publisher. Our songs were published by Sub Pop, whose parent company was Polygram, which had recently been swallowed up by MCA and was now part of a new company called Universal Music Publishing. That's the way things were going in the music business. There used to be seven major labels, but now there were four.

When companies merge, heads roll. One of those heads was Vice President John Baldi's, who was a Luna fan. We didn't have any fans at Universal Music Publishing after that, and they quickly notified us that they would not be picking up the option on the next Luna album.

We could survive without the publishing deal anyway. We still had our deal with Elektra. We made an album called *The Days of Our Nights.* Our fifth studio album, it is possibly the worst of the seven that Luna made. If you study rock-and-roll bands, I think that the fifth album generally tends to suck. Maybe they all hate one another by this point. Maybe they need new ideas. Maybe they're trying new ideas. Whatever the reason, the fifth album is difficult.

The fifth Ramones album, for example, was *End of the Century.* It was produced by Phil Spector, who reportedly pulled a gun on them, and killed their true sound. The fifth Talking Heads album was *Speaking in Tongues.* It has its moments, but it is no *More Songs about Buildings and Food.*

The Beatles are an exception to the rule of the bad fifth album. You could make a case that they sucked *until* their fifth album. We were not the Beatles. No, we were not.

What the hell, most bands are lucky to make it past two albums without breaking up. We should count our blessings.

Your records can't all be great, no matter who you are. If you're talented and lucky, maybe you can put together a remarkable string of records—like Bob Dylan did, or the Rolling Stones, or Stereolab. But it can't continue forever.

It's not for lack of trying that the fifth album is a bloated dud. It's more likely from trying too hard and thinking too much. The day we finished making *The Days of Our Nights,* we decided to track a few B-sides, "Sweet Child O' Mine" by Guns N' Roses, "Neon Lights" by Kraftwerk, and "Emotional Rescue" by the Rolling Stones. These all came out great, better than anything on the album. Perhaps the lesson is that you do your best stuff when you're not worried about delivering a hit single for your record company. Yes, I believe that's it. The record was already delivered, and we could return to the joy of making music just for the hell of it, without anyone asking where the single was.

A hit single. We sure failed at delivering one of those. There are a couple of songs I like on the album, like the really slow one that I sang in German, lazily titled "The Slow Song." Our producer, Paul Kimble, said that the song was so pretty I should sing it in German, to fuck it up. This was the kind of thing we occupied ourselves with.

Of course, my least favorite song, "Dear Diary," was picked as the single. I came to hate singing "Dear Diary." The stupid "baa-baa" section. The bad lyric—"then you blew my mind." I hated that lyric. It was one of those things that comes out of your mouth when you're singing gibberish, before you've written the lyrics proper. But then you find it's a phrase that you are incapable of replacing. You're stuck with it.

Renée had been warning us, for about five years, that Elektra would drop us if we didn't come up with a radio hit. And then, one day in March, she called and said that we had in fact been dropped. She had been right all along.

That's what happens to bands. It wasn't fun, but it wasn't a huge surprise, either. The music business is driven by hits. The hit records, the ones that sell millions of copies, pay for everything. When all is said and done, if your record is not a hit, it's a miss. We had missed four times in a row.

The timing wasn't good. Claudia was pregnant, and I was now without a steady source of income. Luna's upcoming U.S. tour was scrapped.

But there was an upside to being dropped. We could now escape the $1.2 million in phony record company debt that we had racked up over the course of making five albums. We were free to start over at a new label.

Many items factored into our debt. There were the recording advances, averaging $200,000 for each album. We generally spent half that money on recording and pocketed the rest. There was the tour support, something like $20,000 per tour. If we made a $50,000 video, then 50 percent of that cost was added to the pile. If Elektra hired an independent radio promoter to work our record, that fee was also added. This was a brilliant stroke from the record companies. Payola was officially illegal, but hiring the independent promoters to do the exact same thing was now an aboveboard item that they could charge back to the artist.

The record companies had managed to hold on to this old-fashioned system of stacking your releases on top of one another, treating all your records as one big account. This way, even if you had a gold record on your fourth album, they didn't have to pay you, because you still owed them money from those first three albums, the ones that didn't sell so well. You were in the hole, and it was hard to climb out.

Hadn't we sold a couple hundred thousand CDs for Elektra, and also licensed some songs to TV commercials for Calvin Klein and American

Express (those monies going straight to the label)? Wouldn't that even things out? If they sold two hundred thousand CDs, making a profit of $6 per disk, that was $1.2 million right there.

But the math didn't work like that. The account had to recoup only out of the artist's portion of the profits, our 14 percent of the retail price (which amounted to around $2). If we sold two hundred thousand records, our account would be credited only $400,000.

It didn't matter anymore. We were free. Free to start digging another hole.

I'd never heard of a band being dropped by their accountant. You figure that your accountant will do the work and take their five percent. But Siegel, Feldstein, and Duffin was bought by American Express, and they were told to eliminate the acts that weren't making big money. We were one of those acts. Somehow this was more insulting than being dropped by Elektra. It seemed plain rude.

At least we still had Beggar's Banquet in Europe. For the first time, our record was released in Europe before it was available in the United States. Renée worked on finding us another deal at home, and we went off to the Old World for a five-week tour.

Claudia gave birth to a perfect little boy on June 16, 1999. Jack was born via C-section at St. Vincent's Hospital. Some people say that this is the greatest day of your life, but I found it just a bit terrifying. Not just when the doctor lost the baby's heartbeat on the monitor and opted for the emergency C-section. Not just when the nurse asked me if I needed to see a priest before the C-section. Why would I need to see a priest? Was someone about to die? Around 4:00 A.M. my baby boy, covered in blood, was handed to me for a minute. Fortunately I had watched videos of babies covered in blood, so I wasn't too shocked.

I was a father now. It was exciting and scary. There was a little creature in our lives. I spent the night with Claudia and Jack in a room with a view at St. Vincent's. While they slept, I watched the San Antonio Spurs defeat the Knicks in game one of the NBA Finals. I was glad Jack didn't have to see that.

The Slow Ride Down

*What if some day or night a demon were to steal after you into your loneli-
est loneliness and say to you: "This life as you now live it and have lived it,
you will have to live once more and innumerable times more; and there will
be nothing new in it." Would you not throw yourself down and gnash your
teeth and curse the demon who spoke thus?*

—Nietzsche

The 1999 European tour started with a week in the United Kingdom.
Justin, Sean, Lee, tour manager Evan Player, and I took the red-eye
from JFK to Heathrow. I skipped dinner, because I wanted to take an Ambien
to put me to sleep, and they work much better on an empty stomach. The
only risk was what I call Peter Buck syndrome (PBS). He once got in trouble
on a flight to England; they say he was abusive to a flight attendant and
damaged the British Airways crockery, and he was arrested upon arrival in
London. He pleaded not guilty, due to the combination of Ambien and wine
that made him temporarily insane. I believe him. I've seen people act nutty
on Ambien. Some people get up in the middle of night and eat everything
in the fridge while tripping on Ambien. Others go for a midnight drive. And
they wake up with no memory of these things.

Stephen Joyce met us at Heathrow with a van and equipment. Here we were
again—six grown men sharing one van and three hotel rooms for five weeks.
This close proximity to one another was infantilizing. It encouraged us to
behave like children instead of men. I used to share a room with my older
brother when I was eight years old. And now I was sharing a room with Justin.

Our first stop was the Travelodge in Sheffield. It was unusually hot and
humid, and the rooms were not air-conditioned, because this was England.

We had time for a quick nap, and then drove over to the Leadmill. I was there once before on a Saturday night in 1991 with Galaxie 500. Justin had played there, too, with the Chills.

"Sold it out!"

He liked to say that, in a disgusted tone, on nights where we didn't have a good crowd. Okay, so the Chills sold out the Leadmill in Sheffield. I bet they never sold out the Fillmore in San Francisco.

We were exhausted in Sheffield. We didn't play our best. But Luna was a well-oiled machine, and things never went horribly wrong. That's what comes from having a good rhythm section, and we always had a good rhythm section. It's what made Luna different from most indie bands. When you are playing with a good drummer, you are happy. When you're playing with a drummer who changes speed and can't remember the songs, you worry.

Sunday night we were at King Tut's Wah Wah Hut in Glasgow. We had been there in 1995, opening for the Auteurs. What a miserable tour that was. Their first album had been a big success, but no one much cared for the follow-up, and they were playing to about fifty people each night. We could have done that all by ourselves. Sean begged us to blow off the rest of the dates and go home, mostly because he was having a tough time with his girlfriend, Vanessa. Terry Tolkin had been entertaining her while Sean was out of the country, treating her to dinner on his expense account, calling her a car service if she was going to the airport. Sean called Vanessa every night, racking up a huge phone bill. Stanley complained that he had to listen to the nightly phone conversations. He would mockingly imitate Sean's conversations in the van the next day.

"Baby? Baby. Daddy's coming home soon!"

This time, King Tut's had that Sunday night feeling. Sunday night is not a good night to rock. Afterward I went out for a Scotch with Stephen and Katrina of the Pastels. Stephen Pastel was trained as a librarian, and worked as a buyer in a bookshop, John Smith's, that was also the coolest record store in Glasgow.

Tuesday night was Leicester. The Princess Charlotte is one of the most hated gigs in England. Everyone says ahead of time that the sound will be awful. Everyone warns you that the house soundman is a bastard. There was something wrong with the room. They needed to bulldoze it. The Princess Charlotte was the low point of the tour so far. We moved on to London.

Sean and I went over to radio station GLR to perform a couple of acoustic tracks live on the air. The DJ said that Glen Campbell had been sitting in my chair an hour ago. The Rhinestone Cowboy. The Wichita Lineman. We used to watch his TV special when I was young. I didn't know that he had said that anyone who burns his draft card should be hanged (this after his own fans got angry at him for recording the anti-war "Blowin' in the Wind"). It's disappointing when you hear stuff like that, but still, his voice is beautiful, and he's a great guitarist, too. I don't have to like his politics.

Sean and I bumbled our way through an acoustic version of "Dear Diary," and made some stupid, nervous small talk on the air before heading over to the club for sound check.

"Do you think Roger will take us out to dinner?" Lee asked. Roger usually took us out to dinner in London.

Beggar's Banquet had pledged more than $20,000 in tour support for this trip to Europe, but once again insisted that they could not pay us each a weekly salary on top of that. This time, Sean decided that he would not be silent. A week before we went on tour, he wrote an angry e-mail to Roger Trust, pointing out that we still had to pay the rent while we toured around Europe, and ending with the words "give me a break, man!"

"At first I wrote 'give me a *fucking* break,'" said Sean. "But I decided that was rude."

This kind of exchange wouldn't have happened before the Internet revolution. Maybe Sean would have called Roger on the phone to express his feelings. They might have had a cross word or two, but it would have been forgotten soon enough. Not this time.

Roger wrote back to Sean. "Dear Sean, I wish I could say I hadn't read your e-mail."

Roger did not take us out to dinner.

We drove down to Dover and caught the ferry to Holland. The following day was day one in our run of ten shows in a row, from the top of Europe to the bottom, without a day off. Malmö, Oslo, Stockhoim, Copenhagen, Hamburg, Berlin, Cologne, Marburg, Munich, and Bologna.

As we drove off the ferry, our van was stopped at customs by a couple of cute Swedish lady customs inspectors. We were happy to let them search wherever they liked. They could give us the hose, for all we cared. There is probably no such thing as the hose, but we were always talking about it.

After sound check at the KB in Malmö we met one of our Swedish fans. He wandered into the dressing room to chat with us.

"Dean! You are my heroes. I want to kiss you, while Sean fucks me in the ass. . . . Ha! Ha! Just kidding!"

Later he was thrown out of the club; he must have pissed someone off. He was sitting outside crying as we loaded the van.

The Berlin show was at the Knack Club. The crowd was full of guys with beards, standing there with their arms folded. Not many young hipsters, though. Maybe that's the way things are heading for Luna, I thought. The kids in Berlin were probably dancing the night away to techno music, leaving the New York art rock to older guys with beards. This did not bode well, on a couple of different levels.

Lee almost got into trouble that afternoon. He was in an army-navy store, and there was a cute teenage girl working behind the counter.

"Do you like music?"

Lee was single, and that was his way of saying hello to pretty girls.

He invited her to the show, but was immediately chased out of the store by the girl's fat mother, who yelled at him in German. The mother had enormous swollen legs. The German medical phrase for that is *"dicke Beine"*—fat legs.

We were in Cologne the following day. Another Ibis hotel. Another basement club. Another crowd of approximately one hundred. We closed the set with our rendition of "Sweet Child O' Mine." This song was only on our record because Nancy Jeffries really liked it. She told me it was the best vocal she had ever heard me do. I had no objection to that. I figured if someone at Elektra was excited about the song, then that was a good thing. Justin was dead against it—he hated Guns N' Roses. I didn't like them, either, but it's a great song. I am of the opinion that a bunch of pigs can occasionally write a beautiful song together. Oasis did it, too, with "Wonderwall."

Nancy was excited enough to send the song down to the experts in the alternative radio department, down on the sixteenth floor of 75 Rockefeller Plaza.

"Too mellow," they said. "It will never play on alternative radio." So Nancy sent us back into the studio to vibe it up a little. We spent $4,000 of Elektra's money doing a remix with Bryan Malouf, who recently had a hit with Harvey Danger or something. See, what they figured is this guy mixed a hit single last year, so maybe if he mixed our song, it would also turn into a hit single.

We tried to add a little extra guitar, but frankly the song didn't need it. They say a song is finished when you have trouble adding another instrument to it. This one was finished. There was no need to pour gravy on the meat.

The song was added to our album. Then Elektra dropped us, and our record was delayed six months. Sheryl Crow had a big hit that summer with her lame version of "Sweet Child O' Mine." We thought to ourselves, That could have been us. But she's Sheryl Crow, and we are not. Good things happen to Sheryl Crow. Still, I'd rather be me than Sheryl Crow.

Saturday night we arrived in Marburg, a quaint little university town high on a hill. It was a bright, sunny day, and I wandered alone all over town, wondering what the hell I was doing in Marburg. Thirty people came to see our gig at the university, the Philipps-Universität Marburg. I don't think any of them had ever heard of Luna. Some nights I was up there singing my songs, but I wasn't really there. I was just dreaming. My fingers played the chords and my mouth sang the words, but I was thinking about other things. Thinking, I'm wasting my life. Or, I wonder if Immanuel Kant ever lectured here?

I took a course on Kant's Transcendental Deduction when I was a sophomore at Harvard. We spent the whole semester going over twenty crucial pages, and now I couldn't for the life of me tell you what it was about. What a waste of my parents' money.

Kant probably didn't lecture in Marburg anyway. But Vice Chancellor Von Papen gave an important speech here in 1934, urging Hitler to control his rowdy brown-shirted storm troopers. Hitler promptly obliged, throwing a little party they called the Night of the Long Knives.

We were getting lost on some of these drives. It's hard driving to strange new cities, and there is nothing more annoying than driving around for an extra hour when you desperately want to get out of the van and check into a hotel room.

Sean had a habit of yelling at Evan from the backseat. He was quite the backseat navigator. We gave him a new nickname that week: the Scolding Navigator. For the ride to Munich, Evan made Sean the deputy navigator, so he wouldn't be able to scold. We got lost, as usual, and we made sure to scold Sean.

Sean had many nicknames, acquired over years of playing in the band. Some were funny. Some were mean:

Lightbulb

Mrs. Eden

The Lady

The Noodler

The Waffler

Meanderthal

Empty-Faced Eden

The International Party Animal

"Mrs. Eden" was coined by Stanley, who noticed that on travel itineraries, Mr. S. Eden could be read simply as Mrs. Eden. From there it was a short step to "the Lady." If he was late to the van in the morning, Lee would say, "Where's the Lady?" Or, "Where is she?"

Sean didn't appreciate being called the Lady. He struck back with his own names for us, like "You cock!" or "Cockface!"

I'd heard wonderful things about Bologna—the food, the cathedrals, the university, the red rooftops. We saw none of it. Our hotel was located in an industrial park outside the city. We were playing the final night of a two-week festival sponsored by the DS (Democrats of the Left), a party descended from the ashes of the Italian Communist Party. Bologna was sometimes referred to as *Bologna la rossa,* not only for the rooftops, but because the socialists and communists have long been strong there. Did our participation in this festival mean that we would be on an FBI list when we get home? Not likely. The cold war was over, and Italian communists have long been communists in name only—they broke from Moscow in the '70s. Now they had gone so far as to replace their hammer and sickle logo with a red rose.

We were sharing the bill with the Selecter, the ska band from the '80s. I was not sure if they had re-formed, or perhaps they just never went away. They looked old and tired and grumpy. They probably hated one another. We played our show, quickly packed up, and got the hell out of there as the Selecter took the stage. We were pooped, and frankly a little depressed.

We saw prostitutes along the side of the road as we drove back to the hotel, waiting with their car doors open. It was as if we had wandered into Fellini's *Nights of Cabiria.*

We finally had a day off after Bologna. In reality it was a travel day, because we had to drive all the way to Lausanne, Switzerland. The day started off well, with a spectacular drive through the Italian Alps, and a delicious lunch at a roadside cafeteria. Later that afternoon, as we got closer to the Mont Blanc tunnel, we noticed how little traffic there was on the road. We found out why when we reached the tunnel. It was closed, on account of a tragic tunnel fire that had occurred a few months before. It was a shame that no one told us. Or maybe they could have put up some signs on the highway. One might have read MONT BLANC TUNNEL CLOSED—GO BACK!

Z urich was the new low point of the tour. The club we were playing was an illegal squat, a performance space located on the top floor of an old four-story house. As it was illegal, they were not allowed to advertise the shows, and depended instead on word of mouth. For dinner they cooked us a big piece of roast pork. A strange punk-rock girl on crutches was hanging around, bumming cigarettes in a heavy accent. It felt like a David Lynch film, till a guy from our record company showed up with Swiss Army knives. Just like last time.

"We're expecting two hundred people," said the promoter.

"Where will you put them?" I asked.

Forty people showed up, and the poor promoter must have lost money. He tried to negotiate with Evan to pay us less.

"Well," said Evan, "you can pay us less if you like, but it will probably come back to bite you next time you try to book a show with Luna's booking agent." He paid up.

We headed to our two-star hostel. This was possibly the worst hotel we ever stayed in—and we had stayed in some nasty ones. Tiny beds. Dirty sheets. Bathroom at the end of the hall. No toilet paper. No towels. Some junkie prostitutes hanging out in the lobby. We considered getting in the van right then and there and just driving to France, but decided against it. Thank God I had an Ambien to knock me out.

Maybe you think that we were living like rock stars. Out every night, partying with beautiful ladies who waited for us after each show. But it was not like that. Not for Luna. If you wanted to try to pick up a girl, you had to make an effort. You had to wade out into the audience immediately after the show, pretend to look busy, and then answer a lot of stupid questions from guys who wanted to know what kind of distortion pedals we use. Some bands designate a crew member to hand out backstage passes to cute girls during the show, but we thought that was crossing the line. We may have been dogs, but we were not pigs.

In Paris I had time to walk around alone, which felt good. Good to be alone, good to be out of the van, good to be in Paris, good to have lunch at Les Deux Magots, where Jean-Paul Sartre used to hang out, and Oscar Wilde and Ernest Hemingway. All those dudes. After lunch I went and got myself some of the world's most delicious ice cream, on the Île Saint-Louis.

Our Paris show at La Maroquinerie was sold out. This was a good sign.

Next up was Bordeaux, where we played in a legendary little punk-rock club called Le Jimmy. A punk-rock club can become legendary just by having booked some cool bands back in 1980, and then staying in business. If the toilets don't flush, so much the better.

Our hotel was a little odd. It had a nautical theme going, and the little rooms were decked out like a ship's cabins, with round portholes instead of windows. I had my own room that night, and watched an excellent pornographic film on the free TV. Everyone was wearing masks and white wigs, and they were dancing and singing madly and having anal sex, and it was really very funny. It's fun hanging out in the hotel room, drinking a cold Kronenbourg and quietly watching French porn.

The next morning we all had breakfast together, talked about the porn on TV, and signed our new recording contract with Jericho Records.

Renée had been soliciting American offers for the album that Elektra didn't want, and she thought Jericho was the best option. Jericho was small but they were enthusiastic about Luna. Jericho was owned by Internet pioneer Rick Adams, and the label had a distribution deal with Sire Records, which meant we were back under the Time-Warner umbrella.

We were excited to be heading to Spain, where we were actually popular. First stop, Bilbao.

"Bilbao is a shithole," said Stephen.

He was from Newcastle, so he should know.

Kafe Antzokia was a restaurant by day and a nightclub come nightfall. Hundreds of Luna fans came to the show, and then afterward two girls came backstage and offered Sean and me a line of coke.

"Sure," we said. There was an unusual stinging sensation in my nose.

"That was coke, right?" I asked.

"It was *speed*."

Shit. We went out drinking with our new friends. Everyone cheered when we walked into one little bar, and then all wanted our autographs. Nothing like that had happened in Hamburg or Leicester.

The promoter in Valencia put us back at the Hotel Sol Playa. We stayed there the last time through Valencia, and vowed never to return. We couldn't understand why they had put us back in that horrible little hotel, miles from the club, when we had sold eight hundred tickets to the show. We fully expected to be treated like shit in Leicester and Zurich, but not in Valencia. We were pretty pissed off about it, and then when we got to the Roxy, the opening band, Scott 4 (named for Scott Walker's beautiful fourth album), had eaten the food on our rider. In addition, the club was supposed to provide a room with a phone so I could do some important interviews that had been set up, but they told us that I couldn't possibly use their phone. Justin was particularly disturbed by the whole scene, and told Evan that he needed to open a can of whoop-ass. So Evan opened it.

"This is how it's gonna be! You're going to get the opening band out of our dressing room! And you're gonna bring us some more food! And you're going to provide a telephone! And that's how it's gonna be, or there isn't going to be a Luna show!"

A tour manager has to do that sometimes. It wasn't in Evan's nature, but he pulled it off when he had to.

Justin had been in a foul mood for a few days now. At least once per tour,

Justin would go into one of his special black moods. They generally lasted for about four days, during which time he barely spoke. He still supervised the packing of the van, and he still wrote the set lists, but his lips were sealed. He would sit there quietly, but his quietness was very loud, like a little black cloud hovering inside the van. No one ever asked him what was the matter, and he didn't volunteer any information. Then one day he would wake up and the black cloud would be gone. This is how New Zealanders deal with depression.

Justin seemed to be depressed more often on this particular tour. He was finding the whole situation increasingly intolerable, probably because he had decided to move back to New Zealand with Lisa. He wrote a long e-mail to Renée from Germany, explaining that he never wanted to tour Europe again. He was tired of pushing a rock up a hill year after year.

We flew from Valencia to Majorca, once again at the perfect time of year. The peak summer season was over, so it was no longer mobbed by middle-aged English and German tourists, but it was still warm enough to sunbathe and swim in the Mediterranean and enjoy the typical Majorcan wine and the typical cuisine—*arroz brut*—a dish of rabbit, sausage, and partridge stewed with saffron rice, mushrooms, and vegetables.

The Sonotone in Palma was a dive. The stage was five feet off the floor, and was accessed by a rickety wooden ladder. Behind the stage was a filthy dressing room with one virtue—a toilet for the band. So at least I didn't have to stand on line in the public restroom before the show, which is always a bummer. The PA system was underpowered, and they had provided us with some truly shitty equipment. We didn't mind; the show was packed and it was Saturday night and we were happy to be back in Majorca.

Our hotel was on the beach, ten miles outside of Palma. Usually we didn't like to be ten miles outside of town—that would be cause for much complaining. But no one complained in Majorca. There's a special kind of sunshine there, a better-quality sun than they have in Brussels. It was nice to be on the beach, and to each have our own hotel room after four weeks of sharing.

People in mainland Spain asked us, incredulously, why we played in Majorca. Most bands didn't bother with Majorca. Because they invited us, of course, and because we loved it there. The promoter always put us in a decent hotel on the beach, with our own rooms, and then treated us to a great meal. And there was always a wild crowd. Who cared if the PA system only worked on one side and the lights kept going out? The Majorcans enjoy life, and we enjoyed their life, too.

As I stood onstage that night, a hot Spanish girl swayed gently in front of me. She had long eyelashes and dark hair and olive skin and a great chest. She wore a revealing sweater. It was distracting. You can be playing to a thousand fans, but if there is a pretty girl in the front row, that's all you see. The rest of the crowd is a blur. Sometimes, the pretty girl is standing with her stupid boyfriend and he has a hairy arm draped over her protectively, just to make sure the band doesn't blow kisses to her from the stage.

I was enjoying myself a little too much. I had had one too many beers before taking the stage (at midnight), and was a little tipsy. I was still perfectly able to sing and play guitar, of course. After four weeks on tour, I could play those songs in my sleep. But halfway through the show I realized that I had to pee, and that feeling was not going away any time soon.

There I stood onstage, singing my songs, but really thinking about the pretty girl with the fantastic chest, and whether I could make it to the end of the set without peeing. During "23 Minutes in Brussels" I made my move. The long, slow instrumental section at the end of the song gave me a chance to bolt from the stage, down the ladder to the bathroom in the dressing room. Sean, Lee, and Justin finished the song without me. This was the first time in my life that I had left the stage during a song. I liked it. I had a relaxing pee and lit up a cigarette, then sauntered back onstage in time for "Moon Palace," feeling much better about having to hit those high notes— "nyah, nyah, nyah, nyah."

After the show we sat in the dressing room and finished off the bottle of Stoli on our rider. It used to be Jack Daniel's, but Sean's ex-girlfriend Maria told him that bourbon made his breath stink. Stanley (Sean's old roommate on tour) also complained of this, so Sean switched to vodka.

Two precocious English girls barged into the dressing room. They looked to be about seventeen years old, and had that self-assuredness that comes from being filthy rich and privileged and beautiful and seventeen. They had not in fact seen the Luna show. I got the impression that they made a habit of showing up in the dressing room of the Sonotone, that it was a routine stop on their usual Saturday night out. It was *their* dressing room, and we just happened to be in it. Right behind the English girls, looking a little nervous, was the lady who had been standing in front of me during the whole show. Her name was Mariana.

Cordelia, one of the cheeky, leggy, rich, spoiled seventeen-year-old English girls, promised to find us some coke, and took us all to a bar. The bartender said that the dealer hadn't been in yet. I sat at the bar with Mariana, drinking gin and tonics. In Spain they give you just the gin in a glass, with a little bottle of tonic on the side.

Mariana was from Malaga. She was about thirty-five years old, and worked as a flight attendant for Iberia. Her younger brother, a big Luna fan, had told her to go to the show.

Three o'clock came and went. The coke dealer hadn't materialized, and I was tired. I decided to head back to the hotel. But first I kissed Mariana good night. It's rude if you don't kiss a Spanish girl good night (unlike in Japan, where a girl would be horrified if you kissed her on the cheek). The kiss lasted a bit longer than I thought it would. Mariana asked me to come for a walk down by the harbor. Palma was still bustling at four that night—everyone was drinking and eating and having a good old time.

We stopped at the top of a steep stairway, overlooking the harbor. I kissed Mariana again and she invited me back to her place. She lived in a modern apartment complex in downtown Palma. Modern and small—this was her Majorca pied-à-terre, just a little studio. There was nowhere to sit but the bed.

"Would you like me to dress up in my uniform?"

This is the kind of thing that you might imagine happens every night to the singer in a rock-and-roll band. You'd generally be mistaken. But not that night. That night it actually was happening.

Mariana had one of those lower-back tattoos. I had never met a girl with a tattoo like that. We rolled around on her bed till the sun came up, and I have to say it was all very nice. Yes, it was.

Then we talked about music. Mariana offered to sing her favorite song for me.

"Do you know it?" she asked, and sang softly into my ear.

Oh, no. I did know that song. "More Than Words," the ballad by those dudes with the really long hair—Extreme. I hated that song. I remember the video that went with it—I hated that, too. Yet there I lay with a stupid smile on my face while she sang for me. This was my punishment. Or at least the beginning of it.

I grabbed a taxi back to my hotel and crept into bed. It was eight in the morning. I was exhausted, but I lay there awake for an hour, staring at the ceiling, thinking.

I am not a good person. I am a bad person.

I thought about my wife and my little baby boy, asleep in New York City while I was getting it on with a hot Spanish flight attendant who liked Extreme.

Here's the thing about a little fling on the road, which is an occupational hazard for a singer in a rock-and-roll band: It is overrated. You expend a lot of energy on it, and sure, it's exciting and it's fun for a little while. But then it's not fun. You have to pay for the good times. When the fun was over, I would be visited by low self-esteem, crushing guilt, and doubts about what kind of person I really was. I was now a cheat and a liar. Okay, maybe I hadn't told any lies just yet. But I wouldn't be talking about my night in Majorca when I got home.

Couldn't I just be a better person? Couldn't I just immediately jump in a taxi after the gig, and hurry back to my hotel room to watch television? That's what I should have done. But I didn't always have that kind of discipline.

My mind didn't always listen to reason. It actually *urged* me to do the wrong thing. To make questionable decisions. That was how I came to be there. Tipsy, up onstage, with a pretty Spanish girl smiling at me all show long. An hour and a half of her making eyes at me. And then suddenly she was hanging around after the show, wondering where I was headed. And frankly, it had been awhile. And I went wherever she wanted me to go. I went with the flow of the evening.

Cheating on someone can sure make you feel horrible. Especially if you've hardly slept, and you have a headache, and you're riding in a stinky van, wondering what you're doing with your life. It almost makes you feel like crying. I once brought this up with my analyst.

"Everyone does it," he said. "If it makes you feel guilty, and you can't deal with that, then don't do it." He was pretty smart, my shrink.

It did make me feel guilty. I would spend the whole next day thinking that I was not a good person and all wasn't right in my world. But those feelings would likely pass in a couple of days. It was like some strange miracle. I'd find a little place in a corner of my head and I'd stow them there. And then I'd be back to my regular old self. Pretty much.

We moved on to Barcelona and Madrid, where we were sharing the bill with Stereolab, Scott 4, and Gorky's Zygotic Mynci. Stereolab was one of the best live bands in the world, one of those bands that comes along once in a while and changes the whole music scene. They opened people's ears to forms of music that had previously been discarded as kitsch. They were derivative on the one hand, but also startlingly original.

We were told that we were the co-headliner with Stereolab, but really there is no such thing. If you play last, you are the headliner; if you play second to last, you are not. They cut you off after forty-five minutes and your fans yell at you for playing a short set. I could have been upset about the short set, but I didn't really give a shit. It was nice to be finished early for a change.

Exit Justin

On November 15, 1999, at the Troubadour in Los Angeles—the final show of our West Coast tour—Justin sold his Gallien-Krueger bass amp to Steve LaFolette, the bassist in Beulah, for $150.

Justin never said that he was leaving the band, but the signals were there. He had sold his guitars, his espresso maker, and his favorite chair. He had moved out of his apartment and into the Cosmopolitan Hotel on Chambers Street. He was spending more time in New Zealand with his formerly estranged wife. Lisa and Justin had been separated for two years, but now they were an item again, and were expecting a baby.

Our November tour of the States had done well. We were now at the point where many more people attended our live shows than actually bought our newest records. Lots of people get to that point—Nick Cave, Sonic Youth, the Rolling Stones. It means people want to see you live. It also means that you have made a lot of records, and the best one isn't necessarily the latest. If people wanted to buy a Luna record in 1999, they had five to choose from, and the word on the street was that *Penthouse* was the one to get.

Our live audience was holding steady. We continued to pack them in all across the country, but we weren't about to make the jump from large clubs to small theaters, which is what bands eventually try to do. Still, we were selling out the clubs, and staying in decent hotels most of the time. Life on the road was almost comfortable.

Justin, however, was fed up.

Sometimes we would stay at a motel a few miles outside of town, to save money. Justin would grumble about that.

"Nice one, Evan. Out by the motorway! Put that one on the list!"

The list Justin mentioned didn't really exist. It was a mental list of hotels that we would never stay at again. Like the hotel in Seattle, where there was blood on the bathroom floor in my room. Or the Hotel Sol Playa.

The idea was to give the list to our travel agent, who would then make sure that we never wound up at these places again. But the list was virtual. It was never compiled, never given to the travel agent or our manager. The Days Inn in Cambridge, Massachusetts, was on that list, but we stayed there at least once each year. It was on the list but wasn't as bad as the Susse Chalet, out on the Concord Turnpike.

Justin was tired of being in a rock band. His mind was elsewhere, and who could blame him? It's easier to leave if you complain all the time about how awful things are. You make the situation untenable in your mind. Then it's obvious that you have to get out of it.

He was tired of treading water. He was bored with playing the Fillmore in San Francisco and Irving Plaza in New York City.

"I've already done that," he said. "Things should be building. We should be playing bigger places. We should be taking the next step."

After we had finished recording *The Days of Our Nights,* Justin had taken Lee aside for a talk. Justin was considering an ultimatum of sorts—he wouldn't make another Luna album with Sean. He liked Sean personally, but they clashed frequently in the studio.

Justin liked to do things and do them quickly. He was tired of Sean's songs always taking up far more studio time than his songs or mine. He called Sean the squeaky wheel.

Justin never mentioned the proposed ultimatum to me. His final show— on December 13, 1999, at the Higher Ground in Burlington, Vermont—was a whimper. Vermont is Phish country, the land of Hacky Sacks and Frisbee and Tevas. We played to a small crowd of jam-band fans.

We drove to Burlington in two vehicles. Lee and I rode in the van, and we got good and lost on the way. Evan and Sean and Justin rented a car and drove up one day early so they could hit the slopes—Evan and Justin were snowboarders, while Sean was an excellent skier.

Justin's final act, the morning after the show, was to board a plane to New Zealand inadvertently carrying the keys to the rental car in his pocket. Lee and I were halfway to New York by the time this was discovered, but Evan and Sean had to spend half a day waiting for a locksmith.

Justin was gone. He was going to have a normal life, get a job, have kids, and buy a house, instead of struggling to make a living as an almost rock star in New York City. He didn't come right out and quit the band, but then he always had a hard time telling people things that they didn't want to hear. Anyway, he didn't really have to announce that he was quitting—he was now living twelve thousand miles away.

Maybe Justin was the smart one. We had been dropped by our publisher, lost our major-label deal with Elektra, and been let go by our accountant. The music headlines were dominated by Britney Spears and the Backstreet Boys and Ricky Martin and J. Lo. You started to hear that rock was dead again. Rock bands were being dropped left and right, and the A&R people were frightened for their jobs.

I thought hard about whether I wanted to keep Luna going without Justin. Justin had been there since the beginning—for eight years—and I wasn't sure if I could do it without him. It was Justin who functioned as the bandleader during rehearsals, with suggestions on how to translate our recordings to the stage. Justin supervised the sale and production of our T-shirts. He created our Web site, www.fuzzywuzzy.com. He wrote the set lists each night and supervised the packing of the van at the end of the night and did a lot of the driving. Justin got things done in a timely fashion. He didn't get into pointless arguments or complain that he looked weird in photographs or fret that his home demos had a certain special quality that the band hadn't been able to capture. I was going to miss him.

But we had just signed the new contract with Jericho Records, who seemed excited about the band and were working hard on *The Days of Our Nights*. They had hired independent radio promoters and were anxious for us to get back out there and tour some more. I figured we should at least finish out the cycle of touring for *The Days of Our Nights*. And then maybe I would leave Luna, too.

In January 2000 we held auditions for a temporary replacement bassist. One candidate, Joel, lived in Lee's building. His bass chops were undeniable. More than that, he was Justin's size and build, and also shaved his head. We could take him on tour, and our fans wouldn't know the difference. We dubbed him Bizarro Justin for the *Seinfeld* episode where the cast meets their alter egos: Feldman (Bizarro Kramer), Gene (Bizarro George), and Kevin (Bizarro Jerry).

Bizarro Justin was a solid candidate. Except that he showed up with a brand-new G&L bass, in a blueburst finish that allowed the fancy maple to show through. That was a problem. You might think it petty to reject someone just because you don't like the color of his guitar. But these small details are revealing. The blueburst bass looked like something you would see on the Jay Leno show. The blueburst bass was a slap in the face.

The job went to Matt Quigley, formerly of Skunk and Vaganza. Quigley played three shows with us, and he was a lot of fun, but after those three shows we decided he wasn't the right bassist for Luna. Not because his favorite band was Cheap Trick. Lots of people love Cheap Trick. Not because he was an old friend of Billy Corgan's and Courtney Love's. Perhaps it was the pleated khakis that he wore onstage at our show in Park City, Utah. Months after the fact, Sean was still talking about those pants.

"He wore pleated khakis!"

Quigley was talkative and smart. He summarized my own situation after a sold-out show in Dallas.

"Out here, you're a rock star. But when you go home to your wife, you're nothing."

It was my job to fire Quigley, and I didn't enjoy it, because I was genuinely fond of him. Still, it had to be done. I called him at home.

The Best Visible
Panty Line in Rock

In February we held another round of auditions. Bizarro Justin came back in. We asked Evan if he was interested. Evan knew all the songs, and he used to play bass with Die Monster Die. He said he would rather stick with the job he already had—tour manager and sound engineer. The tour manager may not get to prance about onstage with the band, but he goes home with a lot more money.

"What about that girl that Lawrence mentioned," said Lee, "the one who played bass in Ben Lee's band?"

Britta Phillips drove all the way from Pennsylvania to audition for Luna. She walked into our rented rehearsal room wearing corduroy jeans, her hair cut in a bob. Her bass was a fiesta red Fender Precision, a classic '70s reissue. She played the songs well and she was cute and personable. She seemed like our kind of person. She wasn't a trained professional who could play any musical style under the sun—musicians like that are easy enough to find—but she played the songs well and understood what we were about.

We had one round of callbacks at Context Studios in the East Village. Lee, Sean, and I stood on Avenue A after the auditions and held an impromptu meeting to pick the new bassist. Lee was sure that we should hire Britta. I was leaning that way, too. Sean was on the fence.

"I don't know."

"Well, who do you think we should choose?"

"I don't know."

That was as close to a unanimous decision as we were going to get.

"Listen," I said. "No hanky-panky. If anyone gets involved with her, they're out of the band."

I think I was joking. Perhaps I was half joking. Perhaps I was dead serious. Perhaps it was a joke with a serious underlying message.

This conversation on Avenue A was repeated to me two years later by Pete Kember, who lives in Rugby, England.

"I heard you had a meeting after the audition and said no one was to get involved with Britta, or they'd be out of the band."

He heard that from a friend in Los Angeles. It really is a global village of gossip. It was just Lee and Sean and me standing there, but the conversation traveled from the East Village to Los Angeles and then to Rugby. When you start behaving badly, then people will talk about you.

Britta's first appearance with Luna was our very first network-television appearance after eight years together—*Later with Cynthia Garrett.* Garrett was a former VH1 VJ. We flew out to Los Angeles to tape the show, whose studio was right next door to the Jay Leno show. Our audience was comprised of people who couldn't get tickets for *Leno.*

We played two songs and did an awkward interview. It's hard being interviewed on TV. You don't want to be boring. You want to be charming and funny, but it's hard to be charming when you're nervous. I thought that they might give us some preparatory notes, maybe tell us what kind of questions Cynthia was going to ask. They did not.

"How do you guys keep going?" she asked.

I didn't have an answer for that. It sounded like an insult. Why does Bo Diddley keep going? Why does Jonathan Richman keep going? Wasn't she really asking, "Why don't you just throw in the towel, you pathetic losers? You've never had a gold record—why don't you get a real job?"

I wanted to ask her how a VH1 VJ gets to host her own late-night network-TV show.

After the taping, we went to make a short film, an *art film,* to be directed by Sean's old friend Matthew Buzzell. He wanted to interview me for the film, but first he wanted me to get loaded, so my tongue would loosen. We went to Musso and Frank's for steak and martinis.

"Get the house martini," said Matthew. "It's made with Gilbey's vodka, but it's perfect."

After a couple of those martinis, I was tipsy, but not drunk enough for Matthew's liking. He took us over to the Viper Room, where his friend Linda was the manager. It's a silly place. The first time I was there, Wilt Chamberlain was exiting the club just as we were entering, stooping so as not to bump his head in the narrow corridor.

We arrived back at the Hollywood Roosevelt around midnight and got down to the business of making the film—*Psychobabble.* There was no plot and no script. Matthew made it up as he went along. The premise was that Sean would writhe half naked on the bathroom floor, while I stared into a mirror giving drunken answers to Matthew's personal questions.

Matthew had one other suggestion.

"How about if you make out with Britta, or let her walk on your back?" he asked. "And I'll film it."

I didn't think that was such a good idea. Not filming it, anyway.

Britta's first real show with the band was on March 23, 2000, at Axis in Boston. She was perfect, and the Luna fans seemed to think so, too.

The next day we drove to Amherst College and played to a small but appreciative crowd, except for the two guys standing in front of me the whole time performing magic tricks for each other. Students are weird. Why don't they stay in their dorm room if they want to do magic tricks? Or do a magic show and put up flyers announcing it?

After Luna, it was karaoke in the student cafeteria. Seven girls got onstage and performed "Holiday" by Madonna. Maybe they were majoring in Madonna studies. It was a legitimate field a few years ago, but it has fallen from favor lately. You studied gender and empowerment, asking, What does it mean to be like a virgin, and yet also a material girl, living in the material world?

Our show at the Black Cat in D.C. got a good review in the *Washington Post* the next morning. They noted the "beguiling Britta Phillips" on bass. I liked that they called her beguiling. It made me feel proud.

From D.C. we flew to Seattle, where we stayed at the Travelodge by the Space Needle for the hundredth time in our lives. On our day off I saw *Erin Brockovich.* It made me sad. I was feeling a little lonely and fragile and I missed Jack, who was now eight months old.

Calvin Johnson drove up from Olympia to see us at the Showbox. Since he was attending a rock show, he wore a pair of industrial earmuff-style hearing protectors, like the guys you see at the airport. I invited him to sing "Indian Summer" but he said he'd rather just sing the "baa baa" part of "Dear Diary."

Canadian customs and immigration officials gave us a good going-over on our way to Vancouver, keeping us at the border for two hours. They acted real friendly while they searched the van for drugs and counted all our T-shirts.

They must have thought we were stupid. Why would we bring drugs into Canada? Canada is where drugs come *from*. It is a source nation for cannabis. The moment we arrived at the famous Starfish Room in Vancouver, a club staffer gave us some weed, and later a fan donated some brownies loaded with magic mushrooms.

I sat in my room at the Chateau Granville and wrote up the set lists. I had promised Britta that I would deliver one to her, because she liked to go over the songs before we got onstage. I knocked on her door, a little nervous, I confess, and she opened it all covered in sweat because she was working out. I handed her the set list. Then I went back to my room and thought about how sexy Britta looked in her workout clothes, her face bright red and shiny with perspiration.

April Fool's Day found us in San Francisco for two beautiful days and two nights at the Fillmore. Sean received disturbing news from home that day. There had been a fire in his apartment building at 78 Second Avenue, causing serious smoke damage. Sean's roommates were out on their asses and said that they might not be able to move back in. It being April 1, Sean was suspicious. Maybe someone was playing a trick on him.

No such luck—Sean was now looking for somewhere to live.

Saturday night we were two minutes into our first song, "Bewitched," when the power went out in the Fillmore, and on that whole San Francisco block. We waited in darkness for an hour. A free round of drinks was given to the audience. Somebody's friends had taken over the green room and there was nowhere for Lee and me to sit, which pissed us off. The power finally came back on, and we picked up right where we left off, going into Sean's awesome guitar solo in "Bewitched."

That night we broke out "Bonnie and Clyde," having practiced it each day at sound check, with Britta singing the Brigitte Bardot to my Serge Gainsbourg. It sounded great.

Howard Thompson was at the show with a friend, and he quietly told me that Britta had "the best visible panty line in rock." He was not wrong. I felt proud again—proud of her VPL. Most women are under the impression that the visible panty line is something to avoid. Not so.

After our Sunday night show, we went out drinking with Howard and his friend and Graham Poor, who now lived in San Francisco. We wound up at a club named Sixteen, which was not unlike the Friday evening scene at Don Hill's in New York, with the glam music, men dressed as women, go-go dancers kissing each other on the bar, and so on.

Howard and his pal had dropped acid and decided to leave. I bid them a good night, and hung out with Graham, who had landed himself a job as a computer programmer in the new Market Street. Graham and I saw each other once every year or so. Things had been strained between us in our early twenties, as he used to insist that I was going to burn in hell for eternity unless I accepted Christ as my savior, but he soon mellowed, even as he remained a Christian himself. Graham had now started his own company, and wrote programs for a new PDA for Motorola. He was doing well. In fact, he was a millionaire—on paper. Stock options. In 1999 and early 2000, Bay Area tech companies had thrived. But the high-tech bubble had burst in a major way just a month before I saw Graham. He remained optimistic. Little did I know that the tech stock collapse was soon to have a direct effect on Luna.

I got tired of the drag queens and the AC/DC, and took a cab back to the Phoenix, but my feet didn't take me straight to my hotel room. They took me to the New Century, a strip club just up the block, where I found Howard and his friend tripping their brains out, watching the dancing girls. I looked into Howard's eyes and told him, "I'm not here."

The Golden Buff Lodge

That's a sexy motel name," I said, as I pulled the van into the parking lot of the Golden Buff Lodge in Boulder, Colorado. Shit, what was that scraping sound? I scraped the roof on the overhang. I climbed up to take a look and found long, deep scratches in the roof. I didn't think the guys at Hertz were going to check up there, and I certainly wouldn't mention it when we returned the van.

Hanging out once more in the spacious green room directly under the stage at the Fox Theatre, we reenacted the scene where Stanley embarrassed Sean in front of the cute cellist that he was trying to impress, and Sean called him a fucking asshole right before we went onstage.

Twenty or thirty people came backstage after the show, brought there by Gerrity, the promo guy. Gerrity was an old pro, fifty-ish, roly-poly with a red beard. Our record company had hired him to travel around with us, vibe up the radio stations, and make sure our record was stocked properly and that the local record stores had all the posters they needed. Sometimes you find yourself stuck in the dressing room after the show, talking to people you'd rather not talk to, answering a lot of questions, but you can't escape because you're waiting for the T-shirts to be counted and the equipment to be packed and the bill to be settled. That's why the big rock acts have two separate green rooms—one strictly for the band, the other for meeting and greeting radio and retail people and fans and all that.

There was a rumor going around that Luna was playing a secret unannounced show at a bar around the corner. Sean decided to go check it out, to see if there was any truth to the rumor.

The next morning he was sporting a new T-shirt. It said BOTTOM. Bottom was an all-girl metal band, and they were the ones playing at the bar. Sean said they were pretty damn good.

After our show in Chicago, we rushed back to our room at the Days Inn on Diversey to watch ourselves on the Cynthia Garrett show. It didn't suck as much as I thought it had. They showed little snippets from old Luna videos, so you got to see some different hairstyles, like Sean with a ponytail and Justin before he started shaving his head.

Sean wore a suit. I wore a bowling shirt. Cynthia Garrett was perfectly nice—I don't know why I thought she was insulting us. Sean and I were funny. Charming, even. We played off each other, just like we did onstage. I pulled out a kazoo. Cynthia said that we could take our comedy act on the road if the music thing didn't work out. She noted that we had made five albums, which is a lot in this day and age.

"What advice would you give to young people about having career longevity?"

"Go to law school," I said.

N ext up was a handful of shows opening for a band called Guster, in Columbus, Detroit, Providence, and Philadephia.

We had never heard of them, but apparently Guster was very popular, and the label really wanted us to do it. They were described to us as a jam band. A few years back, they would definitely have been on Sean's list of bands that he wouldn't open for. But lately we had discussed the possibility of doing some shows with jam bands. Some of our fans liked Phish—Renée thought it might be good for us to push the envelope and play to some of those Phish-heads.

Bob Lawton was resistant to the idea.

"You guys play actual songs," he said. "They won't like it."

We were not really a jam band. What might look like improvisation was always pretty well arranged beforehand.

I got onstage in Columbus and looked out at the crowd. Jesus Christ! Guster had a lot of fans. And the average age of a Guster fan was fourteen, a very straight-looking fourteen—these were preppy, clean-cut kids. These kids didn't like Luna so much. They stared at us, bored, waiting for their Guster. Since they were bored, I was bored right back. Whatever the audience gives you, that's what you give them. Fuck trying to win them over. These kids were evil.

When Guster came on, the crowd screamed like teenage girls watching the Beatles. If the singer from Guster had pooped onstage, they would have squealed in delight. One of the teenage fans stopped by our dressing room. All sweet-sixteen, with long, perfect hair, dressed in American Eagle. She looked at Britta's arms.

"You must work out," she said.

We had an afternoon off in Pittsburgh, where the good people at the Andy Warhol Museum gave us a private tour. We saw a tremendous show of Warhol's early drawings, some of them quite sexual in nature, some of them drawings of shoes.

And we looked at his time capsules, and inspected some lyric and music sheets from the early days of the Velvet Underground—music notated by John Cale himself. You needed the sheet music to establish your copyrights back then. Not anymore. I bought a poster at the museum store, comprised of a series of Billy Name's photographs of people exiting the bathroom at the Factory: Joe Dallesandro, Brigid Berlin, Viva, Ingrid Superstar, Paul Morrissey, and Warhol himself. They all needed to use the bathroom.

I showed my poster to Lee, and he bought one, too. He was going to hang it in his bathroom.

"Why must you parrot me?" I asked him.

"Why must you parrot me?" he said.

I stopped by the hotel fitness center to do some push-ups and curls and whatnot. My doctor told me that I needed to put on some weight, and apparently lifting weights is one way to do it. There I was, lifting those ten-pound dumbbells, and in walked rock star Anthony Kiedis, of Red Hot Chili Peppers fame, with his girlfriend in tow. He had a mohawk, and was much shorter than I imagined he would be. My impression had always been that he was a big, hulking guy, totally ripped. Ripped, yes, but compact.

I moved on to crunches and lateral pulldowns. Anthony worked out on the rowing machine and his girlfriend rode the stationary bike. Just the three of us. It was quiet, till Anthony spoke.

"Baby? Do you think we should get some of these exercise machines for the guest house?"

"I wanted to put a sewing machine in the guest house, honey."

"I think some exercise machines would be cool, baby."

"Whatever you say, honey."

This was followed by a few minutes of silence.

"Why would you say that, baby?"

"Hmmm?"

"Why would you say '*Whatever you say*'? I always listen to you. I listen to what you have to say."

We moved on to Fletcher's in Baltimore—our second Baltimore gig in five months. That was crazy. Why were we back in Baltimore? Just trying to fill a Friday night, I suppose. We had some Polish fans in the crowd that night, a couple of guys in their forties.

"Luna is number one in Poland!" they shouted.

I doubted that very much, but I dedicated a song to Rosa Luxemburg.

"This is for Rosa Luxemburg!"

"She's not Polish—she's Russian!" they said.

"Really? That's news to me." I knew a little about Rosa Luxemburg.

"Play the song!" someone else yelled.

A fan sent an e-mail to our Web site the next day, confirming that Rosa Luxemburg was indeed born in Poland. Perhaps they really meant, "She's not Polish—she's a commie and a Jew!" I don't know. But there was another e-mail, far more important, from Renée. Our record company was filing for bankruptcy.

"The difference between men and boys," business mogul Leonard Stern once said, "is the size of their toys." Stern made his money in pet supplies and real estate. His "toys" were weekly alternative magazines like the *Village Voice* and *LA Weekly*.

Our record company was also a toy, owned by one Rick Adams, a Fortune 400 guy who had founded a company named UUNET. UUNET was the biggest Internet service provider (ISP) on the planet. In 1996, his company was acquired by MCI Worldcom for $700 million.

Rick took some of that money and bought a famous recording studio—Ocean Way, where we almost mixed some of *Pup Tent*. He renamed the studio Cello Recording. In addition to the studio, he created Jericho Records. We never met Rick Adams, though he did let us know that our Web site sucked, and he paid someone to fix it for us.

Mr. Adams wasn't involved in the running of the record company—he hired a few experienced record company people for that, and they were good at their jobs. They had a five-year plan—the company would lose money at first, but they hoped to see profits eventually.

The tech stock collapse changed everything. Rick Adams didn't want this expensive toy anymore. He pulled the plug on Jericho. That's how a company owned by a billionaire comes to file for Chapter 11. He wasn't personally bankrupt. But a company can be bankrupt, even while its owners are rich. Nobody likes to lose money.

Perhaps there's a lesson here—when someone offers you money, examine where the money is coming from. Don't just jump right into bed with some guy who made a fortune on the Internet (unless he's offering a *lot* of money).

After receiving the bad news, I called Howard Thompson to ask for his advice.

"You're out of your contract? Record your live album!"

Howard was right. If you record a live album while you're under contract to a label, then they own those live recordings. The time to do a live album is when you've been dropped, right before you sign a new deal. That's the only time you own your own recordings.

So, we resolved to record a live album. We also decided to downsize. Since we no longer had a label, and most of our income was derived from playing live, we thought we would move forward without management and save a bundle on management commissions. After seven years working together, we said goodbye to Renée.

Our label was going under, but we still had two more shows with Guster. We drove up to Providence, seven hours in the pouring rain.

I had become acutely aware of where I was sitting in the van. I used to think of it as sitting in the front row or the back row, on the left or the right. But lately I was thinking of it as being in front of Britta, or next to Britta, or, on that drive to Providence, behind Britta. There I was, trying to be cool. I felt like I had fallen under a spell, and it had to stop. I took to chanting silently inside my head on these long rides. *No, no, no. No, no, no. Yes.*

You can't just put a beautiful woman in a van full of men and think that there will be no effect. Any scientist or psychologist will tell you as much.

Take three or four male apes, and put them in a cage—or a Ford Econoline van, which is a cage on wheels. Observe their behavior. Now put a desirable female ape in the cage and observe some more.

The Guster tour ended at the Electric Factory in Philadelphia. We last played the Electric Factory in 1996, opening for Lou Reed on his Hooky Wooky Tour. He called it the Hooky Wooky tour because he had a song called "Hooky Wooky," which was his own slang term for sex. At least I think so. I was backstage with Lou, waiting to use the men's room, and he sarcastically said, "This is so glamorous, huh?" It *was* glamorous for me—I was backstage talking to Lou Reed. And the Electric Factory was pretty glamorous compared with some of the places Luna had played, like the Jewish Mother in Norfolk, Virginia, or Sudsy's in Cincinnati.

Tonight we were playing to two thousand Guster fans. It was like a dream. We were up on the big stage performing to a big crowd, but the people could have cared less about us. They were waiting for Guster. It was like we were not even there. I decided to test this theory. After our second song, I made an announcement through my microphone.

"I wish I were dead."

Silence. Or rather, continued chatter. No change. No one heard, or no one cared, except for the guys in Guster, who were standing at the side of the stage. They thought it was funny.

N ext we flew to New Orleans, where the Jazz and Heritage Festival was starting up. They call it Jazz Fest but they have a loose definition of jazz, loose enough to let Luna in.

Grasshopper showed up at the Howlin' Wolf. He was there for the jazz. He said he was mugged at gunpoint two days ago, standing outside one of the clubs talking to one of the guys in Counting Crows. Maybe he'd be more careful about who he talked to next time. Another cool guy showed up at the Howlin' Wolf—riding into the club on an old bicycle with big handlebars and a banana seat. He said he could get us anything we wanted. We ordered eight hits of ecstasy, and all four of us dropped it after the show.

We tried going out on the town on the ecstasy, hanging out at a cool bar with our friend Wade. But we soon started acting a little strange, rolling our eyes and taking deep breaths.

"What are you guys on?" asked Wade.

We moved the party back to my spacious hotel room. I was the DJ. First up on my portable speakers was "Girl," a pretty little waltz by Papas Fritas. It calmed me right down, except that I looked at Britta and she looked at me and something passed between us.

Girl, don't be afraid
Say what you wanted to say
Boy, stay
Don't be afraid
Don't walk away from a girl in love

We stayed up all night. Each of us threw up at least once. Lee excused himself at around 3:00 A.M. Sean followed at around four. It was just Britta and me, listening to music. I wanted to kiss her, but I knew that wouldn't be appropriate. Come to think of it, it wasn't appropriate for me to be alone with her in my hotel room.

We flew home the next day, and had a connecting flight in Atlanta. Britta's boyfriend lived in Atlanta, and he came to visit her during the hour we had to change planes. The Atlanta airport had a filthy little room for smokers. I sat there and smoked my cigarette and stared at the other smokers through a thick cloud. This was the room from hell. Hell is other smokers and airports. Especially when you are only half alive from staying up all night.

The Dorm Room Jukebox

The act of sex may be nothing, but when you reach my age you learn that
at any time it may prove to be everything.

                                                    —*Graham Greene*

M y life unraveled in the summer of 2001. I no longer lived on
Bleecker Street with Claudia and Jack. I was splitting time between
my parents' loft apartment on Twenty-first Street—they were away for the
summer—and my own tiny one-hundred-square-foot studio at 373 Broadway, where I kept my recording equipment and spare guitars. I bought a
futon so I could sleep there, too, if I had to. A small window opened onto an
air shaft and a brick wall two feet away. The toilet was down the hall, but
the paint-splattered sink in my room, which ran only cold water, was perfect for peeing late at night.

M y affair with Britta began at the University of Massachusetts at
Amherst. Like all college shows, this one was poorly organized. Bands
played in the courtyard all afternoon, each of them playing a little longer
than they should have. By the time they got to the headlining act—Luna—
there were only fifteen minutes till curfew. We didn't much care—they still
had to pay us.

After the show we were invited to a dorm room party. A Napster party.
They weren't playing records or compact discs. Instead, they had a high-speed
cable connection, provided free by the university, and they had compiled a
big long playlist on Napster. This was my first exposure to the world of file
sharing, to the dorm room jukebox that would shake the music business to its

core. A funny thing happened in 2001. After years of going up and up and up, record sales dropped 2.5 percent. The following year they dropped 6.8 percent, and they have continued to drop ever since, in ever larger increments.

When I was in college I spent my own money on LPs. That's what the record business was built on—affluent kids, spending their weekly allowances on vinyl and compact discs. But change was afoot. Now students could find any song they wanted on the Internet. What kind of idiot would go out and buy records now? Well, maybe if people knew that vinyl records are vastly superior in sound quality to those MP3s that they play on their computers, they might think about it. But college students don't seem too bothered about high fidelity.

We had been invited to the dorm room party by a pretty blond film student who had been dancing wildly in front of me throughout our fifteen-minute set.

"You can tell how someone is in bed," said Lee, "from how they dance."

She was pretty, but I wasn't interested. I had stopped noticing the girls in the audience at Luna shows, consumed by my crush on the beautiful girl onstage, directly to my right, a crush that wouldn't go away. I knew I should try to control it. But I couldn't control it. I thought about Britta all the time. Especially on long van rides. Some days I sat behind Britta. Some days I sat next to her. Some days I drove the van. It didn't matter. I was riding in a van with Britta. I was singing a song with Britta. I was intoxicated.

I became more intoxicated at the dorm room party after drinking a couple of glasses of student-made punch. We were at the end of a short run of dates, so the party was not unlike one of those end-of-the-year office parties, the kind where simmering tensions boil over and turn into inappropriate behavior.

It was all so predictable.

It didn't help that we sang "Bonnie and Clyde" together—this long, sexy Serge Gainsbourg song, sung in French, about a doomed couple. The song ends with Bonnie and Clyde being mowed down in a hail of bullets, and then descending into hell.

"You should look at each other when you sing that song," Renée told me. I knew I couldn't do that. I would have forgotten the words. And my feelings would have shown in my face. No, I was careful not to look at Britta onstage.

After half an hour at the dorm room party, we drove the van over to the Campus Center Hotel. The Campus Center at U. Mass, designed by Marcel Breuer, is made of cinder block. But it is Bauhaus cinder block. The rooms are elegant and austere.

I deliberately left my pack of cigarettes in the van that night, which gave me an excuse to knock on Britta's door. I could have just lied about not having a cigarette. But I was going to play the charade properly. I wasn't thinking straight.

I knocked on Britta's door and she gave me a cigarette and a kiss.

I shouldn't have done that. It led to a world of hurt. And yet I did it, so perhaps it's wrong to say I shouldn't have. Why, then, did my feet lead me there to that spot in front of her door? Was I just immoral and selfish? Perhaps.

By the next day we were coconspirators. We rode home in the van that Sunday afternoon with a secret. The morning started off well. I was in a semipleasant daze from the night before. But as the van rattled down the FDR Drive I started to panic.

I was shaking as I approached the door of my building on Bleecker Street, wondering how I could possibly walk into my apartment and not have the whole thing written all over my face. But I opened the door, was greeted by my wife and son and dog, and life went on. Only something had changed.

Britta called me on Monday. She had shared a cab uptown with Lee after our return to New York, and she was sure that he knew something. His behavior toward her had changed, she said. Previously he had been friendly and solicitous. Now he seemed distant and annoyed. This was her intuition. I told her she was imagining things.

We are all capable of grand deceptions. Or at least I am. It's difficult at first, terrifying even, but you get used to it. Sort of. Britta and I carried on an affair for months. In Pittsburgh or Nashville—or anywhere—we would rush to our hotel rooms to meet in secret. It was exhilarating. It was also awful. It was not fun to be a terrible liar. I was unhappy. The secrets were killing me. Secrets make you grumpy and distant, because there are secret things on your mind and you stare into space and someone says, "A penny for your thoughts," but you can't speak your thoughts, so you say nothing.

I was lying to everyone around me, to my wife, friends, family, and booking agent.

Interviewers asked, "Has the dynamic changed with a woman in the band?"

Umm, yes.

Sean and Lee called a meeting ostensibly to discuss the making of our next record. Britta wasn't invited, as she wasn't a full member of the band—she didn't have a vote. We rarely had band meetings (though this was something the Weeds of Eden, Sean's side project, did all the time). We met at Sean's apartment on Avenue A, and Lee spoke first.

He and Sean were aware that something was going on between Britta and myself. They were concerned. Sean was mostly bothered by having to pretend that he didn't know anything.

Fair enough. I'm sure that wasn't pleasant for either of them, being lied to, sitting next to me in the van and pretending not to know about it.

Lee was more concerned that all of this would blow up in our faces.

What would you do, he asked, if you had a friend who was engaging in self-destructive behavior, like he had a drug problem? You would intervene. You would feel obligated to point out that this could only end badly.

And I was engaged in dangerous and self-destructive behavior. More important, perhaps, it was behavior that could be destructive to the band. If word got out, said Lee, our whole lives as Luna would end. It would be over.

Of course, I knew this already. But somehow I had compartmentalized that knowledge. I was able to pretend that no one knew and no one ever would. This was part of my grand deception. As Lee and Sean pointed out, I was fooling myself. I was also putting them in the awkward position of having to keep my secret. They had to prevaricate any time anyone asked, "What's the deal with Britta?" or, "What's it like having a girl in the band?"

I was humble and contrite at the meeting that afternoon. They were quite right—it is not nice to make other people keep your secrets. It wasn't nice of me to turn my bandmates into liars, brothers in deception.

"You're right," I said. "It's dangerous. It has to end."

But later that afternoon I became incensed. How dare they compare me to a drug addict? How dare they tell me who to sleep with? I didn't tell them who to sleep with. I'd kept secrets for Sean and Lee over the years—yes, I had. We had an official band policy—what happens on the road is locked in the vault (the idea of the vault was taken from a *Seinfeld* episode).

That's how it was supposed to be. The reality was different, because everyone likes to share a little secret now and then.

The affair continued. I had no intention of leaving Claudia and Jack—the very thought of it struck fear in my heart. And yet I couldn't stop. I've heard preachers say that once you let the devil into your life, it's hard to get him out, and I have found this to be true.

It was hard to travel around the country with the lovely Britta Phillips, getting onstage and singing together and drinking champagne after the shows, and thinking that I was going to just say no. I had all kinds of real feelings for Britta, feelings that were beyond my control.

I promised myself that I would make a move, a decision, do something to fix my life. Soon, I said, soon I will fix things.

The decision was made for me by the maid at the Days Inn in Fredonia, New York.

We recorded our *Romantica* album with Gene Holder (of the dB's) at Jolly Roger in Hoboken, New Jersey. Each morning, we drove out to Jersey in my purple Subaru. Jolly Roger was located on the top floor of a building that was being converted to condos, like many of the buildings in Hoboken were. Some days we had to stop recording vocals while the workmen pounded nails.

Gene Holder was a great guy and the sessions were relaxed. It's fun making a record when there is no label peering over your shoulders, asking you where the hit is. You make it for yourselves, which is how you should make every record. Or not. But that was the only way I knew how.

We had recently signed on with a new manager, David Whitehead, who generously paid our studio bill while he tried to find us a new record deal. The soft-spoken son of a coal miner, David grew up in the Yorkshire town of Rotherham, before moving to London and working at Stiff Records and Rough Trade. David already represented Laurie Anderson and David Byrne. He said he had an interest in career artists with track records, rather than young bands looking to become rock stars.

Beggar's Banquet, which had been our label in Europe, now made us a

With my mother, 1963

Christmas, 1963

*Me, my mother, Louise,
Jonathan, Anthony*

On my scooter, Wellington,
New Zealand

With my sister, Louise, 1970

Sydney, Australia, 1970

1972

*Anthony and I get ready
for school, 1972*

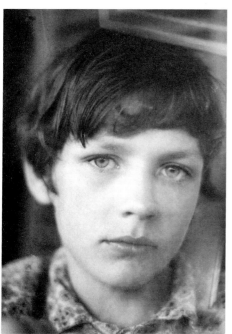

1974

New York City, 1977

With my mother and brother Jonathan, 1978

Speedy & the Castanets

Graduation day, 1985

Galaxie 500 at CBGB

At the Melkweg, Amsterdam

In-store appearance, Amsterdam (Justin in the background)

In the pines, 1990

*Backstage at Town Hall
before Bongwater show*

Claudia at Bleecker Street

Luna promo photo for Bewitched

With Lou Reed and Laurie Anderson after
opening for Lou at the Beacon Theatre (© Ebet Roberts)

Terry at Bleecker Street late one night

Pat and Justin at Pachyderm Studio

On Australian TV, 1997

Luna, 2000

Backstage at Blueberry Hill, St. Louis

At La Zona Rosa, Austin, Texas

CBGB, New Year's Eve, 2001

Backstage, Denver, 2002

Laura, Sean, and Lee in Austin, 2002

With Jack at Rockefeller Center

With Britta, downstairs at the Bowery Ballroom

At Trout Recording, Brooklyn, New York

At the Knave Club, Osaka, Japan

Promo shot for Back Numbers, *2006*

nice offer for North America. We were on the verge of accepting that offer when Jetset Records countered by offering 50 percent more, not just on this record, but on our next one also.

This offer was too good to be true, and ultimately it was, but we went ahead and signed with Jetset. This was the second time we had rejected Beggar's Banquet in favor of a more lucrative deal, and we came to regret the decision both times.

Sean, Britta, and I moved on to Tarbox Road Studios, outside Fredonia, New York, to mix our album with Dave Fridmann. I had worked with Dave in 1992, on some very early Luna demos, and on Mercury Rev's "Car Wash Hair."

We spent ten days mixing at Tarbox. Rather, Dave Fridmann did the work, assisted by Michael Ivins of the Flaming Lips. I spent my time reading, cooking, and watching Fridmann's laser disc collection. I liked the director's cut of *Once Upon a Time in America,* with its great Ennio Morricone score, better than *Silent Running.*

Sean prepared himself to play a very important guitar solo on his song "Black Champagne." He kept putting it off during the sessions in Hoboken, saying he wasn't ready. The solo had to be truly inspired—"like Zeus coming down from the mountain," he said—and for that he needed to be in the right mood.

Zeus never did come down from the mountain for that song, but Sean played a great guitar solo at the end of the title track, "Romantica." He generally delivered his best guitar solos on other people's songs, when there was no self-imposed pressure to do something amazing. He was relaxed for my songs, and was easily able to summon an interesting texture and add a tasteful or dazzling solo.

To each song, Fridmann did something strange and unsettling to our ears, adding layers of distortion to a vocal, or creating feedback loops, or dropping the bass out of the mix when we least expected it. This is why you pay someone to come in and mix your record, someone with fresh ears who hasn't already heard the songs fifty times.

Tarbox Road is in the middle of nowhere—the sticks, the boonies, dullsville. Sean, Britta, and I took turns cooking.

The studio was residential, but there was really only one bedroom upstairs. I booked a room at the Days Inn in town, a ten-minute drive away. Britta came with me. I didn't feel quite comfortable with this arrangement—it was a whole new level of deception. And yet I did it anyway.

On the final day of mixing, I checked out of the hotel—we were scheduled to fly out that evening. When I arrived at the studio at noon that day, there was a phone call waiting for me. It was Claudia, who had just called the hotel. The receptionist had put Claudia's call through to my hotel room, where it was answered by the maid.

"Oh, no," she said, "they just left."

With that utterance, I was cooked.

Claudia ordered me to get my ass on a plane home—immediately.

I felt sick to my stomach. That terrible feeling you get when you've lost something valuable or done something incredibly stupid or bad.

I took that JetBlue plane from Buffalo to JFK, a bundle of nerves, feeling like I was about to walk the plank. Walk the plank I did, through my apartment door into a sea of anger and tears—and questions, questions, questions.

I felt like a criminal.

But as my shrink pointed out, I was not a criminal. I was only a liar and a cheat.

Question: How could I be so stupid as to let myself get caught like that?

Answer: Because I wanted to get caught. I had put myself in an impossible situation. I was miserable. I didn't know how to extricate myself.

Claudia made it easier than it might have been. She gave me two choices, and five days to decide. Either Britta would leave Luna, or I would pack my things and move out.

I was panic stricken. I honestly didn't know what to do.

I called my dad.

"What should I do?"

"You should follow your heart."

"But I don't know what my heart wants."

"You need to figure that out."

Claudia and I had an emergency meeting with our marriage counselor, Ben Marinucci, and his wife, Kay Marinucci (also a therapist—together they ran a weekly group). Ben's office was on Eighty-ninth Street and Lexington Avenue, half a block from my high school, which added to the strangeness of the experience. A friend of mine had lived in this very building. We had both gotten stoned there one afternoon after school.

The two of us sat in the waiting room at 8:00 P.M., waiting for the group session to finish. Once again, I felt like I was about to walk the plank.

Claudia was the one who had been wronged here, and the therapists were generally supportive of her.

"Claudia needs to tell you that it's not acceptable for you to have a girlfriend," said Ben.

Various unpleasant scenarios were discussed.

Maybe Claudia could accompany the band on the road for our next tour (Luna had shows scheduled in Spain the following week—in Granada, Barcelona, Madrid, Zaragoza, and Majorca).

This option did not appeal to either of us.

The only sensible options were the ones that Claudia had laid out—either the band had to find a new bass player, or I had to find somewhere new to live. This was not unreasonable. How could she live otherwise? Could she be expected to sit at home waiting for me while I went on a summer "business trip" to Barcelona and Majorca, with Sean and Lee and Britta?

I hadn't seen Bernie, my shrink, since 1996. I saw him weekly for six months that year, saying that my marriage had lost its passion and that maybe I needed to get out. This was a common complaint, he said, but he knew the cure.

We went through all the usual stuff about my first sexual experiences and my feelings for my mother and what it means to love someone and to be in love, and we talked about how falling in love is easy but staying in love is hard work.

I told him about something that Milan Kundera says, how there are two kinds of women—one that you sleep with, and one that you sleep next to. Bernie liked Kundera's formulation, but he assured me that it was the job of thinking adults to solve that particular puzzle, to fuse the two women into one.

Every week he said that my problems were normal and my marriage could be fixed, and he could tell that I really did love my wife. And then one day, tired of my complaining, he had offered to help me get out of my marriage.

"Yes," he said. "I can see you want to leave. Come back next week and we'll start talking about how I can help you to get out of your marriage."

I walked out of that session and was convinced that he was playing some kind of trick on me.

No, I told myself, I don't want to leave my wife. I love her.

I never went back to Bernie. Not until I was caught in an affair with Britta, some six years later.

Y ou have been running away from this problem for a long time," said Bernie.

"What should I do?"

He couldn't, or wouldn't, tell me. He said I had to figure it out for myself.

"If I knew the answer," he said, "I would tell you. But I don't."

"But I have to decide by Friday whether to ask Britta to leave the band."

"I think maybe you should consult a lawyer before you do something like that."

He had a point. In any other job this would be an obvious case of sexual harassment—you can't have an affair with an employee and then fire her when your wife catches you. But these things happen in rock-and-roll bands. It had never happened in Luna, but it was not to be the last time.

I called Britta.

"I'll leave if you want me to," she said.

I called Sean and told him that Claudia wanted me to find a new bass player for the band.

"Well, Lee and I don't want that," he said.

No surprise there.

The Worst Moment
of My Life

How do we make the important decisions in our lives? I'm not sure when I actually decide to get out of bed in the morning. One second I'm lying there thinking, the next I'm walking to the kitchen to grind the coffee beans.

I was at a crossroads. I had no idea what I would do come Friday. I didn't want to leave Claudia and Jack. But neither did I want to kick Britta out of Luna, and out of my life.

Friday rolled around, and I still hadn't fired Britta. Which meant that I was leaving. I pulled my suitcase down from the closet shelf, stuffed it with summer clothes, grabbed my '58 Les Paul, and walked out the door.

My feet took over. They walked me to the street and out of my marriage. I cabbed it down to my horrid studio at 373 Broadway, where I lay on the floor and cried.

I went out for a tuna melt and a chocolate shake at a greasy diner on Broadway. It was a gorgeous summer day. I managed a few bites of my sandwich, and then walked up Broadway all the way to Fourteenth Street, then east and south to Tompkins Square Park. I had no destination that I was aware of, but at four in the afternoon I found myself wandering aimlessly down Second Avenue, arriving at the basketball courts at Houston Street. I had unconsciously wandered very close to home, if I was still allowed to use that word.

At that moment I looked across Second Avenue and saw our babysitter, Nicoleen, pushing Jack along in his stroller, heading west—home for the day. I froze. I wanted so badly to run across the street to Jack. He was only a couple weeks shy of his second birthday, and was talking now. He didn't know many words yet, but his vocabulary was increasing each day. I wanted to say hello, but I couldn't. He was on his way home, and how could I explain to him that as of noon that day we no longer shared a roof?

There I stood, frozen on Second Avenue, watching my son being wheeled away and feeling as if he no longer belonged to me, as if he was being wheeled out of my life, unable to do anything about it.

This was the worst moment of my life. Of course I know that other people live through much worse. Mine were the problems of a spoiled and self-indulgent singer/songwriter. Still, this was my moment, and it hurt. Never mind that it was self-inflicted.

I gathered myself and walked down Crosby Street, through SoHo, across Canal Street, and back to my studio, where I rolled on the floor and sobbed again. Strange sounds came out of my throat, from deep down inside— guttural, primal noises that I didn't know were in me. But they were there.

Worse, perhaps, was the fact that there really was something I could have done about it. I could have taken the other path, and canceled the dates in Spain. I could have started looking for a new bassist, asking for Lee and Sean's forgiveness and understanding in this, and telling them that this was the only way the band could continue.

I could have embarked on an extensive course of therapy and marriage counseling. Claudia and I could have read books and attended weekly couples' seminars to help us learn where things went wrong. Maybe after a couple of years of this I would be able to rebuild the trust that I had destroyed. I would cast out the bad Dean and work on the kind and obedient Dean. Cast out the liar and the cheat, and become a dutiful husband.

I knew other people who had tried this route. It worked for some of them. Others soon suffered relapses. I also knew, and Claudia did, too, that we were beyond that point. Claudia could be forgiving. But this time I had gone too far.

September 17, 2001

The Brazilian Consulate in New York, closed since September 11, had finally opened for business, and Lee picked up the work visas for our South American tour. Expecting long lines and extratight security, the four of us headed out to JFK a good four hours before departure time, but check-in took a mere ten minutes.

Airports make you alter your behavior. You drink at 11:00 A.M. You buy things you wouldn't normally buy. I bought the latest issue of *Talk* magazine. Apparently Halle Berry was paid a bonus of $500,000 to appear topless in *Swordfish*.

From *Talk* magazine I moved on to *American Pastoral* by Philip Roth, which reads like a great social history of New Jersey in the fifties, sixties, and seventies. The plot concerns a successful Jewish businessman from Newark, whose daughter blows up the local post office to protest the Vietnam War.

What was the world coming to? Terrorist activities were once the provenance of misguided progressives—anarchists opposed to the czar, perhaps, or resistance fighters against a foreign occupation. People convinced that there was no hope, so the only thing left was violent symbolic action. The Weathermen, who aimed to "bring the war home," never hurt anyone except themselves, when they accidentally detonated a bomb in their West Eleventh Street hideout. But the terrorists who took out the World Trade Center were religious fanatics, bent on taking the world backward, not forward.

September 10, 2001, was the only night I ever spent at Britta's apartment on Jane Street in the West Village. The apartment belonged to her roommate and friend Tom Grizzetti. We slept on her European foam sofa bed, which could ingeniously turn first into a single bed, and then into a double.

We woke at eight o'clock on the morning of September 11 and drank coffee in the living room. The living-room windows faced east and south but
the southern exposure was blocked by a taller building across the street.
I was studying the *Times* sports section when something caught my eye.
People were climbing out onto the roof and staring at the downtown sky.

"What are they looking at?" Britta asked.

It was to be a big day. I had my first meeting with a new couples counselor, who was really going to be an "uncoupling" counselor. Claudia and I
knew we had to start talking to each other in a controlled environment, to
figure out what we were going to do about this mess.

I stepped out onto Greenwich Avenue and saw what everyone was staring at. One of the Twin Towers was on fire. The fire department will have
to put that out, I thought to myself. I called Britta to let her know what was
going on. Then I strolled over to Eighth Avenue and caught the L train to
Union Square. The subway riders were abuzz. A plane had crashed into the
World Trade Center.

"That's where I work," said one woman. "That's where I was going
just now."

I didn't have my own place. I had been sleeping in my office, or on my
parents' sofa at their loft apartment on Twenty-first Street, which is where
I was headed. It was there that I watched the towers collapse on television,
along with the rest of the world.

It was not easy to get a cell phone signal, but I managed to get Claudia on
the phone. Our therapy session was canceled.

"Did you call *her*?" she asked.

"What?"

"Did you call her first?"

I walked downtown, across Union Square and down Broadway, against a
growing stream of people coming the other way, some of them dressed in
suits and ties and covered head to toe in gray dust.

I spent the day in my old apartment with Claudia and Jack and Jack's
friends Sam and Eddie and their parents, Ted and Deborah. Claudia was
torn between being glad to see me and being angry with me for not having
been there in the first place.

We tried to figure out what to do. Should I stay the night? It seemed like
the right thing to do. Since the sky was falling, I should be there.

Jack, who had just turned two, was quite unaware of what was going on outside, and we kept him away from the television.

We decided that I would spend the night on the brown leather sofa in the living room. At eleven o'clock I put the sheets on the sofa and lay there staring at the ceiling of the apartment I had lived in for twelve years, thinking, Is this right? I should go. I should stay. I don't belong here.

What was Jack going to think in the morning? It had only been two months, but Jack was already used to the idea that his father didn't live in this apartment. If I came back, even for a night, then how would it look if I left again? How could I explain that Daddy was here today but would be gone tomorrow? He had already asked me about it the week I had left.

"Where's Daddy's toothbrush?" he had asked me, and I had managed to control myself till I walked out the door.

I got up from the couch and told Claudia that I should leave, and she agreed that it was best. And in that instant, our marriage was over for good. While others searched desperately for news of lost husbands and wives, we said goodbye.

D riving into São Paolo from the airport, first you pass the shantytowns, then the high-rise apartments, which stretch as far as the eye can see. New York City feels small by comparison—most of our high-rise buildings are confined to Manhattan. Our hotel in São Paolo had a faded splendor—it must have been beautiful in the 1950s. We each had our own hotel rooms, complete with CNN. We checked in, and I lay down and switched on the news.

George Bush said he was going to smoke Osama bin Laden out. He could run but he couldn't hide.

Five hundred people came to see our first show in São Paolo, which was a nice surprise. The next day, the four of us explored the area around our hotel. I bought a new cigarette lighter and an alarm clock for one dollar each. But I paid far more for the first record by Jorge Ben, *Samba Esquema Novo.* That's the way it is with some classic Brazilian albums. Even in Brazil, they're only available as Japanese imports.

I watched some more CNN in my room. According to a CNN feature, women were oppressed in Afghanistan. Wow! They just discovered this?

It sounded like we were getting ready to bomb them back to the Stone Age. Except the Afghans already lived in the damn Stone Age. I remembered the article Alexander Cockburn wrote long ago in the *Nation*. "If ever a country deserved rape," he wrote, "it is Afghanistan." It looked like they were about to be raped again.

Eight hundred beautiful people came to the second show. We were stunned. I was also stunned by small jolts of electricity from the microphone. They didn't seem to have the grounded three-prong plug there in Brazil, just the two prongs.

Next stop, Belo Horizonte. We ate at a barbecue restaurant before going to some kind of circus festival, where we watched a troupe of jugglers and danced to some bad music in a big tent. I went back to my room and took in some of the American telethon. Will Smith, Mariah Carey, Tom Hanks, and Tom Cruise were on parade. Was that the best they could do? Listening to these celebrities made me embarrassed to be an American. Was this how we were going to communicate with the rest of the world? By trotting out these loopy actors and singers? Next to these idiots, Osama bin Laden looked like a philosopher. Not the kind of philosopher I like, mind you. I'd probably rather hang out with Mariah Carey.

That afternoon I did four straight phone interviews, for our upcoming dates in Argentina and Uruguay. It seemed like all the journalists had been given the same talking points.

"What do you think of the Strokes?"

"Have the Strokes saved rock and roll?"

"Don't you agree that rock and roll was dead, but now it has been saved by the White Stripes and the Hives and the Strokes?"

I loved that first record by the Strokes. But rock and roll is always being saved. Two years earlier it was all Backstreet Boys and 'N Sync and Britney and Eminem, and rock was dead. The A&R people were scared for their jobs, if they still had jobs. The "tweenie" was calling the shots in showbiz.

The death and rebirth of rock music over the last fifty years is cyclical. Rock is periodically pronounced dead by clever rock critics—killed by world music, or by hip-hop, or electronica, or the Backstreet Boys. But if you wait a year, it comes back to life. That enables you to get excited about it all over again, because it's new. Never mind that people have been making garage rock in cities all over the world since about 1966—now the kids think it was invented by the White Stripes and the Hives.

After we talked music, each interviewer asked me about the attack on America. What was my opinion?

I thought back to my days at college in the early 1980s, during the heyday of the cold war. The Soviets were in Afghanistan, and U.S. dollars poured into religious camps in Pakistan, funding Islamic fundamentalists who we hoped would give the Soviets their very own Vietnam War.

Jimmy Carter reintroduced draft registration and boycotted the Olympic Games. Ronald Reagan gave money and Stinger missiles to the freedom fighters, and Dan Rather appeared alongside them, with a turban on his head. The owner of a club in Boston ostentatiously smashed two cases of Stolichnaya (making sure to call the TV stations first).

My anthropology professor at Harvard had spent years living among the Pashtun tribesmen and had written a book about tribal life in Afghanistan. The Pashtun tribal society was virulently patriarchal, as was indicated by Pashtun proverbs like "A woman's place is in the home or in the grave," and "Women have no noses, they eat shit."

Women were physically fenced off from men, and were not allowed to learn to read. They were required to wear burkas, to be covered head to toe, even in the heat of summer. There were charming Pashtun customs like the *levirate* (if your husband died, you had to marry his brother), the stoning of women accused of adultery, and giving daughters away as compensation if one's son commited murder.

My professor explained that the women in these tribes actually wielded significant "power," even though they might have appeared oppressed to us Westerners. I remained skeptical.

Is it okay to stone adulterous women if that is just part of your culture? Shouldn't everyone be allowed to learn how to read? These were the kinds of moral problems that Captain James T. Kirk faced in his travels around the galaxy.

My own take: I never liked those freedom fighters, and I still didn't like them. I wouldn't want to live in their feudal theocracy—it would surely create a problem with my own lifestyle.

But wasn't it strange? For years our government had channeled guns and money to these lunatics—even after the Soviets withdrew from Afghanistan, and after Benazir Bhutto warned George Bush Sr., "You are creating a Frankenstein." With the Russians long gone, the new target was the United States of America. The attack on 9/11 was a perfect example of what the CIA calls "blowback"—the unintended consequences of their cold-war policy.

W e checked into a hotel in Goiânia. Marco, our tour manager, informed us that there were only three rooms for the band, and asked who would be getting the double.

"Just give us the keys," I said.

Britta and I would share a room, but it was a secret. Lee and Sean knew, but no one else did. It wasn't public knowledge. Our fans didn't know. Our friends didn't know.

It's amazing that I could have been so stupid. People knew.

Back in São Paolo, we had a late-night radio session for Brazil 2000, where we played eight songs live in the studio and chatted about Echo and the Bunnymen, who had a new album out. I saw them at Bond's in New York in the early '80s. Alan Vega opened for them and people booed him off the stage.

After the radio session we went to a party that had been organized by a friend of the promoter's. Actually, it was a very small party—one guy who used to be a Brazilian pop star back in the '80s, the pretty daughter of a prominent politician, the four of us, and Marco. We entered a high-rise apartment building right on the Rua Oscar Freire, the fanciest shopping street in São Paolo. We rang the doorbell and were met at the door by the ex-pop star, his nose and upper lip covered in white powder.

"No!" he said. "You cannot come in!"

Then he opened the door a crack.

"You are from New York? I like Jack Kerouac."

He let us in. The apartment was unfurnished save for a bed, a computer, a dog bowl, and a cute Labrador puppy.

He chopped out some lines on his copy of *The Dharma Bums*. I did a line of coke and stood outside on the balcony, pretending to feel good.

I couldn't decide if I was having a great time or a terrible time. On the one hand, it seemed like one of the worst weeks of my life. Every morning I woke up and remembered that I had ruined everything. There was a heavy feeling accompanying everything I did, from morning till night. But I was enjoying myself, too. I was operating on two levels. On some level I could still enjoy myself, enjoy the meals, and the band, and Britta, and Brazil. I convinced myself that I was not having a nervous breakdown, because there I was in Brazil, able to eat and sleep and get up onstage singing "nyah nyah nyah" and "baa baa baa." And the food was good and the shows were well attended, and it was fun being with Britta, and I was crying a little less each day. But I wasn't exactly having a blast.

Each day I called home to speak to Jack. But it wasn't my home anymore. "Why are you calling here?" Claudia would ask. There was no correct answer to that question. I had always called home. Claudia would probably rather I didn't, but she also would have been angry if I didn't call. She'd be angry either way, and I didn't blame her.

I had stopped wearing my wedding ring. I stowed it in the zippered side compartment of my toiletry bag. I could have moved it, but where would I move it to? Perhaps the sock drawer. What are you supposed to do with these things?

The events of the last few months still felt like a bad dream. There was guilt and anguish, like in a bad dream. And I had nowhere to live, like in a bad dream. But there were good parts, too. The dream had its sexy moments. I woke up each morning and the dream continued.

It continued via bus to Curitiba. We shared a bus with the opening band, Pelvs, a word that seems to be missing something. They told us it's pronounced "Pel-vis."

The old-style bus was more Partridge Family than Willie Nelson. It got a flat tire an hour out of São Paolo, but luckily we were right by a truck stop. What was for lunch? Meat, of course. And corn juice, sweet and milky. On my way to the bathroom, I saw a truck driver walking very deliberately with a gun in his hand. They have a little problem with highway robbery in Brazil, and the truck drivers are armed.

Our show in Curitiba was at one of the smallest rooms we have ever played. The club had a second room where you could watch the show on a video screen, at a reduced rate. As I was setting up my equipment, just before taking the stage, I got in an angry exchange with a journalist. He said he was supposed to be there at sound check to do an interview, but he was late, and so he needed to do the interview *after* the gig.

"No." I said. "I don't do interviews after the show."

It's a little rule I've always had. I know I have to do telephone interviews in the daytime, and interviews at sound check, but I figure that when the show is over I can relax and have a couple of drinks and not answer any more questions. But the journalist insisted that I must do the interview, because he had traveled four hours to be there.

"I don't care!" I yelled at him.

He threatened to write this in his newspaper. The horror! Despite this annoying exchange, the show was a lot of fun. The journalist came up to me after the set was over and made a grudging and insincere apology. I accepted.

They put us onstage at 2:00 A.M. in Londrina—so named because it was originally settled by the English. We got out of there at 4:15. By the time we reached the airport that morning, we all felt like death. It was a good thing we were getting out of Brazil.

A fter a night in Montevideo, we flew on to Buenos Aires. It was cold and rainy and we were still exhausted—there had been no time for sleep in Montevideo.

Being completely exhausted increases the chances of an incident—of forgetting something important or walking into a glass wall or getting irritated with one another.

A few years back, Sean dated a lovely girl from Uruguay named Maria. He was still in touch with Maria, and when her mother, who lived in Montevideo, found out that Sean was visiting, she met him at the airport and gave him a package of tea and cookies to carry back to her daughter in New York—special cookies filled with *dulce de leche,* which is very popular in Uruguay and Argentina.

"Goddamn it!" said Sean. "I have to carry this stupid fucking crap for the rest of the trip!"

I agreed with him. It sucks when people give you big heavy items to carry on the plane, only because they're too cheap to take them to the post office. When our taxi arrived at the hotel in Buenos Aires, Sean realized that he had accidentally left the care package sitting by the airport baggage carousel. I had to laugh. I laughed out loud. I thought it was funny. I thought it was ironic. Wasn't that ironic? You curse and complain about having to carry the package, and then you lose it. Maybe it wasn't ironic—but it was just a bit funny.

Sean took issue with my laughter. He read it as schadenfreude.

"What the fuck are you laughing at?" he said. Then he kicked my suitcase into the gutter.

"Watch it!" I said.

I shoved him in the chest. It was beginning to look like the San Diego shoe incident—the silly night in 1994 when I had held Sean's shoe out the window of the van while he grabbed my backpack, and we had punched each other, one of Sean's punches accidentally hitting his girlfriend, Vanessa, who was not amused.

Sean went straight back to the airport, but the package was long gone. I saw him a few hours later at sound check, and he was limping ever so slightly. He had injured his toe while kicking my suitcase.

We didn't get a big crowd on that rainy Sunday night in Buenos Aires. The economy was in terrible shape there after three solid years of recession. There had been mass street protests, the currency had been devalued, and bank assets had been frozen. In light of all that, tickets to a Luna show were a luxury. Never mind. We had the best barbecue of the whole South American trip, and washed it down with Argentine cabernets. We didn't finish eating till 2:00 A.M.

Our flight to New York City was canceled, and we were sent to Miami instead. We had ample time for duty-free shopping. Britta and Lee and I bought sunglasses. Mine were Dolce & Gabbana, but I called them my Mastroiannis, because they made me feel like Marcello Mastroianni. Sean bought two jars of *dulce de leche* sauce.

Corrupt Contract

Bernie liked to analyze my dreams. I liked this, too, especially on the days when I didn't want to be there. It seemed easier to talk about my dreams than to talk about my problems. I could linger over a dream, and it might take up half the session. On Tuesday nights I made a special effort to have a good dream. On Wednesday mornings, I would write my dream down and think about it as I rode the express bus up First Avenue to Bernie's.

One night I dreamed that I was sleeping in my parents' bed and they told me to get out.

"You need to leave home! You need to grow up!" said Bernie.

"But I *am* living in my parents' apartment and sleeping in their bed. They're away for the summer and I'm staying at their place."

Once I dreamed that I was back in windy Wellington, New Zealand, and that I drove out to my granddad's big old Victorian house at 140 Queens Drive, a house that has since been cut in half and moved to a country vineyard. I rapped on the white front door with the gold knocker. I ran from room to room, but the house was empty.

"You're trying to go home."

"I want to see my grandfather. He was divorced, too."

I also dreamed that Bernie committed suicide after a tidal wave hit the East Coast. Claudia appeared in that dream, too, and told me that her shrink said my shrink was crazy. And the reason he took his life, she said, was because he was tired of listening to my whining, and disappointed that I couldn't get my marriage to work.

In October I moved into a tiny one-bedroom apartment at 110 East First Street at Avenue A, directly across the street from Katz's Delicatessen, where I often found myself eating a gigantic brisket sandwich with mayo on rye. I would eat half of the sandwich for lunch and save the rest for dinner. Sometimes I shared the brisket with my dog, Samantha, who was now going back and forth between Claudia's place and mine.

The best features of my pad were the brand-new stove and the brand-new dishwasher—my landlord owned an appliance store in the East Village.

Claudia and I divided the stereo system. I took the receiver and the CD player, and she kept the big speakers. I treated myself to a good pair of B&W bookshelf speakers from Stereo Exchange. I hooked the speakers up with the high-grade speaker cables that the salesman had convinced me were essential, and positioned them on the bookshelves. Nice. The living room was cozy, just like the Realtor said, because it was only one hundred square feet.

There are certain advantages to living alone, I told myself. I could listen to music as loud as I wanted, whenever I wanted. I decided on some Glen Campbell, to test the new speakers.

I got comfortable on the futon and cued up "Mary in the Morning," which opens with Glen on acoustic guitar and a bouncing bass line from Carol Kaye. Then the strings come in, along with Glen's perfect, golden American voice.

Nothing's quite as pretty
As Mary in the morning
When through a sleepy haze
I see her lying there

Shit.

My Mary's there, in sunny days or stormy weather
She doesn't care, 'cause right or wrong
The love we share—we share together

The speakers sounded great, but Glen's golden voice reached right into my soul and slew me. I cried into my hands.

I skipped ahead to "Gentle on My Mind." Glen's twelve-string picking took me back to my parents' living room circa 1974. Carol Kaye again. How different our lives would be without Carol Kaye, who played the bass on all the big hits: "Elusive Butterfly," "Something Stupid," "Bernadette," "River Deep Mountain High," "Good Vibrations," "What the World Needs Now."

And "By the Time I Get to Phoenix." I knew better than to try to listen to that. I put on "Where's the Playground, Susie?" But this, too, was more than I could handle—Glen, standing in a box of sand, wondering what had gone wrong.

I wasn't ready for Glen Campbell. The day would come when I could listen to Campbell's greatest hits, but it wasn't that day.

I told Bernie about my Glen Campbell experience.

"I bought some new speakers," I said.

He was pleased for me. He was always pleased when I did something nice for myself—Bernie stressed the importance of being your own best friend.

"But then I played 'Mary in the Morning,' and I started to cry."

"You stacked the deck."

"What?"

"You stacked the deck. What was it about the Glen Campbell?"

Long pause. There were frequent long pauses in therapy. I knew I was supposed to be the one talking, but I'm not good at talking about my feelings, because I'm a New Zealander. Descended from the Scots and English to begin with, with the added strain of being a frontier people. This is a recipe for stubborn and silent types, people who don't complain, but instead keep things bottled inside.

"Glen is singing about how wonderful his life is when he wakes up in the morning and sees Mary there . . . and it made me feel like a failure. I tried other Campbell songs, but they made me cry, too. Maybe it's his voice. Or the string arrangements."

Another long pause.

"My parents had the album of duets that Glen Campbell and Bobbie Gentry did together. We used to listen to 'Little Green Apples' and 'Elusive Dreams.' And on Sunday nights we watched *The Glen Campbell Goodtime Hour* on TV."

B ernie wanted to charge me $200 a session.

"Two hundred? You charged me one twenty-five back in the nineties."

"Well," he said, "what's better for you?"

"One twenty-five is better for me."

"How about one fifty?"

Separation was expensive. Two apartments, two phone bills, two frying pans. I bought Martha Stewart plates at Kmart. I ordered flatware from Target. There was one bill for the analyst, and another for the couples counselor—Marlene, on Twelfth Street.

Claudia and I had started with Marlene on September 13.

As we sat in the waiting room, Claudia asked me if we were there to save our marriage or to end it. We were there to end it. Marlene was our uncoupler.

Claudia made every effort to save our marriage. But I was out of the house now. It's hard to leave, to put your belongings in a bag and walk out. But once you're outside, it's just as hard to go back.

Our first session with Marlene was tearful and polite. We were in a state of shock. We were nice to each other. Marlene urged us not to rush into anything—maybe she could save us.

"Do you take vacations together?" she asked.

"Not just the two of us. There were family vacations, with the in-laws and the nieces and nephews," I said.

"That doesn't count."

Marlene laughed, but it wasn't funny. She said we had behaved like children.

Things turned from nice to nasty within weeks. We met on November 21, the day before Thanksgiving.

"Do you know what today is?" Claudia asked angrily while we sat in the waiting room.

"No."

"Today is our anniversary."

Since our wedding anniversary happened right around Thanksgiving, we often forgot it.

"What are you doing for Thanksgiving?" asked Marlene.

"I'm taking Jack to my folks' for dinner," said Claudia.

"My friend Sisha is a chef at Gramercy Tavern. He's cooking for a bunch of us," I said.

"Really? Who's going to be there?" asked Claudia.

"I don't have to answer questions like that!" I snapped. "I don't have to tell you where I'm going or who's going to be there."

We were now using these sessions to denounce each other.

It came to a head one day when Claudia proclaimed that our marriage had been a "corrupt contract," where she did all the work while I had all the fun, traipsing around the world in my rock-and-roll band. Adults who work in the arts get real jobs when they have kids, she said. Wasn't it time I put away childish things?

Corrupt contract? She had been seeing a therapist, too. She didn't come up with that phrase on her own. It was good, though. It stung. *Corrupt contract.* It was now clear to me that we could never get back together. My position would be thoroughly compromised. I would return as the naughty boy, chastened and disciplined.

Perhaps marrying a musician is always a corrupt contract. But I never promised anything different—I was always a musician. Still, the cheating and deception I did not promise.

Sisha cooked a fantastic meal for Thanksgiving. The walnut soup and duck liver wrapped in bacon were superb, but I felt like a loser because I wasn't with my son for the holiday. Christmas wasn't much better. Valentine's Day was strange. Every holiday and anniversary and birthday was now a day to feel inadequate. Was I going to be sad on Christmas for the rest of my life?

In March the band flew down to Texas to play shows at South by Southwest in Austin and at the Ridglea Theater in Fort Worth. It was our first time at SXSW and we didn't much like it. First of all, they don't pay you for performing there. We could earn $5,000 doing a show in Austin at any other time, so why were we playing there for free? Second, we were treated rudely by the staff at Emo's. They refused to give us any beer, and they rushed us off the stage just as we were hitting our stride.

Fort Worth—the following night—was more fun. The Ridglea Theater is a lovely old venue located in a strip mall, and they do these great projections on a screen behind you while you're playing. After the show Britta and I took ecstasy, and stayed up all night listening to music. We had planned to go to the Kimbell Art Museum the next day, but we weren't feeling 100 percent. Instead we visited the Target next to the hotel. Britta looked at summer dresses. I looked at the toys.

We went back to our hotel, took a Vicodin, ordered some bread pudding from Applebee's, and watched *Shallow Hal* on Spectravision. This was a nice way to spend a Saturday night in Fort Worth.

I t was good to get away for a couple of days. We flew back to New York on a rainy evening, flying directly over the Ground Zero site and on to LaGuardia. And then I came back to my empty little apartment. This was a new feeling. I was used to coming home. This didn't feel like home yet.

Jack spent the weekend at my apartment. On Sunday we rode the subway up to the Metropolitan Museum of Art and studied the knights in shining armor, which was his favorite part of the museum, and then we wandered around Central Park. Jack collected sticks from the ground and we took them back to my place. We read *Robert the Rose Horse,* and he enjoyed it. I enjoyed it, too, just like I did when I was four years old.

On Monday morning Nicoleen came to pick him up and take him back to Claudia. I carried him downstairs and out to the sidewalk. I strapped him into his stroller and turned and walked back up the steps to the door of my building. I turned and waved to Jack and he gave me the biggest smile and waved back, and then I went inside and lay down on the bed and cried.

"Jack has this incredible ability to enjoy the moment," I told Bernie. "He's always smiling and laughing and having a good time, while I'm sad about the past and worried about the future. The more fun we have together, the more devastated I am when the babysitter comes and takes him home. I feel like I'm just borrowing him for a day or so, like he doesn't belong to me."

"You're pissing on the present."

"What?"

"If you have one foot in the past and one in the future, then you're pissing on the present."

This saying may have contained the truth, but some days nothing Bernie said really made a difference. Sure, I was pissing on the present. And I was going to continue pissing on the present for some time, until this rotten present faded into the past.

Bernie had more witty lines for me that day, too. He had clipped an article from the *Times* with lyrics from various country-and-western songs.

They know all about divorce and heartbreak and cheating and drinking and lying and leching down there in Nashville.

> *I keep forgetting I forgot about you.*
> *I guess I had your leavin' comin'.*
> *If you leave, can I come, too?* [This one made me sad.]

> *If the phone doesn't ring, it's me.*
> *I'd rather be picked up here than put down at home.*

I could have sworn that Bernie fell asleep on me during one of these Wednesday sessions. There I was, revealing my innermost turmoil, when his eyes closed for a minute and his head drooped. He had nodded off.

Two days later, I learned that Bernie's wife had died that Monday. At first I was hurt that he hadn't told me. But I realized that he couldn't have shared that news without altering our dynamic. How could I sit there complaining about my wife (we were separated but still married) while he grieved for the love of his life? I felt like an idiot.

Lovedust

When we were with Elektra, some publicist was always telling us that they were talking to the people at *Letterman,* or the *Dennis Miller Show,* or *Conan.* But it never happened. I told Renée to stop telling me that we might be on TV. I only wanted to know if it was actually happening. Until then, it was just talk. Finally, after ten years together, Luna was booked on *Late Night with Conan O'Brien.*

Now that we were on an independent label instead of a major, we were getting on TV—playing the Craig Kilborn and Conan O'Brien shows. Why now? Was it because we had a sexy blond girl in the band? Or because Jetset Records hired a guy who got paid a commission if he booked us on a TV show?

It was really cold in the *Conan O'Brien* studio. Sound check was rushed, and I couldn't hear my vocal so well. We had elected to perform "Lovedust," which is at the bottom of my vocal range. I felt that I was singing a bit flat, and asked for more vocal in my monitor, but I didn't get it. Sure enough, I sang a little flat.

After rehearsal the previous week, Lee and Sean had called an impromptu band meeting. All four of us attended this meeting, which took place in my '93 Subaru Impreza (some days I gave everyone a ride after practice). Lee and Sean were not happy that Britta and I were a couple, and wanted to express their frustration. This was the legacy of my misbehavior— meetings and more meetings. Couples meetings, divorce mediation, emergency counseling—and band meetings.

"It's frustrating for us," said Sean. "And there's nothing we can do about it. Except maybe quit."

I was not particularly sympathetic. Sure, I could understand why they didn't like being in a band with a couple. I hadn't particularly liked it myself. It alters the supposedly democratic structure of the group.

But Britta didn't vote in Luna. She carefully abstained from the decisions on album track sequences and artwork. So she and I were not a voting bloc. But I suppose we were a bloc of some sort. And if you get back to the four monkeys in the cage, in terms of status I was Monkey #1, the only monkey who had been there right from the beginning of the band. When Justin (Monkey #2) left the band, Sean (#3) could rightly expect to slide up to the #2 spot. But if #1 and #4 (Britta) were sleeping together, it screwed everything up.

Lee and Sean said that people were sure to notice that half the lyrics on the album focused on my personal life, in songs like "Lovedust," "Swedish Fish," and "Renée is Crying."

"Lovedust" was all about the stupid and crazy things you do because you can't think straight—because you're in love. Everyone else is telling you how stupid and annoying your behavior is, but you don't see it the way they do because you can't see anything much at all:

I set a trap for you
But I'm the one who's all caught up
Blinded by lovedust
This is what I saw
A million, a billion, a trillion stars
A million, a billion stars

"Swedish Fish" continued in that vein:

Apricot candles and blackberry pie
Is it a time bomb I see in your eye?
I want you forever, forever tonight
Pullin' your hair and holding you tight

"Renée is Crying," too, seemed to tell a story of heartache and obsession:

Salt-and-pepper squid
And Singapore noodles
I could look at your face

For oodles and oodles
In bamboo chairs we'll sip through straws
As Scott goes up, Renée is crying

Renée, our ex-manager, was annoyed about this song title. She felt sure that people would think the song was about her. But it wasn't. I had clipped a story from a back issue of *Life* magazine that I found at the flea market, a story about astronauts' wives. Scott was an astronaut, and Renée was his wife. The *Life* magazine headline read AS SCOTT GOES UP . . . RENÉE IS CRYING.

Perhaps it was insensitive of me to use that story. I tried singing a different name, like Susie or Josephine, but the lyric didn't flow as well.

I never consciously set out to write songs about my life. But when I examine the songs after finishing each album—specifically when journalists start asking questions about the songs—I realize that they are revealing. So yes, the lyrics for the new record contained scenes from my life, or sometimes just my fantasy life. They had to come from somewhere—and real feelings are often more memorable than phony ones. But no one noticed much. It was standard stuff for rock lyrics. Certain music critics were annoyed by the food references, though, like in the title track "Romantica":

Raindrops in Boston
Warm in Toledo
There's blue in my red
Wine spodyody
Ginger is burning
A hole in my head
While I was sleeping
She came to my room
And borrowed my eyes
How can I know what I think till I see what I say?

I'm in a jam, you're in a pickle, we're in a stew
The airplane is coasting, the pilot is sleeping, there's nothing to do
How will I know which way to go?
Who has the answers?
How can I know what I think till I see what I say?

The *Daily News* gave *Romantica* two and a half stars and complained, "Wareham seems to have something of a food obsession. Which would be fine if the songs resolved with some of his typically wry insight, but instead we get doublespeak, such as 'How can I know what I think till I see what I say?'"

There is no pleasing some people. I had borrowed the line about not knowing what I think till I see what I say from E. M. Forster, I think. The point being that I was confused, that I didn't know what I thought. Which is why we write things down or talk about them. In the act of articulating your thoughts, they become clearer. That's not "doublespeak"—it's psychobabble.

Spin gave us 7 out of 10:

> *"Once we had dreams, now we have schemes," croons Dean Wareham on Luna's sixth studio album,* Romantica. . . . *The lines read like a reality check for mid-'90s modern rockers. After the grunge rush, as label budgets shrank, the "prestige act"—the cool, commercially underachieving band major labels kept around because its presence classed up the roster— became an endangered species. . . . There is no avoiding* Romantica's *sad, sad heart. (Whether Wareham's hurting over a woman or a coldhearted multinational corporation is another story.) Fizzy delights like "Black Champagne" and "Renée Is Crying" greet the sunset with a Sex on the Beach in one hand and a freshly served divorce summons in the other.*
>
> *(Andy Greemwald,* Spin, *June 2002)*

Did he know something? Of course he did. Everyone knew. I didn't need to go on pretending.

Now We Are Five

We added auburn-haired twenty-five-year-old Australian keyboard player Lara Meyerratken for the 2002 *Romantica* tour. Lara had played with Britta in Ben Lee's band (the young Australian singer/songwriter who was, quite famously, Claire Danes's boyfriend). Lara grew up in Sydney, where I spent the years 1970 to '77, and she went to high school right next to my old house in Hunter's Hill. Lara was there to help us capture the sounds on our new record, to play the fake strings, sampled trumpets, mellotrons, and other keyboard sounds.

We now had two pretty girls in the band, bookends on opposite sides of the stage. Britta stood next to me at stage right. Lara stood next to Sean at stage left. Lee was in the middle, on his drum riser.

We began at the Paradise in Boston. The following day started with an in-store appearance at Borders, in the mall at Chestnut Hill. Jetset had struck a deal with Borders, who had ordered an extra couple of thousand CDs in exchange for our doing a series of these in-store performances. The idea was that the personal appearances would bring customers into the store. But who would show up at one o'clock on a Friday afternoon, at a mall in Chestnut Hill? The label and the store were supposed to place a little advertisement, a co-op ad, in the weekly press. Someone forgot to do this, and we ended up replaying that scene from *This Is Spinal Tap* where no one shows up for the signing.

Total attendance at the in-store was four Luna fans. Two of them were infants in strollers, wheeled in by their mom, who couldn't believe that Luna was playing at the mall. One other Luna fan worked upstairs at Abercrombie & Fitch, and happened to see a sign in the store window that morning.

Sean and I played a few songs for our fans, and then the store manager gave us each a little bag of goodies: jelly beans, chocolates, and Rice Krispie's

Treats. This was infantilizing. The in-store out of the way, we drove on down to our real destination, Providence, Rhode Island. Providence is sometimes referred to as the armpit of New England. I've played there twenty times in my life and I've never had fun. There's always an incident. Like some drunk guys trying to pick a fight with me while I'm loading the van.

"Where's the party?"

"What party?"

"He won't tell us where the party is."

We left at nine the next morning to make it to another Borders bookstore in Philadelphia. In-stores were a pain in the ass. They robbed us of our sleep. They took away the precious hours that we might have had to take a nap or watch TV.

At least there were some Luna fans in the bookstore this time. The Borders manager got the word out. I didn't love playing acoustic guitar in bookshops. It wasn't what I envisioned when I started a band. In fact, it was not unlike an anxious dream. I felt half naked without the lights and ambience of the rock club. But I was getting the hang of it.

We moved on to Washington, D.C. Sean and I visited a satellite radio station called XFM, whose multimillion-dollar facility felt like the set of *The Truman Show*. XFM was funded by General Motors and Clear Channel. We walked down a long hallway with dozens of DJs behind glass windows, which were labeled with names like "The 70s," "The 80s," and "Liquid Metal." These DJs were playing and programming music that you could get all over the country if you subscribed to their satellite system. It's still unclear if satellite radio is going to take off, but about a billion dollars has already been spent on it. People who work at radio stations are scared for their jobs.

Everyone in the band seemed to have new gadgets for this tour. Britta had one of these new iPod things, which everyone wanted to borrow. The iPod had only been around for six months at that point. None of us could possibly have predicted the revolution in music-listening and purchasing habits that would ensue. We had, however, noticed kids on airplanes loading homemade CDs into their portable disc players, either whole albums their friends had copied for them, or playlists of songs ripped from the dorm room jukebox.

All this file sharing didn't seem to have impacted our own lives yet. It was more of a problem for acts like Metallica and Madonna, who immediately recognized that they were losing millions of dollars, that they were being attacked by pirates. It was the big albums that would feel the pinch in the years to come, those multiplatinum records that had kept the major labels in business.

It was raining and cold in Toronto. Lee's Palace was a nice place. We were first there in 1992, opening for the Screaming Trees. It looked much bigger then. A fan pointed out to me that it had been ten years of Luna. He said we should have made an announcement, or made special commemorative T-shirts proclaiming TEN YEARS OF LUNA.

I received a gift from another Canadian fan—ten hits of LSD. Actually, he handed them to our guitar tech, who was named Lawrence, to give to me, and then they fell out of Lawrence's pocket, but I was able to find them on the stage after the show. I hadn't taken acid since 1985, and I was not quite in the right frame of mind to take it again, as I was still a little fragile from the divorce. Or maybe I was just fragile, period.

I left the acid in Canada.

Perhaps I was afraid of confronting my own mind. My old friend Graham used to drop acid once a year and do battle with Satan. He told me it is much the same trip each time. He takes the acid. Hours later, he finds himself staring into the mirror. Satan appears and makes a case for the dark side, and Graham's good self does battle with his evil self and emerges victorious. He turns the bad trip into a good trip.

I'm not sure it would work out that way with me. Evil might triumph over good. Or I might just look in the mirror and start to cry.

Our tour moved on to the Midwest. In Cleveland, we met up with Sonic Boom, who was going to be opening for us for the next couple of weeks. His music works in narrow parameters, long, slow, drony songs with minimal chord changes—but that's what makes it so compelling. Sonic Boom is most definitely a hedgehog.

In Chicago, we picked up a tour bus. I was the first on the bus that afternoon, but I didn't pick out a bunk for myself. I figured the polite thing to do would be to wait till we all got on the bus, and let everyone draw straws. This was a naive and foolish mistake. When I came back twenty minutes later, everyone had picked their beds. The good bunks are the middle ones, easy to get in and out of, and slightly larger than those on top or below. Which is where I was stuck—on a low, loud bunk on the bottom, right by the engine. I tried to switch with Lara later in the tour, but she wouldn't have it.

"I'm a Taurus," she said. "We don't like change."

In Seattle, Sean and I performed in the cafeteria at the headquarters of Amazon.com. They set us up right next to the refrigerators. There was no microphone, so it was a bit of an effort to be heard over those humming fridges. I doubt that anyone heard me. I couldn't hear me. We lunched with my old friend Mike McGonigal, who now worked at Amazon. Mike paid me back the $20 he had borrowed from me years ago, in his dark days.

We talked about old times, like the time I played the benefit show for *Chemical Imbalance* with Kramer, when Damon and Naomi got so angry with me, and I got angry right back.

After two nights at Bimbo's in San Francisco, we moved on to L.A. Britta and I had brunch at Swinger's on Beverly Boulevard, where we spied Tricky. Lee was there for lunch a bit later, and he sat one table away from Dave Navarro, who talked loudly on his cell phone about a song he was going to write with the guy from Matchbox 20.

"I figure, why not, dude? This could be my country house, you know?"

We left the hotel at 8:00 A.M. the next morning to perform on *Morning Becomes Eclectic,* at KCRW, before rushing across town to tape the Craig Kilborn show. This was our second time on. Kilborn loved us. He even came to our dressing room to say hello.

"Hey. I hear you guys are good."

We got the booking on *Kilborn* because Lee's brother, Stacy, was friendly with Craig. They liked to talk hoops together.

"Any of you guys like hoops?" he asked us.

The *Kilborn* producers had us perform our song first before any of the guests went on, even though they would run our performance at the end of the show. We ran through "Weird and Woozy," and left immediately for our gig at the El Rey.

We rushed back to the hotel just in time to view our brief TV appearance. It was exciting to be on TV. Millions of people might be watching. The last time we were on *Kilborn* our weekly sales actually went down. That's what our sales rep at Jericho said. Lee had asked him to check the SoundScan reports to see if maybe there was a bump in sales the week we played. Not a bump—a dip.

We rolled on across the country, through Arizona and New Mexico and Texas, all the way to New Orleans.

Our friends Lisa and Katy threw us a little party in the penthouse suite of their swank hotel in the French Quarter.

Byron Guthrie was there, our first drummer. Even though ten years had passed, he was still mad about being asked to leave the band.

"Why was I fired from Luna?" he asked. "I didn't appreciate Justin telling me what to play. I'm a good drummer. I'm better than Stanley was."

"Maybe you are, Byron."

"I'm better than him."

I see him once every few years, and he always asks the same question.

It was 4:00 A.M. and I had had enough of this. I decided to get into the bus.

I could see why Byron was upset. He worked as a bartender in New Orleans, just like he did in New York. And he saw us coming through there in a big old tour bus, and having a party at the swank hotel, and it all must have seemed pretty glamorous. And he was probably thinking about how close he was to being the drummer in this band, and how much better his life would have been and all that. Life could have been one thing but instead it was another.

We Won't See That
Band Anymore!

In October 2002 we set out on a secondary-market tour. That's where you go back to these less important cities that you missed the first time—like Pittsburgh, Columbus, and Columbia, Missouri.

Everyone went out dancing after the Columbus show, but I went back to my hotel room and read fan e-mails, including one from an ex-fan in Pittsburgh, with the subject "We Won't See That Band Anymore!"

This one fellow was furious at me. He had written "IHOP" on a paper napkin at the show in Pittsburgh and passed it to me onstage. I told him that we didn't play that song anymore, which was the truth. But apparently he wasn't satisfied with that answer. He wrote that he was going to sell his copies of *Penthouse* and *Pup Tent* and use the money to buy Phish concert tickets. He assured me that Trey Anastasio would have played "IHOP," because he cared about his fans, while I, on the other hand, had an attitude problem.

I wasn't sure how to respond. Should I write back to him? Apologize? Or explain that we were not trained monkeys, performing tricks for peanuts? I could tell him that we hadn't played "IHOP" in over a year, and would have wanted to run through it a couple of times before playing it in front of an audience. I decided to just let it go, and posted his e-mail on our Web site for all our fans to enjoy.

At the Empty Bottle in Chicago we practiced "IHOP" at sound check, and decided to make it the encore. It was hot as hell onstage, and we were all soaking wet by the end of it.

After a nine-hour drive we arrived quite late in Columbia, Missouri, where we played at Mojo's Roadhouse. They fed us barbecue for dinner, and it wasn't half bad.

Our hotel had an Indian restaurant in the lobby and a nightclub next door. After the show we rode back to the hotel with Mark and Michael Holland of Jennyanykind (our opening band).

"This looks thuggish," said Mark Holland as we pulled up to our hotel to find some people screaming at one another and one guy holding his bleeding nose. There was a wild party going on at the disco.

We hurried into our rooms. Moments later I heard more screaming and looked out the window to the street below, where a full-scale riot had broken out. Dozens of people were running all over the place, punching and kicking one another. Soon after, the cops joined in, ten squad cars showing up together, and the crowd dispersed.

I woke up early on Sunday morning and walked around Columbia, which is actually a pretty little college town. It was dead quiet, with no sign of last night's madness.

We next played the Alley Katz club in Richmond, Virginia. A strange girl wandered into our dressing room.

"Have you noticed," she said, "that when you break crack down and shoot it up, your sweat smells like balsamic vinegar?"

Somewhere in Nebraska I got into this thing with Britta where we were barely speaking to each other. I must have done something wrong, but I really had no idea what it was. This not-speaking thing happened once in a while; it would last for two or three days until neither of us could take it anymore.

It's hard not speaking. It requires effort. But we got over it, and then the tour ended.

L'Avventura

Despite our extensive touring that year, Luna wasn't quite paying the bills. I decided to record an album of cover songs—the dreaded solo album. I figured that it would be easy enough to do and no one could accuse me of taking valuable songs away from the next Luna album. I recorded "Indian Summer" by the Doors and "Random Rules" by the Silver Jews. I recorded Madonna's "I Deserve It," and "Moonshot," a great protest song by Buffy Sainte-Marie, the Native American singer who had married Jack Nitzsche. This was my second time trying "Moonshot." Galaxie 500 had done it, too, at Naomi's suggestion.

I recorded basic tracks for a dozen songs in two days at Stratosphere Studios, with Matt Johnson on drums and Britta on bass. At night I recorded guitars in my tiny living room on First Street. Some nights Britta came over and helped me with keyboard parts. She also played me a couple of songs that she had written—"Your Baby" and "Out Walking"—which she sang just beautifully, like a sultry Dusty Springfield.

The concept for the record expanded. David approached Jetset about Britta and I doing an album of covers and duets instead of a solo album. No one else was doing anything like that.

David got us a meeting with Tony Visconti, the legendary record producer behind the best Bowie and T.Rex albums. I always figured that Visconti was English, but discovered that he was born and raised in Brooklyn. Tony had moved to England in the '60s, hoping, he said, to become the fifth Beatle. He lived through all the excesses of the '60s and '70s—drugs, spirituality, and rock and roll. He spoke with just a hint of an English accent after his years in London, and sported close-cropped gray hair and spectacles.

We spent three weeks with Tony in his studio—Studio B at Philip Glass's

Looking Glass Studios on Broadway and Bleecker—in late November and early December.

Tony's schedule was different from the usual rock-studio hours. Instead of working from noon to midnight, we started each day at 10:00 A.M. and were finished by six or seven in the evening. Instead of procrastinating for half the day, we got right to work. We started with the basic tracks that had been recorded at Stratosphere and at home, and now added vocals, bass, and electric guitars. Tony himself played the mellotron and a five-string bass on one song. Tony and Britta worked out string arrangements on keyboards and Tony conducted the Scorchio String quartet. On that day, he wore a tie and jacket to the studio. The strings sounded silky and luxurious.

The record had been a mess when we brought it to Tony, but it soon started to sound really special. This was the most fun I had had in a recording studio in years. Tony worked quickly. He didn't ask me to sing anything more than three times. Admittedly, it was easier singing covers than singing my own songs, because I didn't have creeping nagging questions about my lyrics and melodies—these were already decided.

We did not argue or have pointless discussions about tempo and groove. We did not procrastinate. We did not retrack songs from scratch, or get stuck for hours on one guitar solo. If we were at an impasse, Tony would urge us to move on to something else and come back to the problem later. Or he would pick up his twelve-string guitar and build us a perfect little bridge.

I remembered that making records could be easy and fun. It didn't have to be painful. We didn't have to drive ourselves crazy.

Recording with Tony was cathartic and romantic. We felt safe in his studio. He didn't judge us or resent us—he had lived through a few things himself. I wrote my first disco song, "Ginger Snaps," which was inspired by George McCrae's "Rock Your Baby":

When the cowboy sings
When the Saturn rings
When the ginger snaps
When the thunder claps . . .

I'm a wayward tom
I'm a silver streak
And the walls have ears
But the walls don't speak
We're going to make it after all

When all was finished, I knew that *L'Avventura,* the album we made with Tony, was one of the best things I had ever done. Although it was poorly planned and conceived, and I had no clear idea of where I was headed at first, it was a record I had been wanting to make all my life, informed by Glen Campbell and Bobbie Gentry, Lee Hazlewood and Nancy Sinatra, Madonna and Mary Tyler Moore.

Wednesdays and
Alternate Weekends

As 2002 drew to a close, there was bad chemistry in Luna. On Thanksgiving weekend we performed at Bowery Ballroom. Britta and I had dinner with David before the show, to discuss the record we were making with Tony Visconti. Then David went home, skipping the Luna show because his parents were visiting from England.

Sean was most upset when he heard that Britta and I had eaten dinner with management, and called a special band meeting to discuss his feelings.

We sat around the round wooden table in David's Chrystie Street office.

Luna should be working harder, said Sean—making more money on the road, touring more, selling more records, and making more money.

The longer a band is together, the greater the pressure to make it big. Because if a band doesn't make it big in the record business, then one day the dream will be over. Some record producers relish working with a band on their fourth album for this very reason—they figure the guys are desperate for a radio hit. I was pretty sure we were past that point. It was quite impossible to have a radio hit if you were not signed to a major label.

We were on an independent label now, so getting played on commercial radio was out of the question, as was getting a video in rotation on MTV. We no longer had a publishing deal with EMI or Polygram. We had a cult following. We were not living like rock stars. Certainly, we could pretend to be rock stars on the nights that we sold out the Fillmore or the Cabaret Metro, or did cocaine in the bathrooms of flamenco bars in Madrid. But then we would come home, and there were still bills to pay.

How did other bands in our position survive? Often they got real jobs. Mudhoney, for example, was still a band, but they were a part-time band. In between making records and doing short tours to promote them, they held down day jobs.

We had played more shows in 2002 than ever before—close to ninety dates, from the Borders bookstore in Chestnut Hill to the Boule Noire in Paris. But Sean said we should go back on the road.

"It is crucial for us to do another leg of touring," he said.

I agreed to a third leg of touring—something we had never done before. But I also urged Sean to do something to supplement his income. I was getting tired of feeling that I had to provide steady work in an era when the work was less steady.

I n January 2003 Claudia and I signed our divorce papers. This was not a happy day. Quite possibly we worked harder on our divorce than we had on our marriage. We attended weekly sessions with a mediator, to sort out all the issues that divorce entailed—a weekly schedule for Jack, a summer schedule, who would pay for what, what would happen on holidays, what would happen to our joint assets.

The divorce papers came back from New York State a month after we signed them. This was not a happy day, either. I read that a man is supposed to feel free when he is divorced for the first time. I didn't feel free on this day. I felt free when I left Galaxie 500—perhaps that had been my first divorce.

But after a year and a half of therapy, mediation, anger, and sadness, I woke up one morning and didn't feel like a failure as a husband and a father—I wasn't miserable anymore. Britta and I moved in together, into a cute fourth-floor walk-up in the East Village. One day, the four of us—Claudia and Jack and Britta and I—went to lunch together. This was Claudia's idea, and it was a good one. We realized that we could all get along, and everyone was going to be alright.

Kill for Peace

On the evening of March 20, 2003, as falling bombs signaled the "shock and awe" of the U.S. aerial bombardment of Iraq, Luna took the stage at the Knitting Factory for the first of three shows. It was difficult to stand onstage and sing songs like "Lovedust," "Teenage Lightning," and "Fuzzy Wuzzy" when the citizens of Baghdad were under attack. I felt like an idiot singing "bom bom bom" and "nyah nyah nyah" on this night.

We opened our set with "Kill for Peace," written by Tuli Kupferberg and first recorded by the Fugs in 1966. I had seen Kupferberg speak a few weeks earlier, when I participated in an evening dubbed Songs from the Vietnam Songbook, at Joe's Pub. "The war against Iraq will be a short war," said Kupferberg. "It will be over very quickly. But the war against the United States—that will go on for a long time."

Near or middle or very far east
Far or near or very middle east
Kill, kill, kill for peace
Kill, kill, kill for peace

If you don't like a people or the way that they talk
If you don't like their manners or the way that they walk
Kill, kill, kill for peace
Kill, kill, kill for peace

Perhaps we should have led a march out of the Knitting Factory and down to Ground Zero, chanting, "Kill, kill, kill for peace." But we finished our set, moving on to "Bobby Peru" and "Bewitched" and the usual Luna fare.

I generally shied away from injecting politics into my music, not because

I didn't care about politics, but because it didn't seem to fit with Luna's music—it was not what Luna was about. But it felt weird conducting business as usual, pretending that nothing was happening. This, of course, was to be a defining feature of the Iraq war. Soldiers and mercenaries were paid to fight, but the rest of the country went on about its business as if nothing unusual was happening. I felt compelled to post a few thoughts on our Web site:

> The phrase "kill for peace" is an excellent example of doublespeak, and we have been hearing an awful lot of it lately—like our government's assertion that Saddam Hussein "chose" to go to war on the day we attacked. In fact it is Rumsfeld and Cheney and Bush who chose war, an unprovoked war that is opposed by people all over the world.

I soon received a couple of angry e-mails from Luna fans. One guy called me "a friend of Saddam," and accused me of condoning the rape of his cousin by Saddam's National Guard.

In June I flew out to the L.A. Film Festival for the premiere of *Piggie,* a low-budget indie feature film by Alison Bagnall, who had written *Buffalo 66* with Vincent Gallo. I had met Alison at a New Year's Eve party in 2000. She said she was struck by my way of pouring the champagne that night, and thought I would be perfect for the male lead in her film—a junkie thief whose life is crashing down around him. Alison set up a screen test, gave me the role, and shot the film in Walton, New York, the following summer.

I had read Nick Tosches's biography of Dean Martin. Martin said that acting is dead easy: They write the words for you. All you have to do is memorize your lines and stand in the right spot to deliver them. It wasn't quite that easy. Alison wanted me to cry on screen in the very first scene of the film. She hired an acting coach, Sheila Gray, who lived above the family business, Gray's Papaya, on West Seventy-second Street. My sessions with Sheila were like therapy sessions: expensive and, at times, emotional. We analyzed scenes from the script and she asked me probing questions about my life in an attempt to make me cry. She made me sad, but she never got the satisfaction of real tears.

I knew I wasn't a real actor, someone with great range, but I figured I could just be myself on a grumpy day and that would suffice for the cranky drug-addict thief. While I portrayed a junkie thief in a movie, my brother Anthony checked into a seven-day detox, then checked out and promptly started using again. Anthony had been up and down. There was a period of some years where he held a well-paying job, doing information technology for a prominent luxury-goods company on East Fifty-seventh Street, but that job was lost when the company's IT department was reorganized.

In addition to *L'Avventura,* Britta and I released *Sonic Souvenirs* that summer, an EP of remixes by Sonic Boom of songs from *L'Avventura.* Sonic said that *L'Avventura* was one of the all-time great albums. He flew to New York and remixed his favorite tracks. It was fascinating to watch him work. He removed the drums from the songs, and added drones and delays and the sound of rainfall. He made the tracks sound spacey and new. Sonic is not proficient on piano or guitar, but he makes beautiful soundscapes, one piece at a time. The *Sonic Souvenirs* EP got a nice review in the *New York Times.* They reprinted the cover photo, a still from our video for "Night Nurse," in which Britta is giving me a haircut. In the photo I am shirtless, and she is wearing a sleeveless, strapless shirt that leaves her shoulders exposed. The way the photo was reproduced in the paper, it looked like I was getting a naked haircut. Friends and family called me to ask if Britta and I were naked in the *Times.*

At the end of June, Luna flew to Porto, Portugal, to take part in a summer music festival.

Our first night there we were taken to dinner by a roly-poly young guy named Freddie, whose grandfather had been a Supreme Court judge.

"Salazar was a financial genius," said Freddie. "He was a dictator—but not a fascist."

Freddie may have been right about that—these are complex questions, and not all ruthless, authoritarian dictators qualify as fascists. Some are merely fascist sympathizers. Freddie knew a lot of stuff. He told us that Neil Diamond still snorted cocaine. We didn't quite believe him, but decided that from then on we would refer to cocaine as Neil Diamond.

"Freddie, is Neil Diamond coming to the show?"

He said he would try to bring him. But for now he urged us to taste some of the delicious port wine that the city was famous for. It was very good indeed. We decided to finish every meal in Portugal with a glass of port.

After dinner we went to see Cat Power, driving past a futuristic-looking new building, still under construction, on our way—Rem Koolhaas's Casa da Musica.

Chan Marshall seemed in good form when we arrived at the show, playing the piano and singing beautifully. But things quickly went downhill. She stopped singing and started rambling incoherently.

"I'm so tired. I'm so tired."

She asked her soundwoman which song she should do.

"Give me a song, baby . . . no, not that one. I already did that one."

She picked up her guitar and strummed a few chords, then started talking again.

"I *love* Vincent Gallo."

"I'm sooo tired."

"Someone bring me four shots of whiskey! And I don't care what it is, but there must be no ice and the first four letters of the whiskey must be G-L-E-N."

"Play a song!" one fan shouted.

"You are not invited to my world," she told him. "I love everyone, but I do not like you . . . but I forgive you."

She gave a little speech about being from Atlanta, and asked why Martin Luther King isn't a saint yet, and I was reminded of the amazing concert recording of Nina Simone that was recorded live in Savannah, Georgia, on the very night that MLK was assassinated.

After half an hour of talk, a few audience members started to boo. The club manager had had enough, too—he turned on the house lights and music. Chan stood up and gave the finger to all.

We went backstage to say hello.

"I know you," she said to me. "I saw you once in a Xerox store on Lafayette Street. You came in there with your wife, and your little dog on a leash. And I said, 'I know you.' But you were not friendly, because *you* were the one on the leash. She had you on a leash."

"I have no recollection of that," I said. Then Chan asked permission to

French kiss each of us. Her tour manager said that she had been kissing people all day long—fans, customs officers, and now us. We went along with her indecent proposal, for just a moment.

The following night we performed at the Hard Club. People were still buzzing about the Cat Power show. It may have been a fiasco, but if people can't stop talking about your show, then surely you have done something right.

B ack home that summer, Lee and Sean were anxious to finish a new Luna album by October, so that we could get it out in February and tour again in the spring of 2004.

We rehearsed twice a week at a little rehearsal studio on East Twenty-third Street, to work on songs for our next album. The rehearsal room stank of foul chemicals from the hairdresser's downstairs, but at least it had a view—of the school for the impaired across the street.

The Weeds of Eden—Sean's side project—had also rehearsed here. They had been recording on and off for many years, and had enough songs to make an album, but they were forever arguing, rerecording, and remixing the songs. They had a cool Web site, and played a show or two, but finishing the album eluded them. Finally, they decided to call it quits.

I suggested a new approach to Sean's songs for this record. Maybe Sean could write his own songs from beginning to end, rather than us co-writing them. And maybe he could sing a couple songs himself.

Now, letting the lead guitarist sing his own songs is an indicator that a band is on its last legs. It is an obvious sign that the songwriting team does not see eye to eye. Still, I thought it might make my life easier.

Sean wrote three very pretty songs. But when the time came to play those songs in rehearsal, the mood in the room would change. There was always something that wasn't quite right, whether it was the bass part or the drums or my rhythm guitar. It was never quite what Sean had in mind. Sometimes we played it "too rock" or "too mellow." Sometimes it was too fast, or too slow. Or not psychedelic enough—which was a general complaint that Sean voiced about Luna's albums.

At the end of trying to play "Broken Chair," there would be an awkward silence.

"Is it something I'm doing?" Lee would ask.

"I don't know," Sean would say. "I don't know."

All I knew was that this wasn't fun.

Sean wasn't having fun, either. All summer long he would mention how stressful his life was. He had lost weight. This was due, he said, to "a diet of stress."

"What stress?" I would ask, but he wouldn't say.

"I don't want to talk about it."

O n September 6, we played at the Trocadero in Philadelphia. We had another band meeting before the gig, over Chinese food. Tony Visconti had been tentatively on board to produce the next Luna album, but he had just backed out. He had spent months recording a Danish band, and wanted a break.

"When will the next record come out?" Sean asked pointedly.

"When we finish recording it," I said. "Sometime next year."

I wasn't trying to be smart. But to me, that was the only sensible answer. I didn't want to rush the record. Why did we have to be finished in October? Why did we have to be back on tour again in the spring? It was starting to feel like a treadmill to me, this cycle of writing records and recording them and then touring, over and over again.

"That's a pretty lame output for a band," said Sean.

In the last two years, we had released *Luna Live!, Romantica,* and the seven-song EP *Close Cover Before Striking.* In addition, I had released *L'Avventura* and *Sonic Souvenirs.* I didn't feel lazy.

But a record contract will do this to a band. We were scheduled to receive $150,000 from Jetset upon delivery of the next record—a hefty sum for an independent label. And people were eager to see that money. Maybe that's a very sensible reason to rush into the studio. Still, I wasn't ready. And I was the one who had to stand at the microphone and sing.

If all I had to do was write a few pieces of music and attend rehearsals, then I, too, would have been ready to make a new record in October. But it's not that easy for the lyricist. Songs do not grow on trees. Writing music is easy. But writing an album's worth of lyrics is like finishing a giant jigsaw puzzle.

.   .   .

T he following week Sean called another special meeting. He had something he needed to get off his chest—a "quasi-personal" matter.

"What is it?" I asked him. But he only wanted to discuss it in person, at
the meeting the next day. I lay awake that night wondering what "quasi-
personal" could mean.

Sean sat on our blue velvet love seat the next morning and explained it.
Apparently he and Lara had conducted a secret affair a few months ago, an
affair that had ended badly, with Lara's behaving so horribly to Sean that he
couldn't possibly stand for her to play in Luna—not for a while. He was very
sorry, but asked for our support and understanding in this matter.

"What happened?" I asked.

He didn't want to share any of the sordid details.

"She did things that a friend wouldn't do," he said.

Of course, once you start sleeping with someone, then you are already
doing things that a friend wouldn't do. And feeling things that a friend
wouldn't feel. And sometimes that leads to dishonesty, betrayal, and anger.

Luna was turning into Fleetwood Mac.

I was probably less supportive than I should have been. I found it hard
to be understanding, because I didn't understand—I had no idea what had
gone down between them, how long it had gone on, or why they even bothered to keep it a secret.

But it seemed that Lara had gone off on tour with another band last summer, became entangled with another guitar player, and left Sean twisting in
the wind.

I didn't understand completely, but I did see that he was upset, and that
he couldn't stand to be cooped up in a van with Lara right now. We went along
with Sean's wishes. Lara was out, and we were back to being a quartet—our
natural state.

The bad news kept coming. Shelley Maple, the head of Jetset, informed
us that the label couldn't possibly come up with the advance specified in
our contract, not in the current environment, with CD sales plummeting
(off 15 percent over the last two years, and still heading south) and distributors going out of business.

There it is. Your paper contract may specify a big advance and a high royalty rate, but it doesn't always work out that way. The next record is not guaranteed—it's always an option, to be picked up or not, at the record company's discretion.

Nowadays I smile, or wince, when I read about a band that has just been signed for $2 million. People think that these musicians were just given this huge sum of money. What it really means is that they have signed a seven-record deal, with the total advances adding up to $2 million. But even this math is meaningless, as the label is always free to terminate the contract, or renegotiate.

We renegotiated the Jetset deal, taking a lower advance, one that was still decent in the current marketplace, but left us all a little poorer, and made me think harder about those long Luna rehearsals.

I Don't Want to
Do This Anymore

A concerned fan sent me an e-mail in July 2004. He said Luna was "the greatest band that too many dumb-ass Americans had never heard of," but he sensed that Luna was in trouble. He compared us to the Grateful Dead in 1978, when their audience had dwindled. We shouldn't be afraid, he said. We needed only to take more psychedelic drugs and play long shows filled with "heavy guitar soloing and plenty of feedback." Soon the masses would come around, just as they did for the Grateful Dead, and Luna would be massively famous and I could OD in my BMW outside Golden Gate Park.

Did he know that Jerry Garcia and I shared the same birthday? Had he guessed that Luna had been secretly broken up since April?

I arrived at Charles de Gaulle at 7:00 A.M. on a Sunday morning, September 2004, and took a taxi to my hotel near the Place de la République. My room was not ready. I left my cheap suitcase in the lobby and went for a long walk. It was a beautiful, sunny Paris day. I strolled from the Place de la République to the Conciergerie. I spent a little time in the cell where Robespierre was held before his execution. He wasn't there long—unlike Marie Antoinette, who practically lived there. Marie Antoinette's cell had been re-created, too, but I've never really been a fan of hers. Her head needed chopping off.

I picked up a short history of the French Revolution at the Conciergerie gift shop, and, for Jack, a plastic knight and horse, emblazoned with the fleur-de-lis—the same kind that they sell at the Cloisters museum in New York.

I headed over to the Centre Pompidou, where they had a great exhibit on light and sound. I bought myself *un sandwich mixte (jambon et fromage)* and ambled around the Marais, which was packed with Sunday shoppers.

Soon I was stinky from all this walking—it had been some time since I had showered. I popped into a pharmacy to buy deodorant and shaving cream. French drugstores don't have a dizzying array of twenty different-scented deodorants, like we do at Duane Reade. The choice is between scented and unscented. It was liberating not having to compare all the different brands, not having to decide between clear gel and solid stick. This was freedom—freedom from choice.

After a cheap and delicious Chinese meal near the Place de la Bastille, I finally made it back to my hotel room. There was nothing on the TV, so I settled in for a bit of reading: Eric Hobsbawm's *Age of Extremes,* his brilliant history of the twentieth century. In the chapter on youth culture, Hobsbawm points out that Western youths, with their newly acquired purchasing power, created a boom in the record business during the fifties, sixties, and seventies. A lot of people made a lot of money.

Any fool could see that things were now changing. Teenagers still had the purchasing power, but new technology was making it possible for them to get the music for free. No wonder the record companies were in a state of panic.

I had a full day of interviews on Monday, and for once I actually had something to talk about. Usually you just answer the same old questions. *What comes first, the music or the lyrics? How is this record different from your others? How did you choose the title?*

But none of this mattered just then. Even though Luna had broken up months ago, we had just gone public with the news.

The secret breakup meeting had taken place back in April 2004, at the Cosi sandwich bar on Thirteenth Street and Sixth Avenue. I wish that I had picked somewhere more interesting, like French Roast, just a couple blocks downtown. Even the Dunkin' Donuts on Fifteenth Street would have been more poetic than this sandwich bar. Never mind—that's how life is sometimes. Those Cosi sandwich bars are everywhere, with plenty of free seats at eleven o'clock on a Tuesday morning.

I didn't say why I had called the meeting, and I didn't really need to. No one disagreed. It was time. We would disband, but we would keep it a secret for now, till after the release of *Rendezvous* in the fall.

But we started getting complaints from our record company, who said they couldn't get much press action on *Rendezvous*. Shelley suggested that the music journalists didn't like this new album so much, which perhaps was her way of saying that she didn't much like it herself.

In the end, we got great reviews. You can generally add a star to the review if you announce that the band is breaking up. People are nicer to you when you're on the way out, or dead. Cher, for example, said the nicest things about Sonny Bono after his tragic skiing accident.

Ultimately, we decided that we should announce the breakup before our tour started. It would give the press something to write about, and it would probably help sell more tickets. Not just another Luna tour, it could now be billed as the "farewell tour," or something stupid like that. I called the label and left an urgent message for Shelley, and wrote up a press release bearing the headline LUNA TO DISBAND. We waited a couple of days, and then asked our publicist, Lisa Gothheil, to send it out to a few music magazines.

Shelley called me in tears the day after the press release went out. She said that this move was going to sabotage sales of our new album, and pleaded with me to retract the announcement.

"You mean call everyone who got the press release and tell them we made a mistake, that we're not really breaking up? We'll look like idiots."

We stood our ground. I wanted this information out there before the promo trip to Europe. I figured it would help garner extra interviews. I posted a list of reasons for the disbanding on our Web site, and these made excellent talking points:

1. Rock and Roll is killing my life.
2. The Universe is Expanding.
3. There are too many bands out there, traveling around, singing their songs, etc.
4. Too much time spent in fifteen-passenger vans. According to 20/20, these things flip over.
5. Too many hands to shake—that means germs.
6. Too many dinners at Wendy's.
7. People are dying in Iraq.
8. This is what bands do, with a few exceptions, like R.E.M. and Metallica and the Rolling Stones. Those bands, however, are multibillion-dollar corporations. You don't break that up.

9. Hotel Electravision.

10. Time to Quit.

Those were just the reasons that I posted. I had hundreds more. When I lay down at night, the reasons got busy, they crisscrossed my brain, they fermented, they fomented, they grew, they built on top of one another. Finally, the reasons to break up came to outweigh the reasons to keep the band going. And that's when I knew it was time to quit. It wasn't one thing or another. It wasn't one incident or another. It was a hundred small things that finally made me say *enough.*

You often hear the phrase "personal and musical differences" as the explanation for a band breakup. This is succinct and accurate. It is what happens to a band. You are different people. At first, this works for you. But after many years together, the ways in which you are different begin to bother you.

We tolerate all kinds of flaws and idiosyncrasies in our friends. But those same flaws become intolerable in a business partner, someone you travel with every day. It becomes harder to see the good qualities, the wonderful things that each person brings to the band. Instead you see the ugly, selfish, neurotic parts. If you were just pals, you'd ignore that stuff.

In a band, you get tired of being so intimately involved in one another's lives in so many ways that you never bargained for. But the bottom line is that bands are supposed to break up, and now it was our turn.

R ecording *Rendezvous* had been fun at first. We recorded with Bryce Goggin at his studio by the Gowanus Canal in Brooklyn, in January 2004. The Gowanus neighborhood has made the transition from nothing to something. Soon they'll probably just call it Park Slope. Bryce was an excellent producer, and a very positive person to have around. He really took charge. We all set up in one open room, facing one another. This meant that we didn't have to wear headphones in order to hear one another. It also forced us to play a little quieter than usual. Bryce had seen Luna play live, and he happened to think that we were a good live band, so he wanted to commit our live performance to tape as much as possible. This meant that we had to get the live takes just right, without any glaring mistakes. So we would work each day till we got a really nice take—not just a good drum take, but a take that was good for the bass and the guitars as well. This recording style also allowed us to set up room mikes and capture the intimate sound of the band playing live in a room.

We spent five days doing the basic tracks for fifteen songs. Once the basic tracks were recorded, I would come to the studio at 10:00 A.M. and do a vocal (I liked to sing in the morning because I had "morning voice," which is richer, froggier). Then we'd listen to the song and record a couple of overdubs—an extra guitar part here, a keyboard there. And then Bryce would print a mix right away. The goal was to finish one song a day. The song "Broken Chair" took three days, because it was one of Sean's. For the first time, Sean was going to do a lead vocal on a Luna record. He was nervous about it.

"I don't want people to just think, Oh, that's the guitar player singing a song now," he said.

"But you *are* the guitar player," said Lee. "And you *are* singing a song."

Sean wrote and sang two songs that made the album: "Broken Chair" and "Still at Home." The songs were beautiful, but they weren't easy to record. Sean had his own way of working. I always felt like his first take on guitar was the best, but he was usually not convinced. Once again, Sean put pressure on himself to deliver "mind-blowing" solos on his songs, so he liked to do about twenty different takes for those. By the end of the *Rendezvous* sessions, Bryce had come up with a new way to produce Sean.

"Sean," he said. "You can come in at eleven tomorrow morning and play your twenty guitar solos, and figure out which one you like. Adam [the assistant engineer] will record you. I don't need to be here for that."

"Sean is a brilliant guitarist," Bryce told me. "But he is one of these people who equates the music-making process with a great deal of pain."

When I thought about the eleven years that Sean had been in the band, one of the enduring images I had of Luna was of a group of people sitting in the control room, listening to Sean finish his guitar tracks. The consensus was that Sean would immediately play something brilliant, but would then struggle for half a day trying all kinds of different ideas, often getting further and further away from the initial brilliance, and shouting abuse at those who tried to make a helpful suggestion. Finally, we'd leave the studio one by one and Sean would say, "How come everyone just goes home when it's my turn to play?"

I couldn't stand to listen to *Rendezvous* for months after we finished it. All I could hear were the arguments that had gone into recording it. Now I know it is one of the very best Luna records. Bryce Goggin captured the band as we were, live in the studio, with minimal overdubs. I love the way my guitar and Sean's play off of each other in "Cindy Tastes of Barbecue."

Your electronic billet-doux
It left me scrambling for a clue
North of North Dakota
East of Easter Egg
I made a promise to the hills

Your purple mouth says snicker snack
I'm turning round I'm turning back
Cindy tastes of barbecue
Cindy tastes of cream
I made a promise to the hills

I love Sean's solos on "The Owl and the Pussycat" and "Still at Home" and "Astronaut" (which Lee wrote and produced). I love "Speedbumps," the way the guitar drops out because I stepped on the wrong pedal.

Musically, we went out on a high note, though it wasn't apparent at the time.

My September promo trip continued to Barcelona, where I stayed at the lovely Hotel Jazz, just off La Rambla. Swimming pool, good air-conditioning, nice lighting, soft pillows, and an excellent location. My publicist had set up eleven interviews in a row. Everyone asked me about the ten reasons for disbanding.

"What is Hotel Electravision?"

That was the hotel in Basel on our last European tour. The promoter had assured Evan that the hotel was in order, but when we showed up we discovered that the hotel was in fact his apartment. Personally, I wasn't so upset. I had slept on floors before, and I would do it again. But some of the others were.

"The universe is expanding?"

That's a quote from *Annie Hall.* The young Woody Allen stops doing his homework when he hears that the universe is expanding, asking, "What's the point?"

"Rock and roll is killing your life?"

That's another rock cliché, but the truth is that rock and roll does kill your life, just a bit. It can lead you down the wrong path, into a double life, perhaps, or a life of drink and cigarettes and other vices. To be rock-and-roll is to be self-destructive, right? Think of Gene Vincent, Dee Dee Ramone, Sid Vicious, Brian Jones. You have to take it all with a grain of salt, and not get caught up in it. It can be fun, living a rock-and-roll life, but it's a slippery slope. Some can dabble. Others are swept away.

My final interview of the day was with my friend Ignacio Julia, for Barcelona TV.

"Is it true that you can't sing?" he asked.

"I hate guys who sing good," I said. Dean Martin had once said that. Maybe I can't sing like Joe Cocker or Sam Cooke, but at least I have my own voice, and I think it has character. Other people have beautiful voices—they can sing rings around me—but no one wants to listen to them.

"Is it true that the breakup of Luna started when Justin left the band in 1999?"

Ignacio was on to something. I thought back to when Justin left the band, and remembered that I was on the verge of leaving, too, till Britta joined. Still, I was so very glad she did.

Ignacio and his camera operator, Benet, took me to Las Siete Puertas for dinner, where I had the best seafood paella I've ever had. Paella can be dry, but this one was nice and oily. Afterward, my Spanish friends didn't want to go home. They walked me back to my hotel, but first we had to stop at a few different bars. Benet tried to score some coke, but the dealer was in a bad mood and wouldn't come out. The dealer had just learned that his girlfriend was pregnant, and he was furious. He was certain that he was not the father.

"I do so much coke, how could I fuck her?"

We ended up at a little hole-in-the-wall bar in the Plaça Reial, which was jumping, even at 2:00 A.M. on a Monday. Ignacio's sister-in-law worked there, so we got free beer. We continued onward, strolling up La Rambla, past Pakistanis selling cans of beer, and beautiful Ugandan prostitutes with dark, smooth skin and lips painted silver. Someone at the record company told me that when Moby was recently in town to do interviews, he asked to be taken to a whorehouse because he was doing research on prostitution around the world. I didn't believe that story. It didn't really go with Moby's Christian/vegan image.

Next stop, Cologne. I liked it there. Driving in from the airport, I listened to the Hidden Cameras on my iPod in my Mercedes cab. Most of their songs are about gay sex. They have one particularly beautiful song called "A Miracle," which is about being in love and sharing a disease.

Being all alone in Cologne was making me sad. So I went shopping.

I wandered down to Cologne's magnificent cathedral, ate a potato pancake with apple sauce (like I always do when I'm there), and wandered through the pedestrian shopping zone, where I bought some jeans and a pair of electric blue Puma TX-3 sneakers. They were high-tech looking, and I hadn't seen them in New York. Dinner was bratwurst and French fries at a *SchnellImbiss* near the hotel. Unfortunately they put paprika on the fries. That's how they do it in Germany.

My hotel was located right next to a multiplex cinema, and that night I saw *Resident Evil: Apocalypse,* with Milla Jovovich. It was dubbed in German, but my German is passable, and dialogue is not so crucial in a zombie flick. You can pretty much figure out what is going on—the zombies are trying to eat the living.

German interviews are different from all other interviews. They take ideas seriously.

"What will be your legacy?"

I was getting that question a lot. I didn't have an answer for it. I recently received an e-mail from a seventeen-year-old girl in Sweden who said that she went to a three-day indie-pop festival that ended each night with everyone hanging out, drinking beer, watching the sun come up, and listening to *On Fire* by Galaxie 500. We didn't set the world on fire, but it feels good to think that people are still listening to a little album that you made with your friends back in 1989 fifteen years later, halfway around the world, as the sun comes up. Can that be my legacy?

From Cologne I flew to London. The music business has changed so much in the last fifteen years. One thing that hasn't changed is London's Columbia Hotel. They still have the same grumpy night porter serving drinks, the same haughty Bulgarian witch behind the front desk, and the same nice old lady serving breakfast.

Upon entering room 217, a wave of despair came over me. I had shared this same tiny room with Kramer in 1989. They still had the same little TV, with no remote control, so you had to stand up to change the channel. Even the green bedspreads were the same. The electric kettle was the best feature, and the shortbread cookies, but a kettle and biscuits are de rigueur in English hotels.

I had a drink at the Columbia bar. There is usually a band or three staying there—it is the rock hotel of London. But that night there was just a table of drunken Dutch fishermen on vacation.

I had spent many an amusing night in the hotel barroom. Drinking bitter English beer and smoking English cigarettes. Silk Cut. Hanging out with friends in other bands. Good times. On this night, nursing my half pint of bitter ale alone in the corner, I felt like I had come full circle. And I realized that I didn't ever want to stay in the Columbia Hotel again.

I curled up in my hotel bed and watched Bush versus Kerry in the first 2004 presidential debate. Apparently Kerry won. There was some talk the next day about a strange bulge beneath George Bush's suit.

There were no interviews to do in England. I did have one Scottish phone interview to do, but I could have done that from New York City. *Rendezvous* was getting good reviews in English magazines like *Q* and *Mojo,* but a feature was pretty much out of the question. That's the way it has been since 1991. The music magazines are geared toward teenagers. I thought that the breakup of Luna might get some extra press, but it didn't pan out that way in the U.K. They had more important issues to talk about, like Pete Doherty and Kate Moss. I'd rather read about Kate Moss, too.

I left the hotel bright and early the next morning for the shopper's paradise they call Heathrow. My carry-on suitcase (a $20 special on Orchard Street) was falling to bits. The handle fell off as I dragged it from the Columbia Hotel to Paddington Station, and I had to buy some string to make a temporary fix.

I tried on some boots at the Prada shop at Heathrow. This was the first time I had ever tried on anything Prada. They didn't have my size, which was just as well. Instead I bought a pair of brown suede Clarks shoes. They were a cross between Wallabees and moccasins. Lee Wall later christened them my woccasins. My rockasins.

I picked up *Whatever* by Michel Houellebecq to read on the flight home. It's mean-spirited, but I was in the mood for something mean-spirited.

> I don't like this world. I definitely do not like it . . . advertising . . . computers make me puke. . . . The world has need of many things, but not more information.

November 6, 2004

Death exists not as the opposite, but as part of life.

                        —Haruki Murakami, Norwegian Wood

I bought *Norwegian Wood* before a trip to Japan, and I never did finish it, but this one line jumped out at me. I thought it applied to the rock-and-roll band, and would make a good, pretentious answer to the question "Why is Luna breaking up?"

Because "death exists not as the opposite, but as part of life." Rock-and-roll bands get older and they eventually break up—that's an inevitable part of the story. Luna had now embraced that part of the story, celebrating our very demise by announcing it prior to the tour. Plus, we hoped that our announcement would help sell more T-shirts, which are the lifeblood of the rock-and-roll tour. Selling T-shirts put cash in our hands and cheered us up. There was nothing like a little bundle of bills in your pocket from the sale of T-shirts.

Sean was now in charge of T-shirts, and I appreciated his taking over that thankless task. Before him it was Justin who ordered the shirts and counted them in and out at each club. The worst part of the job was counting them out at the end of the night and waiting to get paid, wasting valuable time that could be spent schmoozing. But Sean seemed happy to be out there counting the money, money that went straight to the band—after the club had taken its percentage.

In recent years, the clubs have gotten wise. They used to just let you sell your shirts, but now they demand a cut—15 percent, 20 percent. Some big clubs now take 30 percent plus sales tax, forcing bards to price their shirts higher than they want to.

The farewell tour began at Maxwell's in Hoboken. This was the site of the first real Luna show, with the original lineup of Stanley, Dean, Justin, and Grasshopper, back in 1992. That night was very exciting. I couldn't believe how good we sounded that first show with Stanley.

By 2004 we had all gotten just a little tired of driving out to Maxwell's, getting stuck in traffic for the Holland Tunnel on Friday afternoons, getting stuck in traffic coming back at 2:00 A.M. on Saturday. At one point we had played more sold-out shows at Maxwell's than any other band. That was before Yo La Tengo started doing their *Eight Nights of Hanukkah* there each year. But they actually lived in Hoboken. Luna will have to settle for having the most sold-out shows at Maxwell's by a band that doesn't live in Hoboken. Perhaps this is like being the all-time home run champion in baseball's minor leagues.

I contemplated these matters as I waited downstairs in the Maxwell's green room, which is also the storage closet for the restaurant. Candles, napkins, detergent bottles, urinal cakes—it was all there.

We drove up to Boston on a cold and blustery November day. Back to the Middle East. Going back to Cambridge is like going back to the old house I lived in as a child, which is somewhat pleasant but slightly depressing, too. I remember my first Middle East show with Galaxie 500, when it was a belly-dancing club. It was an afternoon matinee and I was frightened—frightened of the microphone and scared of my guitar. I was not afraid anymore. I had my bandmates around me and we knew how to do this.

The day before we headed to Cambridge, "Tugboat" was played on VH1 Classic, which may have meant that I was getting old. I was a classic. But I shouldn't have been taking my cue from VH1. They are notorious for speeding up history, and had just started running that *I Love the '90s* show in 2004.

Joan Anderman of the *Boston Globe* had written a big feature article about Luna, titled "Let's Not Stay Together: Wareham, Bandmates Set to Pull Plug after Twelve Years." Anderman spoke to each of us on the phone. She was smart, and dug deeper than rock critics usually do. I picked up a copy of the *Globe* at sound check.

> Dean: *Anytime you make a big change, there are lots of reasons that build up and you keep them at bay, and finally enough is enough. At some point, it becomes more complicated to stay together than to split up.*
>
> Lee: *We've reached a plateau, and that's not a situation that can sustain itself, regardless of the musical situation. It's healthy to move on.*
>
> Britta: *It is sad. . . . It's still new for me, and I'll miss it.*
>
> Sean: *This isn't a criticism, but the dynamic changed when Dean and Britta decided to become a couple. It sort of polarized things. We weren't doing as much as we could've been or making as much money as we could have.*

Every family is unhappy in its own way. So is every rock-and-roll band. I was going to show the *Boston Globe* article to everyone, but I decided to keep it in my bag. The band was soon to be no more. Why argue about what we should have been doing?

I, too, wished that we could have been making more money, but we weren't. CD sales were down—not just for Luna, but across the board. Record companies were merging, laying off employees left and right. Distributors were going out of business. The ones who stayed in business were reducing their shipments drastically.

The concert business, too, was becoming ever more competitive. The marketplace was crowded. There were hundreds of bands out there, booking the clubs months in advance, playing their stupid songs. There is something tribal about it—different groups of men wearing different kinds of rock clothing, descended from different rock traditions, singing their songs and dressing up and dancing around, competing with other groups of men for an audience's attention.

Bob Lawton told us that we shouldn't go to "the well" too often. We could play Washington, D.C., twice in one year and make good money, but we couldn't push it and try for a third gig, because the audience would decrease. And if your audience decreases, then your pay decreases also. Nobody wanted that.

That night's show at the Middle East was the best Boston show we'd ever played. We ended with "Black Postcards." The lyrics hadn't changed since I wrote the song, but they now meant something different.

I'm tired of having no future
I'm tired of pushing my luck
I'm tired of waiting for the endgame
Watching the stars turn black

We pushed on to Buffalo, a beautiful drive through the Berkshires.

It had been three days since John Kerry conceded the election to George Bush. It was depressing to think that we lived in a country full of religious nuts. "How can 58 million people be so dumb?" asked England's *Daily Mirror.*

Ralph Nader gave a scathing and riveting concession speech on ABC News, where he accused George Bush of taking the country "backwards into the future." It was riveting for about forty-five seconds, and then they cut him off.

We visited the Rock and Roll Hall of Fame in Cleveland. It's not unlike a Hard Rock Cafe, or a wax museum. Everything is neatly categorized. They have Memphis, Motown, San Francisco psychedelia, and New York City punk. I didn't see anything on the 13th Floor Elevators or the MC5.

The café food at the Hall of Fame was lousy, but the record store wasn't half bad. I bought *Creedence Country* and a Dolly Parton compilation containing her recording of "I Will Always Love You," which hits me in the gut every time I hear it. Yet every time I hear Whitney Houston sing the song, I get angry. Why did she have to destroy it? She *Whitnified* it, adding extra notes where none were needed.

We had 170 paid customers at the Beachland Ballroom. My friends in Cleveland said that the recession there was real. All the stuff we had seen on TV was real. There was a reason that the Democrats and Republicans had spent so much time and money campaigning in Ohio. People had lost their good jobs and were unemployed or working at Wendy's. They didn't have money for rock shows. Or perhaps they were all at the Helmet show over at the Grog Shop. Sometimes there's only room for one rock band per night in a town like Cleveland.

Lee had coined a new term—"manhive." He observed that Luna's audience was skewed toward guys in their thirties. On certain songs, you could see a group of guys jumping up and down, pumping their fists or playing air guitar. This was the manhive, the Luna mosh pit.

The bouncer at the Blind Pig recommended a greasy spoon for dinner—he said that their hippie hash was famous. After peering through the window, we decided to go to a slightly more upscale restaurant, the kind that serves booze. As we sat eating, Sean was approached by a student wearing a Howard Dean button—perhaps ironically.

"Dude. Are you going to sing 'Still at Home'? That's my favorite song on the new record."

Sean waited till the fan left.

"No way," he said.

Sean preferred to sing "Broken Chair." The song refers obliquely to his former girlfriend, who had bought him two matching vintage leather chairs when they lived together—as a birthday gift. One of the chairs was broken. When Sean moved out, she let him take the broken chair.

Jason Raboin, our tour manager and sound engineer, kept telling me that "Broken Chair" should not be in the set list. He called it "Song for People to Go and Get a Beer To."

I won't miss the Blind Pig. The dressing room is cold, lit by fluorescent light, covered in graffiti, and there is only one real chair and a couple of bar stools. We played a long, slow game of musical chairs in that filthy little room. This is why it's better to tour in a bus—in a pinch, it can double as a dressing room.

We had spacious rooms at the House of Blues Hotel in Chicago, located in Marina City, next to the Chicago skyscrapers seen on the opening credits of *The Bob Newhart Show,* and on a Wilco record. It was bitterly cold at the Abbey Pub, where we were playing the next two nights—so cold that Dr. Sample wouldn't work, and neither would my Butt Face fuzz pedal, which runs on a germanium chip. Germanium is very sensitive to variations in temperature. The Butt Face didn't like it here.

Matthew Buzzell arrived that day with his movie camera. He had come to direct a documentary about the last days of Luna—*Tell Me Do You Miss Me*. Matthew had pitched the movie idea to Robin Hurley at Rhino Entertainment, who provided us a modest budget. This was his second music documentary—he had already directed a great film about the jazz singer Little Jimmy Scott. With his thick black glasses and his woolen Brooks Brothers cap, Matthew had a Michael Caine–*Alfie* thing going on. Matthew and Sean had studied acting together at the North Carolina School of the Arts. He liked to tell us how Sean had been the star pupil, the boy wonder. Matthew also liked to remind Sean that it was he who had dragged Sean to see Galaxie 500 at the Knitting Factory on Houston Street many years ago.

Today Matthew took his camera and followed Sean and me to a pawnshop, where he filmed me haggling with the manager over an old Gibson Falcon amplifier. Then he filmed us cabbing it back to the hotel.

Our Friday night show was very different from the show Thursday. A fan sent us an e-mail on this subject. She said the Thursday night show was one of the greatest live music experiences of her life. But then on Friday she had to contend with rowdy frat boys screaming "Yeah fuckin' rock 'n' roll muthafuckah-frickin' Chicago Bitch!"

The manhive was bumming people out. Thursday night's show was reviewed in the *Chicago Tribune* by Joshua Klein. We read his review aloud as we pulled out of town on the way to Minneapolis.

> *All good things must come to an end, goes the adage. But what of the always pleasant but rarely exceptional? Do they get such a romantic sendoff as well? Luna's repertoire of samey sweet nothings isn't particularly diverse.*

Ouch. Maybe he was right. Maybe it had been twelve years of samey sweet nothings. But is diversity what makes an artist good? Picasso is diverse, of course, but Rothko isn't. You might say that Picasso was a fox, while Rothko was a hedgehog.

Bad reviews hurt more than good ones feel good. I rarely believed the good ones. If a review said I was a wonderful songwriter, I'd think, That can't be true, can it? My therapist was fond of saying that recognition must come from within. He wrote a book about it—*How to Be Your Own Best Friend*. In the book, he writes, "It is up to us to give ourselves recognition.

If we wait for it to come from others, we feel resentful when it doesn't, and when it does, we may well reject it."

Since we couldn't get a hotel room in Minneapolis (the Vikings were playing), we stayed at the Marriott Courtyard out by the Mall of America. We ate dinner at a popular steakhouse chain. Sean's steak made him violently ill—he was up all night vomiting. Then he had an argument with Matthew, his roommate, whom Sean accused of stealing his laundry detergent.

"You took my laundry detergent, you cock!"

"I did not."

"Cock . . . Oh, wait. I found it."

B ritta and I were barely speaking again. She was mad at me for some perceived slight and I knew she was mad at me but couldn't bring myself to ask why—because I didn't want to know. We would stake out our respective positions and sometimes we didn't budge for days.

I went to the Mall of America alone.

There was a nice piece on Luna in the *City Pages:* "He pairs words in Seussian swirls," they wrote, "and unwittingly writes some of dream pop's finest poetry."

"Dream pop" was a new term we were hearing a lot of at the time. It wasn't power pop. It was dream pop, which was related to shoegaze and space rock. Whatever it was, we were part of it.

Jason and I bet on how many people would show up at the Fine Line Music Cafe that Sunday night. He said 250. I said 400. The count was 317. He won the bet, but I declared it a moral victory for me.

Our guitar tech wanted to buy some weed after the show, from a local woman who came to all the rock shows. He called the pot lady on her cell phone, and we drove around in circles trying to find her, finally tracking her down at Ryan Adams's hotel. He was in town, too, playing the State Theater. Two big tour buses sat idling in front of his hotel.

We pulled up with our Econoline van and trailer to wait for the pot lady.

I was reminded of the scene in *This Is Spinal Tap* where the Tap runs into another band in their hotel lobby, a band that is playing the Enormodome and traveling in style.

Matthew was tipsy and talkative that night. Sean told him to shut up. Matthew softly slapped Sean in the face with his leather gloves. Sean didn't like that so much. Especially after his brutal mugging in Fort Greene the previous month, where an unknown attacker bashed him in the face with a brick, fracturing his eye socket and putting him in the hospital. He answered Matthew with a punch in the chest.

It's too bad the camera wasn't rolling for that sequence. It would have spiced up the documentary—a little pushing and shoving between the director and the guitarist, who are the best of friends. But that wasn't central to the story.

Britta and I started speaking again in Madison, Wisconsin. We wondered what we had been fighting about, and decided it was nothing—other than that I am not communicative enough and I resist people's demands on me to be more communicative. Maybe that's not nothing. Maybe I am a withholding son of a bitch.

We moved on to the Highdive in Champaign, Illinois, where we had dinner with my friend Lisa's parents. They were lifelong Democrats who had voted for Bush in the recent election. They didn't actually like Bush, but they subscribed to that whole theory of the impending great clash of cultures, which is why they supported the war in Iraq. I was waiting for them to compare Bush to Churchill, which they did, just before dessert was served.

The next day, Britta and I wandered into a Barnes & Noble in Cincinnati. They had a huge Christian book section there, but I also saw a teenage girl wearing a Larry Flynt T-shirt, which warmed my heart. Wherever you have sanctimonious Christians telling you what's right and wrong, you also have people who despise them.

One gentleman at our Cincinnati show wore a T-shirt bearing an image of George Bush as Lucifer, with a quotation from the Bible on the back, a warning to us all to beware of false prophets who think they are vessels for the Lord. I invited him up to the stage and he received a round of applause.

The day after the show I received an e-mail from a fan who said he felt like he was "watching the Rush Limbaugh show, but just from the other side." I added this to my file of angry letters from fans who say that musicians should just shut up and play the songs.

In Nashville, we checked into the Vanderbilt Hotel, the very hotel where

Al Gore was holed up while he awaited the results of the Florida re-count in 2000.

I called Dave Berman of Silver Jews, who lived in Nashville now.

"Where are you staying?" he asked.

"The Vanderbilt. Do you know it?"

"Yes."

David and his wife, Cass, showed up an hour later with Harmony Korine in tow, and took us to dinner at a nice restaurant. Harmony and Dave had both recently completed rehab for addiction to crack. Harmony said that his crack cocaine problem was far more serious than Berman's. He said that he did unspeakable things to get drugs. They traded stories. Berman told of his own descent into crack hell, which in fact ended at the Vanderbilt Hotel, where he checked into a five-room suite, ingested large quantities of crack and Dilaudid and Xanax, and contemplated suicide.

That was the old David Berman. The new David Berman attended meetings and was religious and talked about his rabbi. He said that Alcoholics Anonymous was not religious enough for him.

"This is music city," said Dave. "Everyone you meet is a musician. Waiters, taxi drivers, bartenders. They're all great players, and they're always hustling you, looking for work, wondering if they can play on your next album. It's a drag."

After the show that night we went to a dive called the Springwater. Berman was there, completely sober, insulting a couple of musicians that he knew. Ordinarily they tell you not to hang out in bars if you're a recovering drug addict. But Berman had it figured out. He remained sober, but could still act like a drunk if he needed to.

The Springwater was located right next to Centennial Park, where Robert Altman's *Nashville* was filmed. Matthew insisted that we stroll over there at 2:00 A.M.—he wanted to film us wandering around the very same park. We grudgingly obliged. He was the director.

The first leg of the farewell tour ended on November 30, 2004, with a sold-out show at Irving Plaza in New York City. This was our first New York show since we announced the breakup. We didn't say it was our last

New York show, but we didn't say it *wasn't* our last New York show. It could have been the last show—which was good for ticket sales.

After the twelfth song—"23 Minutes in Brussels"—the crowd applauded for a solid minute, a continuous swell of applause that hit me right in the . . . well, I'm not sure where it hit me. It was nice, but it hurt, too. It felt like an extended thank-you for twelve years of playing live—just for being Luna. I thought the applause would go on forever, but Lee cut it off by launching into "Tracy, I Love You."

The Right to Work

New Jersey is a right-to-work state. We discovered this when we performed on John McEnroe's TV show in December. It was an odd day for two reasons. First, because MSNBC just announced that McEnroe's show had been canceled. There was something poetic about his having us on his show that week, because we'd been canceled, too. Second, because Lee Wall was out in Los Angeles, looking for a new apartment, we had Matt Johnson fill in for him on drums.

"Don't worry," I told him, "we'll pay you something, but you'll also be paid by the TV studio."

We always got paid something when we appeared on TV. But McEnroe's producer informed us that New Jersey is a "right-to-work" state. I believe this is some kind of anti-union rhetoric—"right to work" actually translates to "we're not paying you."

We performed "Speedbumps," at Johnny Mac's request. It was my new favorite song from *Rendezvous*. It reminded me of something the Feelies might have done—or maybe the Strokes. There is a definite similarity in the sound of those two bands. They both play fast, angular guitar music. But the Feelies were nerdy and suburban, where the Strokes are debonair and cosmopolitan.

I don't wanna take your call
I refuse to climb your wall
I don't wanna ride that bus
I am tired of all of us

I never knew which camera to look at when we were on TV. As a result, I looked shifty-eyed. My eyes darted here and there.

McEnroe didn't seem happy about the show's being canceled, and having to stick around to tape a week of shows with the Sword of Damocles hanging over his head.

To close the show, he strapped on a red Les Paul and jammed with us on "Sweet Jane"—his request. He took the solo himself. The greatest tennis player of his generation really wanted to be a rock star. I taped the show and sent a copy to my grandfather in New Zealand, a tennis player himself, who was suitably impressed that I jammed with John McEnroe.

While My Eyes Go Looking
for Flying Saucers in the Sky

Tine wrote me a letter in 2002. She had recently divorced.

I dreamt about you last night. You were sitting on a bench in
Copenhagen, near the lakes, and not so far from a big cinema. It was
dark and in the evening. I was surprised to recognize you and asked
what you were doing there all alone. You told me, you'd just lost your
band. I asked if you wouldn't like to come along, you could stay some
days and you could join us for the Mercury Rev concert (in reality they
are actually playing next Wednesday). You looked at me, shook your
head and said that you had decided to spend just one night in all the
cities you ever played in, to recover from the loss.

Luna was flying to Spain for one last tour.

We arrived in Barcelona in the afternoon and checked into a rotten little
hotel close to the Apolo. I had requested the Hotel Jazz, the three-star hotel
that I stayed at when I came to do interviews a couple of months earlier. We
had been assured that this one was also a three-star hotel, but much closer
to the Apolo. It was close to the club, but the other part was a bald lie.

I took everyone to Las Siete Puertas for the fantastic paella, and then we
got good and lost on the way back to the hotel. Everyone enjoyed getting
lost in the narrow, winding walkways of Barcelona's Gothic quarter.

We woke up at one in the afternoon. Shit. I cursed myself for sleeping so
late. I had wanted to get on Spanish time. We spent the afternoon with Ignacio, drinking coffee and browsing through the soundtrack CDs at the FNAC.
I found a copy of *Contempt,* Georges Delerue's score for Godard. I love the

Moravia novel, and I love the film, but the beautiful score by Delerue provides the emotional core of the movie.

The FNAC is a huge store, and we got separated from Lee, but he called me on my cell phone to say he was standing in the lobby. He liked to do that, and then I would demand that he reimburse me the dollar it cost me to answer his call. After the FNAC, we hit Vinçon, one of my favorite shops in the world, and I bought the German alarm clock I used to have. I had bought the exact same clock a few years before, but the plastic face got scratched up by something sharp in my suitcase, and I ended up throwing it away when I got home. Now I had a second chance.

Before the show that night I interviewed Ignacio for *Tell Me Do You Miss Me,* which was a switch. He had interviewed me half a dozen times over the years. We talked about Sterling Morrison and the Velvet Underground and General Franco. Ignacio pointed out that it wasn't so long ago in Spain that women had to be covered head to toe, just like in oppressive societies like Afghanistan.

"I am glad that Luna is breaking up," he said. "You don't want to turn into the Flamin' Groovies. It's time for a new beginning."

We had five hundred lovely people at the Apolo. I almost cried when I looked out at the cheering crowd and the lovely chandeliers. Barcelona had long been our favorite European city to play, because they liked us there and we always seemed to have fun. The last time we played in Barcelona it was the summer solstice, and the city was celebrating St. John's Eve (Verbena de San Juan). We could smell the fireworks in the air, and went to a party with Ignacio, up in the hills. It was a great spot and we sat there smoking cigarettes and dipping our feet into a little pool.

Tonight was less exciting by far, a night of quiet introspection. Sean, Britta, Matthew, Ignacio, and I went to a brightly lit little bar and drank beer and ordered a couple of ham sandwiches. We watched the sanitation workers, in their overalls, as they came in for their breakfast.

Lobby call the next day was 9:00 A.M. for the drive to Madrid. As we drove, I listened to "Timestretched" by the Divine Comedy and "Dreaming My Dreams with You" by Waylon Jennings. I started to feel sad. Listening to sentimental songs can do that to me, especially while riding in a van on four hours of sleep.

I'll always miss dreaming my dreams with you.

Here we were, driving the same roads, possibly for the last time. Playing at the same clubs, staying in some of the same hotels. What the hell was I going to do with myself when this was gone?

The drive to Madrid took seven hours. The van rattled loudly, the seats wouldn't recline, and there was no chance of sleep. Luckily I had a Vicodin, the perfect solution on days like this, when my head hurt and the sun was shining in my eyes and the van felt like a cage on wheels. At least it was warm and sunny there in Spain. We stopped for lunch at the side of the road. Turkey, potatos, asparagus, café cortado. The cortado is a Spanish specialty—an espresso with a little splash of steamed milk.

After our show at Arena, we went out drinking with our friends Mark and Jesus and Jorge. They had slowed down in the eight years that I had known them. I remember my first promo trip to Spain, for the *Pup Tent* album. Our label rep met us at the airport on Sunday night and took us out drinking. We sat in a bar watching golf on television—the final round of the PGA championship, live from Winged Foot in Mamaroneck, New York. Colin Montgomerie was fading from contention, and Craig, our Scottish promotions man, was upset.

"Let's get some coke," said the rep, at about two in the morning.

"But we have to do an interview at nine in the morning."

I felt like a lightweight. Luckily, he couldn't find any coke that night, though he did have some in the office the next afternoon. He offered me a line between interviews, but I declined. One of the interviews was on videotape, and I didn't want to appear with cocaine eyes.

This time the coke dealer showed up in a sharkskin suit and someone chopped out lines on a table in the back of the bar. Sean and Matthew had been talking to a nice girl who had been at both the Barcelona and Madrid shows, standing in the front row. Matthew and Sean were getting irritated with each other.

"I think there's a vibe," said Matthew.

"No," said Sean. "It's just like it was in college. Matthew tries to move in on girls who are interested in me, by announcing that there is some kind of vibe."

Jesus drove 140 kilometers an hour all the way to Cádiz. The van shook. Britta sat next to me, feeling ill. She had thrown up that morning.

Sean bitched at Matthew—playfully, of course.

"You're making a living wage!"

Matthew was being paid a small weekly salary out of the film budget. The rest of us were just hoping that we could sell enough T-shirts to go home with a few hundred dollars. The tour manager and driver earned the living wage, but we got the glory of being onstage playing our songs to cute Spanish girls in their pantalones, and talking to the Spanish guys who didn't speak English but wanted to know what kind of effects pedals we used.

At least we were all getting along. Knowing that this was Luna's last time in Europe made us appreciate it that much more. There was no longer any reason to complain about the lack of press or radio play or low sales figures. Sure, we weren't making any money, but no one was screwing us. We were here because we wanted to be here, because we liked touring around Spain, playing our music in these lovely cities.

A na Espina, the Majorcan promoter, met us at our hotel in Palma. She was petite and looked a little like Marlene Dietrich, with white pancake makeup and bright red hair. She was there in 1996 in Pradejón, our first Spanish date. We all thought she was very pretty. We also thought we were going to die. Her English boyfriend drove like a maniac from Madrid to Pradejón, speeding over the hills and hurtling down narrow, winding roads.

In Majorca we were playing the Teatre in Lloseta, which was located near an old cement factory about forty minutes outside of Palma. This was a beautiful new theater complex with a brand-new PA system, a far cry from the dives with wretched equipment that we had played in the past. It's nice to feel that your equipment won't crap out on you, but frankly I liked playing dive clubs. For some reason it felt more authentic than playing a shiny new theater complex. Maybe we were so used to playing in dirty little clubs that we got confused when we were thrown into a comfortable environment.

T he Valencia show was mobbed. We always played Valencia on a Friday night, and Friday night in Valencia was always exciting. Sean and Lee and Jason went out drinking after the show, looking for fun, for whatever might happen. Which turned out to be nothing. I used to do that—spend hours talking to girls and their stupid drunken boyfriends in clubs. And I used to stumble back to my hotel room at 4:00 A.M. and feel wretched the next day. I was glad I didn't do that anymore.

I n Bilbao, Britta and I ate delicious peppered lamb skewers at a crowded tapas bar. The Azkena was a tiny club with a teeny stage, and it was jammed with people. They pack them in like sardines in Spain—they have a different interpretation of "sold out." A club is sold out when they literally cannot fit another person through the front door.

Postshow I found myself talking to a few fans and having my photo taken and being asked lots of questions. I decided to get the hell out of there. That kind of conversation makes me tired.

Britta and I walked back to the hotel, popping our heads into Kafe Antzokia on the way—the large club where Luna played in 1999. I opened the door and it had turned into an indie discotheque, and they were blaring "Pup Tent" over the PA. The song sounded great that loud; we worked so damn hard on it in the studio, and it paid off.

I felt like I had walked through a door and come out six years earlier. Like Tom Sawyer must have felt standing in the back of the room at his own fake funeral, seeing all the people crying and saying such nice things about him.

T ouring is exhausting," said Matthew, as we boarded our 8:00 A.M. EasyJet flight to London Stansted the next morning.

I didn't find it quite as tiring as I used to. It's exhausting if you are out getting hammered every night, documenting the search for postshow fun. It's exhausting if you don't come back to the hotel till five in the morning, but not so bad if you're in bed by two.

But Matthew did get some special footage from the previous night. He filmed one fellow on the street sticking a beer bottle in his ass.

I listened to Caetano Veloso's "London, London" as our plane approached the city.

While my eyes go looking for flying saucers in the sky.

It is a beautiful song, written by Caetano during the period that he had been exiled from Brazil. I thought about the ULU, where we would be playing tomorrow night, the same club where Galaxie 500 played its final show in England, the same club where my Japanese friend slapped me in the face.

"Why you are writing all your songs to me?"

London's Stansted Airport was cute. What wasn't cute was my suitcase coming down the carousel half open. My special black German alarm clock was gone. The horror.

The green room at the ULU was located in an old squash court. It was quite large and had good acoustics. A doctor came to the show, and gave us a packet of Valium. He donated medical supplies to bands in need.

Sonic Boom joined us onstage, playing his electronic tabla and synthesizer on "Fuzzy Wuzzy" and "Indian Summer." The London crowd was very talkative—that's the way it is in England. There are always a couple of English blokes who want to lob funny insults at you.

"Don't let your middle age go to waste!"

I had no response for that. I was in a reflective daze all show long, thinking about the time I was there with Galaxie 500. I had friends there that night who were also at the last Galaxie 500 show, and when you have friends at a show, you spend your time onstage thinking about them, or about the last time you saw them, or about how much your lives have changed. Things you don't think about on your first tour, when you are just amazed that people have come to see you at all.

I was repeating myself. Retracing my steps. And it was better the first time. The room looked bigger. Saying goodbye wasn't as fun as saying hello.

I Love You but I've
Chosen Darkness

Britta and I arrived at LaGuardia in plenty of time for our 8:30 A.M. flight to Austin, and went downstairs to have breakfast.

I had been depressed all week, which had been happening more frequently before a tour. I would get a vague sinking feeling, a feeling that I should be home with Jack, a feeling that something bad was about to happen. But I quickly got into the routine—the routine of not having to face life, or make decisions. You go where you are told each day. You get up when the tour manager says to get up, you eat lunch when he says to eat lunch, you go straight to the club for sound check, run to the hotel to lie down for thirty minutes, write the set list, run back to the club for the show. You wait for the money to be counted after the show, and then you get in the van and go. It could be grueling, but the mindlessness of it was not unpleasant.

"Our flight is delayed," said Britta, looking at the monitors. I turned around and looked at the display. We were flying first to Raleigh, then on to Austin.

RALEIGH 8:56, I read off the departures screen.

We sat down for a greasy egg sandwich and a milky latte. As we sat there at LaGuardia next to the baseball cap shop, where you can customize your own cap, I spied my old marriage counselor, Ben Marinucci, and his wife, Kay.

Ben didn't save my marriage, but that was my job more than his. I'm sure I never gave him the tools, or whatever it is that you need to save a marriage—most important, the will to save it.

Ben and Kay were heading to Tucson.

"What time is your flight?" Ben asked.

I turned around to look at the screen again. This time I looked a bit harder. I had been looking at the *arrivals* screen! Shit. We grabbed our bags and ran to the gate as fast as we could. The woman at the gate knew exactly who we were. She had been calling our names over the intercom in the departure lounge for twenty minutes. We had officially missed our flight.

They found us a couple of seats on the next flight, but they had to split us up. That was probably for the best. Britta wouldn't have to sit next to me in my foul mood, but I was given the very worst seat on the plane, a middle seat in the last row, by the toilets and the roaring engine. My seat wouldn't recline, and I was stuck between two big guys who were deep in conversation.

Why didn't they sit together if they wanted to talk? My foul mood deepened.

I put in some earplugs and took half a Valium and fell asleep. That was lucky. Earplugs and Valium are lifesavers.

This was it. The last leg of the final tour. The last days of our nights. Lee flew in from Los Angeles, his new home as of January 1. Sean had already been in Austin for a few days, spending time with his family. His sister was married to a lawyer. Or a doctor. One of those. They had two children. Other people, people who are not in rock bands, have real lives—lives of quiet accumulation, 401K accounts, Roth IRAs, college funds, retirement funds, and health insurance.

Austin was one of our favorite cities to play, right up there with Barcelona and San Francisco. We were greeted onstage with a one-minute ovation from 1,100 fans, an ovation that washed away all the day's petty annoyances. It was a perfect show. The stage sound was great, and everything was clicking.

On the way to Dallas the next day, we stopped one last time at the Up in Smoke barbecue cafeteria, where we always ate on the way from Austin to Dallas. I had had the same lunch there a dozen times over the years. In 2002 we ran into the Dictators. I remembered watching them climb out of their Ford Econoline van and telling myself that I did not want to be riding around in a van when I was fifty years old.

Maybe I'll feel differently when I'm fifty. Maybe I'll miss the Up in Smoke.

The Sons of Hermann Hall in Dallas was a beautiful old wooden Texas ballroom, like something you might see in *The Last Picture Show*. It had long been a German American hall for drinking, big bands, and bowling. They had old black-and-white photographs showing how things used to be. An elderly woman, the manager, told me about the ghosts. One time she was minding her own business, stocking the bar, when she heard voices upstairs. It sounded like little children, singing and talking and running. But when she ran upstairs to check it out, the children were gone.

I didn't really buy that ghost talk, but right before hitting the stage that night, the power switch on my amplifier broke clean off, which could be considered a little spooky. I borrowed a Vox AC-30 from the opening band— I Love You But I've Chosen Darkness. The show was sold out and had that great Saturday night feel. Britta and I went back to the hotel and watched *I, Robot* on TV. I had unpleasant dreams, in which I yelled at Britta for being late for another flight. I was glad to wake up.

The fans in Boulder were clean-cut. It was like we had arrived on a different planet peopled with mountain-ski types, handsome boys and pretty girls, tanned and blond and wholesome. Sean was sure that some of these wholesome girls would be hanging out after the show, but they were not. The green room was quiet.

"Goddamn it! Where is everybody?"

Riding back to the hotel in the van, Sean took out his frustration on Jason, barking out directions from the backseat. The scolding navigator was back.

Britta and Lee and I flew to Tucson the next day, while the rest of the team drove the van. Club Congress was located inside the Hotel Congress, where we would be staying for the next couple of nights. Except the manager informed us that they were completely booked, on account of the annual jewelry convention, so the three of us would have to share one room with bunk beds.

Long sigh.

We ducked into the hotel restaurant, and Lee called Jason to apprise him of the situation. After dinner the hotel manager called us over. An extra room had materialized.

"Jason is a good tour manager," he said.

Apparently Jason had threatened to pull the show unless they gave us the rooms that we had been promised.

There was a small party in the green room after our show the following night. I didn't stay long, but Lee and Matthew and Sean all stayed up till three o'clock, talking to a cute girl who was a friend of a friend of Sean's. At 3:00 A.M. she announced that she had to go—she had to teach early in the morning.

It would have made a good episode of *Animal Planet.* Here were three males competing for the same female. They played a strange waiting game, a mating ritual of sorts, to see if one of the males would drop out. But none of them did, and the evening ended in a stalemate. Such is life on the road.

We drove Interstate 8 to San Diego, over the hills and along the Mexican border. We took care of some important business in the van. First, we voted on the design of the T-shirt for the last show—this would be a special commemorative T-shirt with a special commemorative price. Then we voted to cancel our early morning TV appearance. That was an easy decision. We had enough to do—three shows in three nights, in San Diego, L.A., and San Francisco—without adding an early morning TV show. And anyway, the band was breaking up. Why go on TV and promote Luna when we'd soon be gone for good?

We needed an official excuse, though. I volunteered to have a sore throat.

"That's lame," said Sean.

But we couldn't think of anything better. I called Robert Vickers at Jetset and broke the news. Robert, a former member of the Go-Betweens, had been the label's publicist for many years, but now he functioned more as the label manager. He warned me that this could have consequences the next time I wanted to be on Fox6 TV in San Diego.

We recently received an inquiry at our Web site, from a woman at the Fox News Channel. One of their Baghdad correspondents was a big Luna fan, and he posted something on the Fox site about how he liked to listen to Luna to unwind after a hard day's reporting. She was thinking we could set up a link from our Web site, www.fuzzywuzzy.com, to theirs, www.foxnews.com. But we didn't want to link our site to their nasty disinformation service.

This was my fourth time at the Casbah in San Diego. The first time was with Galaxie 500 at the old Casbah. This fourth show was sold out, and the crowd was especially drunk and rowdy—a real Thursday night crowd. There was no green room at the Casbah, so after the show we sat outside on the sidewalk, and got to talk to every last one of our drunken fans on their way home. One guy told us that he paid the bouncer $100 to get in the back door of the club.

I will always remember that Casbah show. I will remember all my nights at the Casbah.

I read my horoscope in the *San Diego Times* the following morning.

> Leo: *You understand the law of diminishing returns. A tired scene is now officially beyond your help. You're not sure where you want to go, but you are sure it's time for departure. Start walking, and you'll discover the path.*

We were in Los Angeles, playing a sold-out show at the El Rey Theatre. I was nervous up there in front of all those people. Los Angeles was on the list of cities where I got nervous. I didn't know what to say to all those people. I had nothing. It occurred to me that I needed to write some banter for these last days, something evocative and wistful.

That night was one of those nights where I felt like an impostor, a phony, a pretend singer who had no business being onstage at the El Rey. I guess other people feel that way about their jobs, too, like they've managed to fool everybody.

L.A. shows could be anticlimactic because there's nowhere to go after the clubs shut down. It's not a real city. So it was back to the Farmer's Daughter Motel and early to bed.

The Fillmore was sold out, too. What a great room, with the chandeliers and all the history, and the chocolate-dipped strawberries in the green room.

There was a long round of applause after "Friendly Advice." I could see Angel Corpus Christi dancing on the balcony at stage right—she and her husband, Rich, had seen every Fillmore show we'd ever played, from that exact spot. Angel said that she felt a collective sadness when the lights came on and as people realized that that was it. Luna wouldn't be back. We had played there once a year for the last seven or eight years, but we would not be coming back to play those songs anymore. The lights came on and the people all cleared out and the room was empty.

Britta and I decided to celebrate, swallowing a hit of ecstasy right after the show. We sat in the green room, talking to Ricky from the Brian Jonestown Massacre, when suddenly I started to feel the ecstasy only fifteen minutes after I had swallowed it. I needed to get out of that room *immediately*. I made a lame excuse about being tired, and Britta and I hurried through the empty club, out the side entrance and down the steps to get outside and find a taxi. There on the sidewalk a cool gay Mexican kid with a mohawk was waiting to have his Luna poster signed. It wasn't just frat boys who liked Luna after all.

Back to the Phoenix Hotel. Safety. Britta and I hooked up the iPod to a set of Altec speakers we had bought at the mall in Los Angeles, and we lounged around on the carpeted floor listening to Madonna and New Order and Bobbie Gentry and the Carpenters, Mazzy Star and Julie London and Richard Hawley. What a fun night we had. I was still living the dream.

On Monday we drove to Sacramento for the first and the last show Luna would ever play there. I was still pooped from the weekend. We played in a restaurant/club called Harlow's, and there were some strange fans out there that night. One older guy brought a laminated three-page foldout poster of Britta that had about twenty different captioned photographs of her on it. He had been following her career for years. There she was with Julia Roberts and Justine Bateman in a still from *Satisfaction.* There she was in Ben Lee's band. And there she was with Luna. Matthew decided to put the guy on camera.

"I've been a fan of Britta's for many years . . . and Dean . . . and the Luna band."

I t was cold and foggy damp in Eugene, Oregon, the kind of cold that gets into your bones. I walked a mile to the laundry to wash my clothes. Dryers were free on Wednesdays. Oh, happy day. I watched the clothes go round and round and realized that I missed Jack. Days like this reminded me of why I didn't want to live this life anymore.

On the way back from the laundry I found a vintage-clothing store, with clothes from the seventies and eighties. I tried on a few things, but then

I remembered that I preferred new clothes. I liked Brooks Brothers—new shirts, 100 percent cotton, soft and dependable. I was tired of the indie-rock uniform, the faded corduroys and ironic polyester shirts. Was I turning into a self-hating indie rocker?

The Eugene gig was at historic W.O.W. (pronounced "double-U-O-double-U") Hall, which was built in the 1930s by the Woodmen of the World, a fraternal organization that provided life insurance and burial benefits for its members. We had two hundred people, which was pretty great for Eugene. Apparently Greg Dulli and the Twilight Singers had just been there and they only had twenty. I was reminded of that fanzine dedicated to him in the '90s—*Fat Greg Dulli,* which is not to be confused with *Die, Evan Dando, Die.* I'm glad no one has named a fanzine after me.

Our Seattle show sold out immediately when tickets went on sale, so we added an early show to accommodate the fans who were left out, and also to give ourselves an extra $6,000. Early shows were never much good, though. They lacked energy. You hold back, because you know you've got to do a whole other show, and you need to leave some gas in the tank. This particular early show was the worst show of the tour—all four of us played poorly.

The late show felt like the best we had ever played. I made not a single mistake, and interesting notes flowed forth from my Les Paul.

After the show a woman approached me with a simple question.

"Why are you quitting?"

She couldn't believe it. We had just played two sold-out shows at Neumo's. How could we be walking away from this? It must have seemed pretty glamorous from the audience perspective. It was glamorous. What could I say? This was my fifth time playing a sold-out show to adoring fans in Seattle. I had done it. Yes, it was a rush getting up there onstage. Maybe I was going to miss it. But I decided that I could live without that rush, and the rush of the eight-hour van rides, too.

Crossing the border into Canada was quick and easy. It helped to have a nice clean-cut, baby-faced tour manager. A tour manager with tattoos and a strange haircut always increased the odds of getting the hose. That much we had learned.

We had a young crowd at Richard's on Richards in Vancouver, because it was a nineteen-and-over show. To see shows in the States, you have to be twenty-one years old. Sometimes you can persuade a club to do an eighteen-and-up show, but then they lower your guarantee, because they can't sell booze to the underage crowd. What's the point of letting a bunch of teenagers into the show if you can't sell them booze? None. No point. But Richard's on Richards had done something clever. They scheduled two shows—Luna at eight o'clock and a Latin dance party at ten.

It was a special and exciting night onstage for Sean. He got a great ovation when he sang "Broken Chair," and there was spontaneous applause after each of his guitar solos. When he went out to count the T-shirts after the show, three young ladies surrounded him.

"I want to marry you!" said one of the pretty ladies, before giving him a kiss.

This never happened. This kind of come-on is the stuff of rock-and-roll fantasy. But that night it was happening to Sean. The problem was that our van was scheduled to leave for Seattle in half an hour.

With the Latin-dance-party people coming in, loading out was a little chaotic. We all pitched in, wheeling our equipment out, while Lee stood outside on the sidewalk and made sure that nothing was stolen. As he stood there, he heard Sean's pretty lady yammering on her cell phone.

"Hey . . . you won't believe it, I just met the guitar player from Luna . . . he's really cool. Guess what, he's Canadian!"

At that moment a white stretch limousine pulled up in front of the club, and the three girls stepped into the limo and drove off into the night. This provided us with a good hour of amusing talk for our ride back to Seattle.

"Sean, what are you doing here? You could be riding around Vancouver in a white stretch limo with three hot chicks."

"Guess what, he's Canadian!"

"I want to marry you!"

Our West Coast trip was over. We sat at the Sea-Tac Airport all day, waiting for our plane. Lee pointed out that although it was only a seventeen-day trip, it seemed much longer. We covered a lot of ground— from the Sons of Hermann Hall in Dallas to the W.O.W. Hall in Eugene to

Richard's on Richards. We sold out most of the shows and broke guarantees almost every night.

And we all got along well for a change. There were no incidents. There was very little of the usual complaining about lack of support from the record company, hotels that were located too far from the venues, why we weren't on any TV shows, et cetera.

The end was upon us, and for that reason it seemed like we were all more appreciative of the pure thrill of traveling all over the country, playing Luna's music to thousands of people. Knowing that we were onstage in Seattle playing "23 Minutes in Brussels" for the last time in that city was very different from playing it with the knowledge that we would likely be back a year later, playing the same song on the same stage.

This Is the Day

There were seven days till the final Luna show. I had been daydreaming about this show. I played the scene over and over in my head—playing the final song onstage, singing the last lyrics, playing the final ten seconds, the last note. Of course, all this made me misty. I imagined I'd cry when the final song came, but I thought that I could get it all out of my system in advance if I imagined how sad it would be.

What if I simply didn't attend the last show? Was that an option? I could avoid all the goodbyes. I was tired of saying goodbye to people. I was ready to start my new job—only I didn't have a new job.

I sat in bed that week and watched the Metallica documentary, *Some Kind of Monster*. It was painful to watch. The film shows the worst things about being in a band: the inability to make decisions, the constant voting, talking, and meetings. Metallica writes lyrics by committee. How excruciating. It doesn't help that James Hetfield and his bandmates are not the smartest guys you'll meet. That can be the beauty of a rock-and-roll band—that a bunch of idiots can actually create something transcendent. Metallica doesn't do that so often, but they have their moments.

James Hetfield checks into rehab to deal with his drinking problem, and you would think that he might receive some support from his bandmates, but all he gets is grief. Lars, the asshole drummer, complains that he wasn't consulted—he is annoyed that *the band* was inconvenienced, that Hetfield dared to put his own interests above those of the collective.

I was surprised that Hetfield didn't just tell them all to fuck off. But that would mean dismantling a highly successful corporation. Metallica and U2 and R.E.M. are more than rock-and-roll bands. They are institutions, corporations. And corporations have lives of their own. Because of their immense wealth, they write songs differently from the rest of us. They don't have to worry about keeping recording costs down, so they can write in the studio, maybe a few hours a day, over the course of two years.

I awoke at 7:30 A.M. on February 22, made French toast and bacon for Jack, and took him to school. He showed me what the five-year-olds had been up to—they had constructed a replica of Christo's *The Gates,* with wood blocks and little pieces of orange cloth. I preferred the kids' version to the one in Central Park.

I had a window seat for our flight from LaGuardia to Chicago. As the plane took off I got a look at Rikers Island. The prison was covered in snow, and snow makes things pretty, but not Rikers Island. The barbed wire trumps the snow.

My thoughts turned to my brother Anthony, who would not be attending the final Luna shows. He hadn't seen us perform for some years now. Most of the time, he is out of my mind. I rarely see him, so I forget about how he is living his life. But sometimes I hear a song that reminds me of him, like "This Is the Day" by The The. This great song, a favorite of Anthony's, tells the story of a guy who has been up all night long. His eyes are bloodshot. He opens the window shades and sees a plane fly across the sky, and reflects that he could have done anything at all in this life, and all his friends say how lucky he is. He vows that on this day his life will change.

New York City is not the best place for someone who has spent years buying drugs on street corners all over town. Uptown, downtown, Amsterdam Avenue, Second Avenue, Avenue D, Waverly Place. Giuliani removed some of the dealers from the streets of Manhattan, but a bundle of heroin was always just a phone call away if you knew the number. It was too easy and too cheap. No, Anthony needed another fresh start, and soon found himself on his own flight, heading south and west, far from temptation.

After a final Detroit show at St. Andrew's Hall, Jason woke me up with bad news—the airline had canceled our flight to New York, citing inclement weather. I called Claudia, who told me that it was sunny and calm at home. The airline was fucking us. They couldn't put us on another flight till the following afternoon, which didn't work for us, because we were supposed to be onstage at the Bowery Ballroom by that time. We went to plan B—renting a minivan and driving home. Damn it. I was looking forward to picking Jack up from school.

"I'll drive," I said.

I drove till lunchtime—main course, Taco Bell, dessert, pink Sno Balls from a gas station—and then I drove some more, seven hours total, till we were deep into Pennsylvania. Jason took over and I rode shotgun the rest of the way. As night fell, an effulgent moon rose over the Pennsylvania sky.

"Look," said Lee, "the moon!"

We fell silent for a moment. Here we were, courtesy of a canceled flight, taking one final road trip together under a full moon. We had done this hundreds of times, and the long drives with our knees pushed against the seat in front of us were not exactly fun, but this was the last one, and we were not unmoved.

Bowery Ballroom

Originally, we had planned to do two shows at the Bowery Ballroom, but when they sold out within a couple of hours, a Sunday matinee was added, and then a Monday night, much to the annoyance of those fans who had bought tickets to the original "final" Luna show on Sunday night—now they only had tickets for the penultimate show. There was much grumbling in the Luna chat room online. I didn't visit this room myself, but Matthew Buzzell told me about it. "They're just doing it for the money," someone had posted.

That was true. We were only adding that Monday show for the money. It was also a higher ticket price than usual, which we did just for the money, too.

Lara played with us on Saturday night, and it was good to have her back onstage playing the keyboards. There had been some discussion about this when we were in Spain. Sean said that it was okay for her to play one of the last shows, but he didn't want her there for the very last show. Fair enough.

I suggested that we fly Justin over from New Zealand to play these final shows, but I was voted down. You can't send telegrams anymore—they no longer exist—but I got a fake telegram from Justin, sent via e-mail, and I read it aloud from the stage during the last shows.

TO THE BAND LUNA STOP GOOD LUCK TONIGHT STOP WISH I WERE THERE
STOP TEAR IN EYE STOP BEEN A GOOD RUN STOP CANNOT WAIT FOR THE
BOX SET STOP COUPLE OF TIPS FOR THE LAST SHOW STOP SEAN HAVE
YOU LEARNED THE MEANING OF THE WORD ENSEMBLE YET STOP BY THE
WAY I SAW YOU MOUTH THE WORDS I LOVE YOU TO VANESSA ACROSS THE
STAGE IN NEW HAVEN STOP I FELT UNEASY IF NOT A LITTLE SOILED
STOP ALWAYS FUN STOP LEE REMEMBER DO NOT SPEED UP IN THE MIDDLE

OF FRIENDLY ADVICE IT IS NOT A POLKA STOP TRY AND KEEP THE TOUR
TAN GOING AGAINST ALL ODDS STOP DEAN PLAY ONE FOR STANLEY AND
TERRY STOP IT IS OKAY TO CRY JUST MAKE SURE YOUR OLD MAN IS NOT
AROUND STOP BRITTA ALL MY SECRET SPIES TELL ME YOU DO A GREAT
JOB STOP BASTARDS STOP THINKING OF YOU GUYS TONIGHT STOP WILL
GET MY BASS OUT OF THE CLOSET AND PUT IT ON MY STAND STOP LOVE
JUSTIN.

The thought of Justin's Fender Jazz Bass sitting on its stand, twelve thousand miles away, made me sad.

Jack and Claudia came to the matinee. This was Jack's first time seeing Luna since he was two years old. He sat up in the balcony and waved to me excitedly. He told anyone who would listen, "That's my daddy!"

Britta and I got out of bed at noon on Monday, February 28. We had been up late—it had been crazy at the Bowery Ballroom these last nights, with all those Luna fans packed into the bar downstairs, lots of goodbyes, and questions, questions, questions. It made me glad that I was only a tiny bit famous. It must be exhausting to have people approach you all the time with questions like "What are you going to do now?" I only got it once in a while, often enough to make me feel slightly important, but not so often that I had to walk around in a hooded sweatshirt.

Snow began to fall around two o'clock that afternoon. I sat down for a slice of pizza at the window at Stromboli's on First Avenue. Lee called to talk about our gift for Jason, and when our call was over I cried quietly and quickly into my pizza. When I raised my head again, I saw Sean across the street, checking out a pair of New Balance sneakers in a store window.

I wore a striped purple Paul Smith shirt for the final Luna show, which I regretted when I saw it in the Luna documentary—because it's purple. Our manager worked with both David Bowie and David Byrne, so he received a 25 percent discount at Paul Smith. He said that I could surely get a discount, too, but when we sent a press packet over to the Paul Smith PR rep, I was deemed not worthy of the discount. That put me in my place.

The snow kept falling. I worked on the set list, trying to make it as perfect as possible. Jason had asked me not to put "Broken Chair" in the set.

"The audience loses focus. I feel the energy being sucked out of the room."

I came up with this:

"Chinatown"

"Sideshow by the Seashore"

"Astronaut"

"California"

"Malibu Love Nest"

"Tiger Lily"

"Friendly Advice"

"Bewitched"

"Tracy, I Love You"

"Pup Tent"

"Going Home"

"Time to Quit"

"Moon Palace"

"Black Postcards"

***

"Everybody's Talkin'"

"Fuzzy Wuzzy"

"23 Minutes in Brussels"

"Indian Summer"

I showed the set list to everyone before the show.

"Where's *the Chair*?" said Sean.

I added "Broken Chair."

Our fans seemed excited on that final, snowy Monday night, pleased to be there for the emotional countdown to the end of our time as Luna. At the end of each song, I could feel people thinking, *That's it, they are finished with that song.* I looked out and saw Jen, whom we met at Northsix a few years ago when she barged into the dressing room completely trolleyed. Jen cried through the entire show. It made sense at the time, but really what was there to cry about? No one was dying. It was just that Luna had thrown in the towel and she'd never see us play again and her youth was over.

Her crying was making me sad. I pleaded with her to stop. I gave her my kazoo after the kazoo solo in "Everybody's Talkin'," thinking maybe if she had a kazoo she'd be happy.

I kept asking myself, "How do you feel?" I should have felt sad, right? We played "23 Minutes in Brussels" for the very last time and I thought, We're playing it for the last time.

Enough. I was ready for all this to be over.

We ended with Beat Happening's "Indian Summer," which had been a frequent closer over the years, before it fell out of favor. But that night it was back. I used to really enjoy hearing Sean's beautiful long guitar solo, the way he bent certain notes on his Jazzmaster. This time I moved stage left, so I could hear it better. And then I counted down to the end, the two notes that go back and forth all through the song, and we were done. We walked off the stage, and it was a relief to be walking off the stage knowing that we would not be back the very next night.

The dressing room at the Bowery Ballroom was usually packed with people drinking and smoking after a Luna show. But this last night it was just the four of us, plus Matthew, who had positioned himself in the corner to film these last moments.

I have since seen the Luna documentary, *Tell Me Do You Miss Me,* and in this final scene I appear to be fighting back tears. I can now report that I was victorious over those tears. We had a long, sad moment, but then we went downstairs for the post-Luna party and it was all good.

One guy said that he was from *Spin* magazine and wanted to interview me, so I waived my no-postshow-interview rule and answered his questions. I drank champagne and shook a lot of hands till I had had enough. I grabbed my Les Paul and my coat, and Britta and I reentered the bar wearing our coats and people started clapping, which embarrassed me. It was like that moment at a wedding when the married couple reappears, in different clothes, before taking off.

I hugged Lee goodbye. He was off to L.A. in the morning, and I wouldn't see him for a while. I hugged Sean goodbye. I would see him the next week for his fortieth birthday party, but it was an important goodbye nonetheless. After twelve years of dueling guitars, from that moment on we were two guys who used to be in a band together.

Britta and I trudged upstairs and out into the snowstorm and hailed a cab at the corner of Bowery and Delancey. It felt good to be heading north.

ACKNOWLEDGMENTS

Thank you: Andy Aldridge, Lee Boudreaux, Jason Brody, Autumn de Wilde, Christy Fletcher, Ann Godoff, Darren Haggar, Megan Hustad, Michael Lavine, Gary Mailman, Michael Macioce, Britta Phillips, Mark Rozzo, Kate Scherler, Laura Stickney, Maggie Sivon, Rich Stim, Lindsay Talbot, and David Whitehead.

For their recollections: Renée Lehman, Robin Hurley, Robert McCain, Howard Thompson, and Terry Tolkin, who is alive and well in Stillwater, Oklahoma.

Special thanks to Jane Fleming at Penguin Press for patiently explaining the many stages of finishing a book, to my father for insisting that I take notes on my travels in music, and to my mother for her love and her joie de vivre.

Most of all, thanks to Scott Moyers for making it happen.